# Raising

# Raising ?

# Civil Rights in a New Era

A series of Century Foundation Books developed in conjunction with the Civil Rights Project at Harvard University. The volumes in the series assess the prospects for justice and equal opportunity under law for racial and ethnic minorities in the United States.

## Other books in the series include:

*Religion, Race, and Justice in a Changing America,*
Gary Orfield and Holly J. Lebowitz, editors

# Raising Standards or Raising Barriers?

## Inequality and High-Stakes Testing in Public Education

GARY ORFIELD AND
MINDY L. KORNHABER, *editors*

A CENTURY FOUNDATION BOOK

2001 • THE CENTURY FOUNDATION PRESS • NEW YORK

The Century Foundation sponsors and supervises timely analyses of economic policy, foreign affairs, and domestic political issues. Not-for-profit and nonpartisan, it was founded in 1919 and endowed by Edward A. Filene.

LIBRARY OF CONGRESS CATALOGING-IN-PUBLICATION DATA
Raising standards or raising barriers? : inequality and high-stakes testing in public education / Gary Orfield and Mindy L. Kornhaber, editors.
    p. cm. — (Civil rights in a new era)
  Includes bibliographical references and index.
  ISBN 0-87078-451-X (hardcover: alk. paper) — ISBN 0-87078-452-8 (pbk.: alk. paper)
    1. Educational tests and measurements—Social aspects—United States. 2. Educational equalization—United States.  3. Test bias—United States. I. Orfield, Gary. II. Kornhaber, Mindy L. III. Series.
  LB3051 .R324 2001
  371.26'01'3—dc21

                                                          00-012741

Cover design and illustration: Claude Goodwin
Manufactured in the United States of America.

# Contents

# *Acknowledgments*

The editors are grateful to have worked with the authors who have contributed papers to this volume. Each of them has long been involved in thoughtfully examining the role of high-stakes testing in the context of America's very disparate public schools, and it has been an exciting experience for us to see their newest work and insights take form in their chapters. The ideas behind this book originated at a conference on high-stakes testing and K–12 education, which had many organizational parents to whom we owe our thanks: Teachers College, Columbia University, hosted our original conference. Our meeting there was cosponsored by Teachers College, Columbia Law School, and Harvard University. The Spencer Foundation provided funds to the Civil Rights Project to launch this conference and the chapters stemming from it. We are also grateful to the Carnegie Foundation, The John D. and Catherine T. MacArthur Foundation, and the Charles Stewart Mott Foundation for their support of work on K–12 education issues at the Civil Rights Project. Staff members of the Civil Rights Project, Marilyn Byrne, Lori Kelley, Michal Kurlaender, Suenita Lawrence, and Christina Safiya Tobias-Nahi, have helped in innumerable ways. We deeply appreciate their care, intelligence, and dedication. The Century Foundation invested its energies, support, and staff in this project. We are grateful to them for publishing this book and helping to build greater public understanding of high-stakes testing in our system of public education.

# *Preface*

While this book was in process, a new administration, headed by George W. Bush, came into power after a campaign in which both candidates strongly supported accountability through testing. Over the course of the campaign and thereafter, major battles have erupted in a number of states over the enforcement of testing policies. Some of those policies are being shelved or delayed while others are becoming even more strict. In short, the issue of educational testing has become even more prominent.

The intense focus on testing that George W. Bush advocated in Texas has now become the model for Title I, the federal program for education of poor children. This focus has been underscored by the choice of Rod Paige, the former superintendent of Houston and a strong testing advocate, to head the Department of Education.

In his education policy statement, "No Child Left Behind," President Bush concludes that testing will do much to "close the achievement gap between disadvantaged students and their peers":

> Schools must have clear, measurable goals. . . . Requiring annual state assessments in math and reading in grades 3–8 will ensure that the goals are being met for every child, every year. Annual testing in every grade gives teachers, parents and policymakers the information they need to ensure that children will reach academic success.

The president, like many other test advocates, thinks that the combination of information, accountability, and sanctions will enable students to reach high standards. He feels certain enough about this to justify the imposition of annual testing requirements on the states, even in an administration committed to increasing state autonomy in other areas.

However, as is too often the case, statements like the president's simply assume that testing and accountability systems will lead to educational improvements. Testing advocates take for granted that tests change the behavior of students and teachers in a positive way and that those changes produce more learning. They often equate a given test score with actual academic achievement, despite inconsistencies that occur in scores even for the same person in successive experiences with the same test. They also often assume that policies aimed at producing higher test scores will produce a stronger economy, and they allude to the economic dangers of a workforce whose test scores are lower than those of other nations. Test advocates treat these assumptions as self-evident facts. They are instead issues that should be examined through empirical investigations.

Nearly all of the authors in this volume have documented that certain assumptions used to justify a heavy reliance on high-stakes tests are flawed. They largely find that the evidence is inadequate to demonstrate that test policies will motivate the unmotivated; solve problems created by inadequately trained teachers or weak administrators; close gaps in achievement among students from different racial, ethnic, and economic backgrounds; lead to better job candidate selection; or alter the national economy. Some contributors to this volume go further, claiming that the misuse of test scores to impose drastic sanctions without equalizing opportunity to learn actually can make bad situations worse and can harm the educational attainment of the most vulnerable students. Some studies in this book document that an overemphasis on testing leads to drastically narrowed curricula and to increases in dropout rates.

The stakes, or consequences, for students and schools are very high in the intense but often uninformed debates over testing now taking place in Congress, in the courts, in state capitals, and in many school districts. Too often the complex issues involved in improving teaching and learning are reduced to slogans and sound bites. Assessment is treated as if the right tests and sanctions can solve all the problems. The benefits of high-stakes testing are assumed, and the costs—in terms of money, instructional time, curricula, retention, and dropping out—are ignored.

This volume makes clear that high-stakes tests, even when appropriately used, are not sufficient to promote strong schools. Well-constructed and appropriately used tests can help to detect problems, but they do not, in themselves, solve them. Advocates and critics alike agree that many other factors besides tests are important. States and districts that are regarded as exemplars of achievement gains have implemented a complex set of interacting policies, such as teacher professional development, smaller class sizes, and increased funding. Testing is not the sole or primary reason for actual improvements in learning.

If we are to work toward genuine efforts to foster higher levels of learning on a more equitable basis, the limits of test-driven reforms need to be acknowledged and addressed. We therefore make the following recommendations:

- We urge policymakers to use testing to inform, rather than replace, decisionmaking. A test score reveals only a very limited amount of information about individual students. Therefore, all major professional associations involved in educational testing, as well as the National Research Council, emphasize that decisions about student promotion, retention, program or curricular placements, and graduation must be based on more than a single test score. These decisions also should be informed by "other relevant information," such as grades, teacher recommendations, and results of other tests.[1] It is not objective to rely on a single test score or test scores alone in making important educational decisions; it is a misuse of testing technology.

- If we are going to put a serious emphasis on tests, it is very important that they be good tests and that they assess material that students actually have been taught. Many existing state tests are not valid tools for making decisions about retention, placement, or graduation. In addition, high-stakes tests are often imposed on schools where there is no guarantee that the students have been exposed to the material or have teachers who know the material tested. Minimum scores are often set as a result of political considerations about acceptable rates of failure and without any study of the feasibility of various groups of students and schools reaching the specified levels of proficiency. Students should not be denied diplomas or be retained in grade on the basis of scores from tests that have not been appropriately validated or when they have not been taught the material.

- We urge policymakers to reach beyond test policies to implement reforms that actually build good learning environments. Research shows that poor and minority youths are more likely to be subjected to high-stakes tests, but they are also far less likely to attend schools

---

[1] American Educational Research Association, American Psychological Association, and National Council on Measurement in Education, *Standards for Educational and Psychological Testing* (Washington, D.C.: American Psychological Association, 1999), pp. 146–47; National Research Council, Committee on Appropriate Test Use, *High Stakes: Testing for Tracking, Promotion, and Graduation,* Jay P. Heubert and Robert M. Hauser, eds. (Washington, D.C.: National Academy Press, 1999).

with experienced and certified teaching staffs, adequate libraries, up-to-date technologies, and high-achieving peer groups./ We need policies that increase the pool of highly qualified teachers and that address the shortage of these teachers in districts and schools serving those most in need. Poorly designed test-use policies actually may have the perverse impact of encouraging good teachers to leave already challenged schools. We also need policies that foster smaller class sizes, especially for those most in need; smaller school sizes; adequate libraries; and rich and engaging curricula. Testing policies cannot substitute for, or accomplish the work of, policies aimed at building strong learning environments.

- We urge the media to go well beyond reporting comparisons of test scores and publishing failure rates. The media need to inform themselves and the public about the meaning of test scores, their appropriate use, and the key qualities of schools that affect test scores; for example, the level of poverty and segregation in schools, which students and teachers do not control, but which policymakers, courts, and legislatures greatly influence. There should be special efforts not to show the absolute level of test scores, which is very strongly related to the educational background and resources of a school's parents, but to use assessment to see how much the teachers add to students' knowledge. Otherwise, publicity about test scores can create the false impression that teachers are extremely effective in rich communities and do little of value in poor schools.

Our basic idea in commissioning the studies for this book was to enrich the public discussion of an extremely important set of issues in American education. As part of an organization centrally concerned with equal opportunity for minority youths, we feel the urgent need to improve inadequate and inferior school opportunities. We are sympathetic to the idea that good assessment, high standards, and accountability are essential parts of this process. It would be tragic, however, if these good ideas led to a counterproductive use of tests and sanctions that actually makes things worse for many of the students whose chances for a decent life are almost totally dependent on the schools. We believe that the studies in this book will help generate a more sophisticated and informed discussion.

Gary Orfield
Mindy L. Kornhaber
Cambridge, Massachusetts

# CHAPTER ONE

# High-Stakes Testing Policies
## Examining Their Assumptions and Consequences

MINDY L. KORNHABER AND GARY ORFIELD

We are in the second decade of an educational movement that assumes high-stakes tests are essential for improving educational standards. Most Americans believe that students are not doing well in school. Most also believe that the rewards and sanctions (or "stakes") attached to tests motivate students to work harder, just as profits and losses spur efficiency in the marketplace. Americans generally think that tests are a fair and neutral means of evaluating whether individual students merit promotion to the next grade or merit a high school diploma. They also view high-stakes testing as a way to hold schools accountable for student achievement. Decisionmaking on the basis of test results is strongly appealing given Americans' deep faith in education and individual effort. Americans who were educated in leading colleges and professional schools are, almost by definition, successful test takers, and so they also tend to hold positive views about using tests to judge students, schools, and school systems.

Critics assert that these beliefs are based on false assumptions and misleading analogies. They note that the evidence that tests promote educational gains is not strong. They hold that many students, unlike many business people, are not readily motivated by the rewards and sanctions associated with rising or falling scores (see Chapter 5, by George Madaus and Marguerite Clarke). Even to the extent that testing motivates students, they argue that sanctioning students on the basis of test scores is neither fair nor neutral. The critics point out that sanctions attached to tests have large, negative consequences. Since tests tend to measure unequal backgrounds and opportunities, and not simply an

1

individual's effort, negative consequences are more likely to affect black, Hispanic, and poor youths than they are to affect those whose families and schools offer the richest preparation.[1] They also note that while the negative consequences of testing are becoming apparent in social science research, very few leaders are talking about them.

These different perspectives toward high-stakes testing arise from different roots. To understand the first perspective, it is necessary to consider the political climate that has led to the proliferation of high-stakes testing policies. To understand the second, it is necessary to consider the assumptions underlying high-stakes testing policies and the consequences stemming from them. It is also necessary to consider the recommendations made by professional groups for the use of testing.

The essays in this volume acknowledge the differences in these two perspectives. Each of the contributors believes that high standards are important and that test information, when carefully used in conjunction with other information about students and schools, can help to improve teaching and learning. At the same time, most of the contributors note that high-stakes tests frequently have been misused. Their research, which examines high-stakes testing policies from a wide range of disciplines, largely converges on an unsettling finding: high-stakes tests, even those intended to raise standards for all students, can and have created barriers, especially for the nation's most vulnerable students. This volume presents such findings, while also illuminating policy initiatives and social science research that can constructively address America's achievement gap.

## The Political Climate for High-Stakes Testing

The recent widespread adoption of high-stakes testing has roots in a political rhetoric that emphasizes a decline in the quality of public education and its capacity to educate the nation's young people. President Ronald Reagan clearly articulated this view when he proclaimed in a 1983 radio broadcast that "our education system, once the finest in the world, is in a sorry state of disrepair." Reagan claimed that "the educational skills of today's students do not match their parents'" and that the nation was "failing an entire generation." He asserted that "the quality of learning in our classrooms has been declining for the last two decades" and that when students "graduate from high school, they're prepared for neither work nor higher education." Alongside his assessment of the nation's education system, President Reagan called for "higher goals and tougher standards for matriculation."[2] The 1983 Reagan administration report, *A Nation at Risk*,[3] crystallized this view and created a widespread perception of an educational crisis so severe as to undermine America's economy and future. In that report, the state of our nation's schools was presented as a threat to the country's security, on par with a hostile enemy.

The press and political leaders took up the report's message and underscored its claims of a massive educational decline. In late 1983, *Education Week* reported that fifty-four state-level commissions had been formed during that year in response to *A Nation at Risk*. Within a year of that report, twenty-six states had raised graduation requirements and almost all the rest were considering doing so.[4] Many new student and teacher testing plans also had been enacted.[5] A Gallup poll in May 1983 reported that 87 percent of those familiar with *A Nation at Risk* supported its recommendations and that 75 percent of the public at large favored tests for promotion from grade to grade.[6]

Within three years, thirty-five states had enacted comprehensive reforms. These reforms emphasized increased course taking and testing.[7] Testing was seen as a way to impose standards on schools and students and hold them accountable for achieving results (see Chapter 2, by Gary Natriello and Aaron Pallas).

The trend toward testing continued in Vice President George Bush's presidential campaign. In 1987, when he announced his candidacy, Bush said that he wished to be the "education president." He reiterated this goal as part of his standard campaign speech and promised to work in cooperation with the governors to support state minimum competency tests for graduation and grade promotion.

During his first year in office, Bush held a "Summit on Education" with the nation's governors, headed by Arkansas governor Bill Clinton. This summit helped to forge Bush's major education proposal, America 2000, which was supposed to produce large educational gains by the beginning of the new millennium. One of the program's basic objectives was to develop much tougher tests that were set to world-class standards. These were seen as a means of producing citizens who could hold their own in a competitive world marketplace.[8]

When Governor Clinton and his running mate, Senator Al Gore, were campaigning against President Bush, they affirmed education goals similar to Bush's. In fact, Clinton's language clearly mirrored that used by President Reagan: "Too often our schools move people up the ladder whether they study or not, graduate people whether they know anything or not, and dump people in the workforce whether they have real skills or not."[9] Clinton and Gore pledged to achieve the America 2000 goals, with world-class standards and high-stakes tests as basic components. Thus, the Democratic candidates, just like their Republican counterparts, promised to establish "tough standards." They also pledged to work for a national examination system that embraced such standards.

In the 2000 presidential campaign, Vice President Al Gore called for all states to create high school graduation tests. Governor George W. Bush faulted the Clinton administration for not linking test results to federal aid, promising to take aid away from schools whose test scores did not rise.[10] In the first week of his administration, President George W. Bush called for changes to Title I that would require states to test students in grades 3 through 8 each year in reading and math.[11]

Thus, there has been an unbroken line of rhetoric, extending across six presidential terms, fostering high-stakes testing. For almost two decades, all the national leaders of both parties have embraced the theory that our schools have deteriorated and that they can be saved by high-stakes tests. So have the state leaders in almost all our states. The fact that major politicians have been in agreement about a theory for so long surely means they think that it has electoral advantages. However, that does not mean that the theory holds true.

In fact, many of the negative claims about achievement trends have been shown to be false. For example, economist Alan Krueger noted in a 1998 article that over the past twenty-five years the average student has gained about six percentile ranks on the National Assessment of Educational Progress. "In other words, the student scoring in the fiftieth percentile today would perform as well as the fifty-sixth percentile student did twenty-five years ago." Krueger further notes that "the most disadvantaged students have made the greatest gains. The gap in math scores between students in disadvantaged communities and all communities narrowed by approximately one-half of a standard deviation between the early 1970s and 1990. . . . These findings are inconsistent with the popular stereotype that inner-city schools are in decline."[12]

After reviewing trends on all the major tests, the psychologists and education researchers David Berliner and Bruce Biddle concluded that:

> Standardized tests provide *no evidence whatever* that supports the myth of a recent decline in school achievement of the average American student . . . . Instead, the evidence suggests that average school achievement has either been stable or has increased modestly

for a generation or more. And, although top-ranked students . . .
have tended to hold their ground, those from "less advantaged"
homes have recently shown achievement gains.[13]

The data also show a consistent trend toward higher average IQ test scores.
Berliner and Biddle remark that "the number of students expected to have
IQs of 130 or higher . . . is now about seven times greater than it was for the
generation now retiring from leadership positions in the country and often
complaining about the poor performance of today's youth."[14]

As these reports indicate, minority students on average have made
gains relatively greater than those made by other students.[15] Nevertheless,
the gap in achievement remains substantial, and it now appears to be
widening once again for black students and for Hispanics in some subject
areas.[16] Rather than being informed by such findings, however, the central
role that high-stakes testing currently occupies has been overwhelmingly
shaped by the rhetoric of our political leaders. In turn, the faith placed in
testing has been advanced by the press, which typically describes policy
debates in the terms used by the two national parties.

In contrast, this book offers more grounded bases for considering the
role that high-stakes tests should play. Drawing on research in economics, education, law, political science, psychometrics, and sociology, it
provides data-driven analyses of the assumptions underlying high-stakes
tests and their consequences. Using these sources, it also offers proposals for using tests in ways that reduce barriers to the equal attainment of
high standards. We review these assumptions, consequences, and proposals below.

## THE ASSUMPTIONS UNDERLYING
## HIGH-STAKES TESTING

Several assumptions have played a large role in fostering the rise of high-
stakes testing in K–12 education. Among these are that high-stakes testing will enhance economic productivity, motivate students, and improve
teaching and learning.

### ASSUMPTION I: TESTING WILL ENHANCE ECONOMIC PRODUCTIVITY

In 1983, *A Nation at Risk* indicated that the future economic well-
being of the country was linked to the educational performance of
the nation's schoolchildren. The report highlighted the assertion that

students from countries that were then more economically successful, such as Germany and Japan, had higher levels of achievement. Thus, it was assumed that if the United States raised its educational performance, its economic performance would also rise.

This fundamental assumption does not hold up well under scrutiny. First, and most obviously, the U.S. economy has jumped out of its early 1980s doldrums to surpass the performances of Japan and Germany. This is true even while American students do not appear to be out-performing their counterparts in Germany or Japan.[17] Second, statistical analyses reveal that the relationship between measures of cognitive skills and economic productivity is weak. Extensive analyses reported by the National Research Council in 1989 show that workers' tests scores explain only about 5 percent of the differences in supervisors' ratings of workers' job performance.[18] Similarly, Henry Levin in Chapter 3 asserts: "Traditional tests, including those used for international comparisons, show only nominal statistical links to measures of worker productivity." Levin emphasizes that he supports high standards, and he states that there are many good reasons to pursue them. However, he sees little evidence that either traditional tests or tests based on new, higher standards should be pursued to advance worker productivity or the wider economy.

Levin does acknowledge that researchers have found substantial wage gains of 7 percent for men and 14 percent for women associated with a one standard deviation increase in math scores.[19] An increase of one standard deviation is sizable; it reflects, for example, a gain from the mean score, or fiftieth percentile, to the eighty-fourth percentile, when scores are normally distributed. However, Levin asserts that pegging wage gains like these to any education reform is unrealistic: it is rare for any educational reform to achieve a consistent gain of even 0.25 standard deviation.

In contrast to Levin, John Bishop and Ferran Mane argue in Chapter 4 that testing can promote economic benefits. These authors cite research by Joseph Altonji and Charles Pierret in which an increase of one stan-dard deviation on a measure of cognitive skill was associated with a 16 percent increase in wages some twelve years after high school.[20] (However, as Levin has indicated, school change efforts do not produce test score gains of this size.)

Bishop and Mane's own comparisons of graduates from high schools with or without minimum competency examinations (MCEs) support the positive relationship between testing and economic benefits as well. They have found, for example, that among 1992 graduates from low socioeconomic status backgrounds, the 1993 annual earnings of those who attended MCE high schools were $694 more than for those from non-MCE high schools. This amounted to more than a 10 percent increase. However, while this figure is statistically significant, it still indicates that neither graduation from high schools with mandated exams nor graduation from those without such exams readily lifts impoverished young people out of poverty.[21] Looking further into Bishop and Mane's findings (see Table 4.6, pages 82–83), it is also clear that for neither black nor Hispanic 1992 graduates was the effect of an MCE school statistically—let alone socially—significant. These findings indicate that successfully completing a minimum competency graduation exam is not an economic magic bullet for poor and minority young people entering the workforce. The sweeping claims by many politicians and researchers that high-stakes tests will improve the lot of poor and minority youth must be leavened by such realities.

Moreover, the politicians' claims must be tempered by the possible negative economic consequences of high-stakes testing. Test supporters assert that passing a minimum competency graduation test will signal a job applicant's value to employers. Yet such tests do not measure qualities that often matter most in job success: initiative, creativity, reliability, persistence, ability to work with others, and an understanding of specific job skills and employment cultures.[22] Because such tests are weak predictors of job performance, Levin argues that relying on test scores in hiring decisions bears the "high probability that many workers will be rejected for jobs that they could perform and others will be selected for jobs that they cannot perform." Given the typical disparities in test scores between whites and Asians, on the one hand, and blacks, Latinos, and Native Americans on the other, such practices would damage both the nation's economy and its social fabric.

## ASSUMPTION II: TESTING WILL MOTIVATE STUDENTS

Common wisdom, as well as behavioral psychology, holds that normal, thinking beings strive to gain rewards and avoid painful consequences. It follows that students should study to succeed on a high-stakes test, or at least to avoid being left back or denied a diploma. Certainly, tests will motivate some students and some of their teachers. There is a good deal of testimony about such effects in reports of some highly successful inner-city schools. Yet, there is also a good deal of evidence that the relationship between testing and motivation is in fact more variable than most politicians, and probably most scholars, would wish.

In Chapter 5, George Madaus and Marguerite Clarke assert that "advocates of the motivational potential of examinations have not paid enough attention to who will be motivated and who will not. This point is particularly relevant when the examinations are referenced to 'world-class' standards. . . ." Madaus and Clarke underscore that motivation in students is a complex construct that depends on many factors. Among these factors are the perceived relevance of a reward to the student's own life; the perception of whether the rewards really matter, even to those who might pass; and the student's perception of his or her own capacity and whether, given a variety of obstacles, it is at all feasible to obtain the reward.

Madaus and Clarke also note that there are differences in motivation across social and cultural groups. Sociologist John Ogbu and his colleagues offer one explanation for these differences.[23] Ogbu finds that youngsters from historically subjugated minorities on average score one standard deviation lower on standardized tests than their counterparts from other groups. Given that Ogbu has found these differences even within a homogenous society like Japan, as well as in diverse societies such as India and the United States, these differences are not genetically linked to race, despite claims to the contrary.[24] Instead, Ogbu attributes the disparities in test scores to sociological dynamics that influence motivation: across a wide variety of nations, youngsters from historically subjugated groups tend to identify themselves in opposition to the majority and its behaviors and values. To maintain their peer group and social ties, such youngsters may reject the values that schools—often agencies of the dominant majority—advocate.[25]

This dynamic can hold even when youngsters understand that a high school diploma matters. Madaus and Clarke note in their chapter that "research on dropouts also shows that many, while fully appreciating the importance of educational credentials, do not believe that such credentials are of much help in their social milieu." If this is so, it is unclear how policies promoting more challenging tests, which bear even greater sanctions, will enhance these students' motivation.

Alongside sociological dynamics, psychological responses also help to explain the vexed relationship between testing and motivation. Claude Steele's elegant experimental work throughout the 1990s reveals that among those students from historically subjugated groups who have remained motivated and have succeeded, psychological pressures can undermine their test performances.[26] When such individuals are told that a test shows no differences across racial or gender lines, their performances are far better than when told the same test shows average differences in performance across groups. In the latter situation, the students' efforts to surmount negative stereotypes lead them to overthink problems and to devote excess time to problems they answered correctly. Through such striving, they actually wind up scoring lower than they otherwise would have. Interestingly enough, the same psychological stress affects high-achieving white men in test settings in which they are told Asian men outperform them. This phenomenon is thus a human response, rather than a racially based one, to a testing situation in which others are known, or reputed, to score better. Given that such score differences are well known in this society, it is reasonable to infer that this dynamic disproportionately affects black, Latino, and Native American students.

## ASSUMPTION 3: TESTING WILL IMPROVE TEACHING AND LEARNING

Proponents of higher standards and tests to measure them argue that such policies help create systems that clearly articulate what students should know and be able to do. This clarity makes it possible to hold students and educators accountable for results. Because all students are supposed to meet such goals, testing should improve the educational opportunities for many disadvantaged students, for whom low standards have been norm. Bishop and Mane advocate this position, as have many other scholars and policymakers. Many thoughtful researchers argue that implementing high standards and high-stakes tests will shine a light on students and schools that require additional resources to succeed and that these resources should then be provided.[27]

In a certain sense, such thinking mirrors the assumption that high-stakes testing motivates students. It is a rational line of thinking. On the other hand, there is a good deal of evidence that the systemic effects of high-stakes testing on learning and instructional resources do not play out only in this rational and constructive way.

Some of this evidence leads Madaus and Clarke to assert that "high-stakes, high-standards tests do not have a markedly positive effect on teaching and learning in the classroom." To the extent that score improvements are sought using "increased control of teacher and student behavior through the imposition of rewards and sanctions . . . other undesirable consequences are possible." One of the undesirable consequences is that students' conceptual learning may be undermined rather than developed. Madaus and Clarke find that this potential exists in part because teaching to the test's form and content "can narrow the focus of instruction, study, and learning to the detriment of other skills." They note such narrowing can occur with both traditional multiple-choice tests and with tests that call upon students to produce essays or other answers of their own making.

Linda McNeil and Angela Valenzuela have documented this kind of instructional narrowing during many years of research in schools in the Houston area, particularly in schools serving poor and minority students. These schools have increasingly been geared toward raising scores on the Texas Assessment of Academic Skills (TAAS). In Chapter 7, McNeil and Valenzuela highlight that, especially for minority and poor students, the TAAS system sharply curtails the curriculum. For example, they have found that in schools serving large concentrations of minority students, all teachers—regardless of subject matter expertise—must devote some part of their class time to drilling students in TAAS math, reading, and writing. Thus, because of test preparation requirements, students are shortchanged on instructional time in science, history, the arts, and other areas that the TAAS does not test.

McNeil and Valenzuela argue that instruction also is undermined in subjects tested by the TAAS. For example, the TAAS requires students to answer multiple-choice questions pertaining to short reading passages. Because reading performance of this type is what matters on the test, such readings have displaced from the classroom longer works of fiction and nonfiction. As a result, McNeil and Valenzuela report that in some schools students' ability to comprehend book-length material has declined. In addition, the TAAS system undermines learning in the tested areas because students who are at risk of failing are placed in special TAAS math and TAAS English classes. These classes focus on test preparation, and they do not offer credits toward graduation. Students may be kept in these classes until they pass or until they decide to drop out of school. In either case, their exposure to a rigorous, or even an ordinary, high school curriculum is severely limited.

McNeil and Valenzuela also underscore that, because the TAAS is a high-stakes exam for educators as well as for students, educational expenditures have been siphoned away from substantive educational resources and poured into test preparation purchases. They found that money has been redirected toward consultants who align curriculum and instruction with the test and toward forms of professional development that emphasize score-raising techniques more than teacher's subject matter knowledge or pedagogy. Especially in schools with high concentrations of poor and minority students, TAAS increases expenditures for commercial test preparation workbooks and reduces expenditures for science labs and library books. Such reallocation of resources, alongside the displacement of substantive curriculum, means that the TAAS may actually be widening the wedge between the learning opportunities of majority and minority youth.

As evidence that students are actually learning more, proponents of high-stakes testing, as well as state and district administrators, point out that test scores are rising and that the gap in TAAS scores between majority and minority students has decreased. However, most serious scholars of testing find such arguments unconvincing. Test scores can rise for many reasons that are unrelated to increased learning. For instance, scores can increase by changing the pool of students who are tested, by altering the test conditions, or through outright cheating.[28] Scores may also rise simply because students are being narrowly educated to do better on a test, which still does not mean that students have gained more knowledge and skill.[29]

If students were actually learning more, not just producing higher scores, then they should show increases on tests other than those they have been trained to take. While some test results undermine the notion that Texas students are actually learning more,[30] a recent analysis of National Assessment of Educational Progress (NAEP) test scores, led by David Grissmer,[31] finds that Texas students are making gains. Grissmer associates these gains and similar gains in North Carolina not only with testing, but also with several statewide systemic reforms that were launched in the late 1980s and early 1990s.[32] For example, the Texas reforms entailed lowering class size, increasing spending on schools, reallocating funds to poor districts, and retraining teachers.

In Chapter 6, Monty Neill, with the assistance of Keith Gayler, emphasizes that there is no simple relationship between high-stakes testing and improved learning as measured by the NAEP. Their chapter compares how states with and without high-stakes graduation tests fare on the mathematics portion of the NAEP. Neill acknowledges that the NAEP is an imperfect instrument for this purpose, since not every state participates and, for participating states, the extent to which state-level tests and the NAEP are aligned varies. In addition, state-level data are available only at the fourth and eighth grade levels. But despite such limitations, Neill maintains that the NAEP is a good indicator, in part because it tests some higher-level knowledge and problem-solving skills.

Neill hypothesizes that if a state has a mandatory high school graduation test—by definition, a high-stakes test—and if such a test truly influences learning, then it should be possible to detect the test's systemic effect on learning at the fourth and eighth grade levels. The test's systemic effects should influence instruction at these earlier grades and possibly also motivate students. However, Neill finds little evidence to support this hypothesis. At the fourth grade level, states with a high school graduation test had a small advantage on NAEP scores. This advantage was predominantly in the percentage of students reaching the basic or higher level of math proficiency. However, at the eighth grade level there was no association between such mandatory tests and NAEP gains. In fact, the opposite held true: states without a mandatory high school graduation test were more likely than those with a test to make gains, both in the percentage of students reaching the basic level of proficiency and in the percentage reaching proficient and advanced levels.

Neill argues that for those states with high-stakes tests that showed NAEP gains, it is important to examine how various groups within the state performed. While Texas claimed gains on both fourth and eighth grade NAEP scores, other researchers have found that the gap between whites and African Americans' NAEP scores has increased since 1992.[33] Such findings run contrary to the argument that the TAAS is improving equality in learning across different racial and ethnic groups.

In essence, while long taken for granted by politicians and reinforced by the press, the assumptions underlying high-stakes testing are not supported definitively by research. The economy, student motivation, and improved learning are issues of such scope and complexity that they require far more from policymakers than the ongoing promulgation of higher standards and high-stakes testing.

## CONSEQUENCES OF HIGH-STAKES TESTING

If the assumptions underlying high-stakes testing are flawed, the impact of such testing programs is unlikely to be as rosy as their proponents—or even their detractors—might wish. In this section, we consider the impact of high-stakes testing programs on two important indicators of school success: high school graduation and grade promotion.

### THE IMPACT OF HIGH-STAKES TESTING ON HIGH SCHOOL GRADUATION RATES

Among the leading concerns about high-stakes testing programs is their impact on high school graduation rates. Even test supporters, such as Bishop and Mane, acknowledge that testing will affect graduation rates. In this volume, they argue that failure rates will likely be very high when New York State implements its new Regents examinations graduation requirement. However, these authors assert that over a period of some seven years this problem will largely disappear: "dropout rates will be at or below current levels, and this will be accomplished without making the Regents Exams easier than they are right now." They concede that if they are wrong, then there may be a decline of between 2 and 4 percent in high school completion rates.

Bishop and Mane rely on several assumptions to arrive at this low dropout rate. First, they "expect students to react by studying harder." As noted above, this expectation is not clearly or universally borne out by empirical research, and it may be less likely to hold true for students already at risk.[34] Bishop and Mane also assume that failure rates will return to normal because teachers will either get better at teaching to the new standards or be replaced by those who can teach to them. This claim is clearly at odds with many studies that find that certified and high-quality teachers are in short supply, especially for schools serving disadvantaged youth.[35] Furthermore, their claim that the quality of the teaching force will improve because of increasing competition and the resulting higher wages does not address the maldistribution of qualified teachers. It is instead plausible that qualified teachers will be driven away from the most needy schools because the pressure of teaching to the test and/or sanctions for low test scores will make other professional settings more attractive. A fourth assumption made by Bishop and Mane is that dropout rates will be tolerable because many students who cannot pass the new Regents examinations will either transfer to private high schools (which are exempt from the Regents requirements) or pursue a general equivalency diploma (GED). If so, the new Regents examination system will continue to support the kind of degree system it was intended to counter, namely one divided along racial, ethnic, and economic lines. In all likelihood, private high school diplomas will be disproportionately awarded to more privileged students, while the GED, with its lesser status and earning power, will be disproportionately awarded to the disadvantaged.

Bishop and Mane's optimistic assessment about the effect of high-stakes testing on dropout rates in New York is markedly at odds with the analyses undertaken by other contributors to this volume. For example, Gary Natriello and Aaron Pallas's examination of the relationship between high-stakes testing and the award of high school diplomas in New York, Texas, and Minnesota reveals that high-stakes testing decreases the likelihood that poor and minority students will graduate in all three states. Their analysis of data from New York provides a sharp contrast to Bishop and Mane's conclusions. Their work shows strong negative relationships between the proportion of students who are black, Hispanic, poor, or who have limited English proficiency (LEP) and the proportion of students who receive a Regents diploma under the older, less stringent New York Regents Examination. For instance, in high schools where more than 50 percent of the students are black, fewer than 40 percent receive a Regents diploma. In high schools where 40 percent of the students are Hispanic, again fewer than 40 percent obtain the Regents diploma. In schools where half or more students receive free or reduced-price lunches, fewer than 35 percent earn such a diploma. In short, in schools where even half the population is made up of poor or minority students, far fewer than half the students attain the old, optional Regents diploma. Given that the new Regents exams are both tougher and required, there is little reason to be sanguine about poor and minority students' chances of receiving a high school diploma under New York's revamped high-stakes system.[36]

The situation in Texas also calls into question Bishop and Mane's assertion that dropout rates will fall over time. In Texas, a high school exit exam has been in effect for a decade. Walt Haney of Boston College found that in 1989, the year before TAAS was implemented, about 70 percent of whites and 58 percent of blacks and Latinos had progressed from grade 9 to their high school graduation. After the TAAS was implemented, progression rates for whites declined for one year and then bounced back to pre-TAAS levels. The rate for African American and Latino students also decreased, but it never recovered. It now stands at about 50 percent.[37]

Although TAAS proponents highlight that gaps in test performance on TAAS have diminished between whites on the one hand and blacks and Latinos on the other hand, marked differences in test performance still persist. Thus, of those minority students who remain enrolled at the end of their senior year, one in six do not pass the TAAS exit-level test, while fewer than one in ten white students do not pass. Haney associates the TAAS with the loss of diplomas to one hundred thousand Texas minority students.[38] Given such findings, Natriello and Pallas assert in their chapter that "these tests are, and will remain for some time, an impediment to the graduation prospects of African American and Hispanic youth."

In sum, evidence from Texas's longstanding high-stakes exit test yields a much more realistic, and less rosy, picture of graduation rates than advocates of high-stakes testing suppose. The evidence indicates that it is unclear just how long it may take to travel the route between the implementation of high standards and high-stakes testing to equally high educational attainment among all groups. If Texas is any indication, equal attainment of the high school degree is certain to take substantially longer than the seven years Bishop and Mane predict for New York. One estimate for closing the racial gap in measured achievement—an estimate not specifically geared to high standards and high stakes—is seventy-five years.[39] It is unclear whether high standards plus high-stakes testing will in any way speed this up; there are indications that the gap has in fact widened since the late 1980s.[40] In the meantime, and for the foreseeable future, high-stakes testing programs increase the chances that poor and minority students will be denied a high school diploma.

## The Impact of High-Stakes Tests on Retention

As part of the drive to raise standards and hold students and teachers accountable, a good deal of political rhetoric—widely aired at the national, state, and local levels—has advocated an end to social promotion. Not surprisingly, an increasing number of states are turning to tests to make decisions about promoting or retaining students. Several large school districts, including New York City and Chicago, also have implemented such programs.

In Chapter 8, Robert Hauser investigates the impact of such policies. He notes that while high-stakes testing may be associated with increased retention rates, this is detrimental only if retention ultimately fails to benefit students. Unfortunately, as Hauser notes, there is an abundance of research that links retention to such failure. He cites Charles T. Holmes's meta-analysis of sixty-three controlled studies, which concluded, "On average, retained children are worse off than their promoted counterparts on both personal adjustment and academic outcomes."[41] Retention further harms students' learning and future chances in the workplace by greatly increasing the likelihood that they drop out. Hauser finds that more recent studies claiming that retention improves academic success do not hold up under either a close reading or a reanalysis of their data.[42]

Contrary to the ongoing clamor to end social promotion, Hauser's analysis of data from the Current Population Survey of the U.S. Bureau of the Census reveals both that retention is already widely in use and that African American and Hispanic students are more frequently retained than white students. By ages fifteen to seventeen, 40 to 50 percent of black and Hispanic youth are a year or more overage for their grade, while only 35 percent of white students are. At ages fifteen to seventeen, nearly half of black males are overage for their grade, while fewer than 30 percent of white girls are.

In sum, the consequences of high-stakes testing on retention, graduation, and educational attainment are very commonly deleterious and discriminatory. They have obviously disparate impacts, which will continue for the foreseeable future. As noted above, the assumptions underlying the tests are also problematic: there is evidence that testing is not going to lead the nation to greater productivity. There is also evidence that the tests do not motivate a great many students to work harder. Furthermore, testing does not necessarily lead to improved learning. Achieving transfer of knowledge and skills from one test to another, or from the school to the world beyond, has long been a central and difficult problem in education.[43] This problem is hardly alleviated when teachers and students must focus so much attention, time, and resources to prepare for a high-stakes test.[44]

## REDUCING TEST-RELATED BARRIERS TO THE EQUAL ATTAINMENT OF HIGH STANDARDS

Clearly, American policymakers and the public want to see the nation's young people educated to high standards and become thoughtful and productive adults. Given this, what kinds of constructive roles can testing play, and how can we ensure such constructive roles?

Jay Heubert, in Chapter 9, notes that "tests do not produce improved teaching and learning, any more than a thermometer reduces fever." However, he also argues that "when good tests are used properly" the information they produce, alongside information from other sources, can be helpful.

Drawing on the most recent version of the Standards for Educational and Psychological Testing as well as the National Research Council's volume, *High Stakes: Testing for Tracking, Promotion, and Graduation*,[45] Heubert first underscores key principles for appropriate test use. Among these principles are measurement validity, attribution of cause, and effectiveness of treatment.

In order to have measurement validity, it is crucial that a test actually measure constructs that are relevant to making a high-stakes decision in a reliable and accurate way. For example, if a test is supposed to inform decisions about the mastery of high school math, then for students with limited English proficiency both the test and the instruction preceding it must not be dependent on English. This is because English is not relevant to the mathematics reasoning in question.

The principle of proper attribution of cause requires that inferences drawn about students' scores be appropriate. A decision that relies on a test score should therefore take into account the causes for the score, and not just the score alone. A low score should not be attributed to a student's capacities or knowledge unless plausible rival interpretations have been examined and ruled out. Rival interpretations might include the quality of instruction, limited English proficiency, and the student's health. Such plausible interpretations provide information that can be used to ameliorate educational problems rather than compound them through retention or other inappropriate score-based decisions.

Finally, for test use to be appropriate it must support effective treatment. Heubert asserts that "test use is appropriate only if test scores lead to placements and other consequences that are educationally beneficial for the students. . . ." Thus, Heubert emphasizes that using scores to justify "simple retention in grade and placement in typical low-track classes" is wholly inappropriate, since such treatments do not advance academic achievement and often harm students.

While these principles are well known and well accepted throughout the testing profession, Heubert notes that there are no serious mechanisms for enforcing them. At present, enforcement relies on test developers' and test users' "good faith and good judgment." Unfortunately, voluntary adherence to appropriate test use is too often undermined by financial pressures on test developers and political pressures on states, districts, and schools.

In contrast, Heubert notes that federal law offers enforcement mechanisms for addressing the discriminatory effects that may follow from the improper use of high-stakes testing, but it does not have "specific standards defining the appropriate use of educational tests." To correct this situation, Heubert proposes that federal civil rights laws should be linked to the standards for appropriate test use that have been promulgated by the testing profession. This linkage would provide teeth for enforcing appropriate test use and clear standards for the courts to call upon when addressing cases of possible test misuse and discrimination. To be effective, this linkage would have to be both issued and enforced by the federal government.

Alongside clearer standards and better enforcement, what else might be done to ensure that tests do not create additional barriers to learning? One approach, noted in Hauser's chapter and highlighted in Neill's, is for test information to be used to enhance classroom instruction. As it stands now, the particulars about a student's test performance—for example, patterns of problem-solving successes and difficulties or areas of content that are clearly mastered or missing—are often not delivered to a student's teachers in time to modify instruction. In essence, test information is used to determine placement and other high-stakes decisions, but it is not necessarily used to improve classroom learning. Instead, Hauser advocates early diagnostic assessments and intensive early intervention. Similarly, Neill argues for much more "formative assessment." Formative assessment practices are intended to provide information that can be used to improve instruction. These practices include providing students with ongoing information about their performance and teaching students to evaluate their own work for quality. Neill cites a study by Paul Black and Dylan Wiliam indicating that such assessment practices are associated with improvements on standardized tests that are markedly greater than the typical education reform.[46]

Information from tests also can be used to reflect back on educational policies and systems. As Natriello and Pallas suggest, test scores could be used as one source of information for exploring the educational processes and opportunities that are provided to students and for making educational resources more equitable. It is becoming evident that several states have looked at test results to modify their own high-stakes systems. For example, many states implemented demanding test requirements to demonstrate their enthusiasm for high standards. However, these test requirements often were not clearly linked to the curriculum or pegged to feasible levels of achievement. As the time came to use test results for high-stakes purposes—for example, to retain thousands of students or deny them diplomas—a number of states modified their exams, the scores required for passing, or the use of high-stakes consequencs.[47]

As the scholarship in this book makes clear, it is evident that test information can and must be used far better than it frequently is. As Madaus and Clarke note, the goal of enabling the nation's young people to reach higher standards requires much more "than mandating tougher standards and an external examination referenced to them." Test results embed inequalities of race, ethnicity, and poverty. Enabling a more equal attainment of higher standards therefore requires policymakers to tackle the disjunction between a single, high-stakes test standard and the array of disparities that students encounter in education and elsewhere in society.

# CHAPTER TWO

# The Development and Impact of High-Stakes Testing

## Gary Natriello and Aaron M. Pallas

Throughout the twentieth century the use of formal standardized testing has grown in the United States and permeated most major sectors of life. From the use of such tests to classify personnel for the armed forces and regulate immigration early in the century,[1] to the application of testing and assessment in schools and colleges[2] and in workplaces[3] as the century unfolded, to the institutionalization of widespread testing as government policy in more recent years,[4] the use of testing technology has expanded at an unprecedented rate. Indeed, formal testing has become the kudzu of modern American society—a healthy, vigorous grower penetrating all available space.

In the last quarter of the twentieth century, testing was developed as a major tool of policymakers for the governance and regulation of education. Beginning in the 1970s with the growth of the minimum competency testing movement, numerous states turned to the widespread, formal testing of students as a mechanism to place a performance floor under the educational enterprise. With the development of the contemporary school reform movement following the release of *A Nation at Risk* in 1983, widespread standardized testing, increasingly connected to consequences beyond the test report alone, became a staple of educational policymakers in their quest to raise and maintain high standards. Such standards and the testing practices thought to signify and support them enjoyed continued currency among both members of the educational policy establishment and leaders of the broader political order in the 1990s as an element of a systemic reform movement that seeks to align curriculum, standards, and assessments to achieve a powerful

19

impact on the educational system. Finally, the information on student performance made available through widespread testing, if not the technology of testing itself, has been incorporated into the arguments of school finance reform advocates, who point to the poor patterns of performance among students in certain groups and locations as evidence to support claims that certain public schools, typically those serving urban and minority youngsters, are inadequate to meet the needs of the students they are supposed to provide with genuine educational opportunities.

In this chapter, we first review the recent developments in the growth of testing as a requirement for high school graduation for K–12 public school systems throughout the United States. We then examine the performance patterns on such tests of students in different racial/ethnic groups by focusing on several states for in-depth consideration. Finally, we consider the multiple meanings of the movement to require students to pass formal, statewide tests in order to receive a high school diploma.

## THE GROWTH OF WIDESPREAD TESTING IN K–12 EDUCATION

Formal testing of students in K–12 schools has enjoyed popularity among policymakers for several decades because it is viewed as addressing a number of goals. First, programs of formal testing controlled by state government agencies allow the level of government with the legal authority for schooling, the state, to exercise control over the activities of the local schools and districts where schooling actually occurs. As such, formal state testing programs can be a part of the monitoring process used by states to ensure that appropriate educational activities are occurring and, along with funding and regulation, are among the most important methods of exercising state influence. In an educational system that is among the most decentralized in the world, such devices are particularly attractive to state leaders whenever they feel pressure from the citizenry to maintain and enhance the quality of education.

Second, statewide formal testing of students has the potential to influence the behavior of all major actors in the educational system. Testing can be interpreted as causing students to pay greater attention to the demands of the educational system and to devote greater effort in meeting those demands. Testing may also be viewed as a mechanism to influence the behavior of professional educators, teachers, and administrators by exposing the results of their performance to public scrutiny in a comparative framework. Finally, testing may be seen as a device to influence the way the public perceives public schools. Particularly when testing is attached to the awarding of high school diplomas, it may be viewed as a way to guarantee to the public some basic level of accomplishment for high school graduates. Indeed, it may be the goal of offering quality assurances to the public that most clearly motivates high-stakes testing.

Another appeal of widespread testing to the policy community is the inherent efficiency of testing as a performance-monitoring process. Testing student outcomes offers a more favorable ratio of information gathered to expenses incurred than most other supervision strategies. Formal testing programs attempt to arrive at assessments of performance based upon severely limited samples of performance under restricted conditions. Moreover, such testing programs carry the mantle of science and are thereby legitimated. Finally, testing programs can be portrayed both as monitoring devices and as educational reforms themselves and thus do not lead, at least initially, to substantial new expenditures for additional changes in the system.

All of these factors suggest that there are compelling reasons why policymakers, oriented toward the exercise of rational measures to improve school bureaucracies, look favorably on widespread testing programs. In addition, there may be powerful social forces leading to the adoption of such systems. In light of the rise of testing technology in the early part of the twentieth century and its use to respond to and control the perceived threat posed by massive immigration and the possible displacement of advantaged classes in American society,[5] it is worth considering whether the current boom in testing is more than coincidentally arising in the wake of both the civil rights movement, which liberated millions of American blacks from strong social restrictions on their advancement in society, and the massive movement of new immigrants into the United States over the past twenty years. In other words, the current testing boom may be viewed both as an attempt to control the educational bureaucracies and to slow the rate at which new groups enter positions of power and influence in U.S. society.

Whatever the cause or causes, there is no denying the broad use of formal testing tied to high school graduation. The 1998 report by the Council of Chief State School Officers, *Key State Education Policies on K–12 Education*, indicates that twenty-two states currently have required examinations for high school graduation.[6] An additional five states are in the process of developing examinations that will be required for high school graduation.[7] The Education Commission of the States reports that three states offer endorsed diplomas to students who not only pass an exit test, but also score at a level higher than the minimum required for a regular diploma.[8] The same report also notes that three states offer honors diplomas to students who pass a more rigorous test.[9] These reports are, however, moving targets, as state-level policies regarding graduation tests can shift rapidly.

## IMPACT OF HIGH-STAKES TESTING

There is little consensus on the impact of high-stakes testing on students, teachers, schools, and the general public's perspective on education. Proponents of high-stakes testing argue that such tests alert parents and the public to the performance of individual students and the system over-all. These proponents suggest that such tests cause students to devote greater effort to their schooling and that they also orient schools to the goals for education adopted at the state level. Indeed, there is some evi-dence that formal state testing programs do influence the activities of teachers and school administrators by directing their attention to a cur-riculum linked to the tests.[10]

Opponents of high-stakes testing policies argue that such policies, and indeed the entire standards movement, are based on faulty assump-tions about human motivation. Kennon M. Sheldon and Bruce J. Biddle argue that rigid standards, narrow accountability, and tangible sanctions may reduce the motivation of teachers and students.[11] They note that stu-dents who are focused on tests and sanctions may lose intrinsic interest, learn only superficially, and fail to develop a desire for learning. In addi-tion, they observe that while reforms that include standards, account-ability, and sanctions may raise test scores, they may at the same time impede progress toward creating a population of life-long learners who can adapt to changing needs and conditions.

As Jay Heubert and Robert Hauser note, proponents and opponents of graduation testing can argue about the issue precisely because there is relatively little research that addresses the consequences of such test-ing.[12] Without pressing the issue of the *ultimate* impact of high-stakes testing, in the next section we consider the *immediate* impact in terms of the test scores of students from different racial and ethnic groups in Texas, New York, and Minnesota, three of the twenty-two states that now have high-stakes testing programs.

# HIGH-STAKES GRADUATION TESTING IN TEXAS

In the late 1980s, the Texas legislature mandated a new criterion-referenced testing program, dubbed the Texas Assessment of Academic Skills (TAAS). The tests are used to gauge individual students' academic progress and to evaluate the performance of schools and districts for statewide accountability purposes.

There are two ways of satisfying the testing requirements for a high school diploma in Texas. The first is to pass all three parts (reading, mathematics, and writing) of the exit-level TAAS. The exit-level TAAS is administered initially in the spring of the tenth grade, and then in the spring, summer, and fall of each subsequent school year. Students thus have eight opportunities to pass each part of the exit-level TAAS. TAAS tests are also administered in grades 3 through 8, and the state board of education has set the level of satisfactory performance so that the passing standard in reading and mathematics in grades 3 through 8 is equivalent to the passing standard at the exit level (that is, answering approximately 70 percent of the items correctly).

The second way of satisfying the testing requirement is to pass end-of-course tests in algebra I, English II, and either biology I or U.S. history. The end-of-course tests are administered in the last two weeks of the course, and students who fail to attain a passing score can retake the test each time it is offered. It is not possible to satisfy the testing requirement by mixing scores on the exit-level TAAS and the end-of-course tests.

## EXEMPTIONS

Students receiving special education services may be exempted from the TAAS and end-of-course tests if their admission, review, and dismissal (ARD) committee determines that these tests are not appropriate measures of the student's academic progress. An exempt special education student who successfully completes an approved Individualized Education Plan (IEP) can receive a high school diploma. Students with learning disabilities such as dyslexia who are not exempt from testing by virtue of their special education status may be eligible for testing accommodations. Although students of limited English proficiency may be exempted from the TAAS assessments in grades 3 through 8 on the recommendation of the student's language proficiency assessment committee (LPAC), there is no such exemption for the exit-level TAAS or end-of-course tests. A student with limited English proficiency who has entered the United States within twelve months of the initial administration of the exit-level tests may postpone the initial administration once but subsequently is subject to the usual testing requirements.

The Texas Education Agency reports the proportion of students not tested across all of the TAAS tests (that is, grades 3 through 8 and the exit-level). In 1997, 9.4 percent of the students eligible for participation in the TAAS testing program were not tested. African American and Hispanic students were much less likely to be tested than white students. Of the 11.6 percent of African American students who were not tested, more than 80 percent were exempted by their ARD committees. Of the 13.8 percent of Hispanic students who were not tested, approximately 40 percent were exempt due to limited English proficiency, and an additional 40 percent were exempted by their ARD committees. (As noted above, limited English proficiency is not a legitimate exemption for the exit-level tests.) In contrast, only 5.2 percent of the white students were not tested, and nearly 80 percent of these were exempted by their ARD committees.

## RACIAL/ETHNIC DISPARITIES IN PERFORMANCE

There are substantial differences across racial/ethnic groups in performance on the tests required to obtain a high school diploma in Texas. Table 2.1 shows the pass rates for several such tests administered in the 1998–99 school year: the TAAS exit-level tests in reading, mathematics, and writing, administered in the spring of 1999, and the end-of-course tests for Algebra I and Biology I, administered in the fall of 1998. These results pertain to students not enrolled in special education and include both first-time test-takers and students retaking the test. In every case, the pass rate for white students greatly exceeds that for African American and Hispanic students. These gaps have, however, shrunk

### TABLE 2.1. 1998–99 TAAS PASS RATES BY STUDENT RACE/ETHNICITY, ALL STUDENTS NOT IN SPECIAL EDUCATION (PERCENT)

|          | TAAS | | END-OF-COURSE | | |
|----------|---------|------|---------|-----------|-----------|
|          | READING | MATH | WRITING | ALGEBRA I | BIOLOGY I |
| White    | 97      | 91   | 97      | 52        | 92        |
| Black    | 85      | 69   | 88      | 20        | 64        |
| Hispanic | 82      | 75   | 86      | 26        | 67        |

*Source:* Texas Education Agency, Division of Student Assessment, available at http://www.tea.state.tx.us/student.assessment/reporting/results/swresults/index.html.

slightly over time, as the pass rates of all groups increased markedly from 1994 to 1999.

Perhaps more revealing are the TAAS exit-level cumulative pass rates. These rates are the percentages of students who first took the exit-level TAAS test in the spring of their tenth-grade year and who successfully completed all three parts of the exit-level TAAS by the spring of their senior year. Table 2.2 shows the TAAS exit-level cumulative pass rates for the classes of 1996 through 1998. The results reported in the table show that, by the spring of their senior year in high school, a substantial fraction of minority students—more than one-sixth—did not successfully complete the TAAS exit-level tests required to obtain a Texas high school diploma. In contrast, fewer than one in ten white students in the classes of 1996 through 1998 failed to complete the exit-level TAAS successfully. Although increases in cumulative pass rates from 1996 to 1998 are encouraging, overall these tests are, and will remain for some time, an impediment to the graduation prospects of African American and Hispanic youths.

TABLE 2.2. CUMULATIVE PASS RATES ON THE TAAS FOR THE
CLASSES OF 1996–98 BY RACE/ETHNICITY (PERCENT)

| | ALL STUDENTS | WHITE | BLACK | HISPANIC |
|---|---|---|---|---|
| Class of 1996 | 84.7 | 91.7 | 76.0 | 76.2 |
| Class of 1997 | 86.6 | 92.7 | 78.9 | 79.3 |
| Class of 1998 | 88.7 | 93.9 | 82.4 | 82.6 |

*Note:* Includes only those students not in special education.
*Source:* Texas Education Agency, Academic Excellence Indicator System.

## LEGAL CHALLENGES

In December 1995, the Texas branch of the National Association for the Advancement of Colored People (NAACP) filed a complaint with the U.S. Department of Education's Office of Civil Rights (OCR), alleging that the group disparities in performance on the exit-level TAAS are evidence that the test discriminates against minority youths. In 1997, OCR determined that the complaint did not warrant a finding of racial bias.

The Mexican American Legal Defense and Educational Fund (MALDEF) filed a suit in a federal district court against the Texas Education Agency in October 1997 on behalf of seven students who did not pass the TAAS exit-level test. MALDEF's press release on the suit

states that "approximately 7,500 students each year do not pass the
TAAS test and are denied a diploma . . . . Over half of Texas' minority
students in the sophomore year do not pass one or more parts of the
TAAS test, and approximately 85 percent of the students who do not pass
the TAAS in May before graduation are Mexican American or African
American." However, on January 7, 2000, the United States District
Court for the Western District of Texas upheld the use of the test and
stated that the "TAAS examination does not have an impermissible
adverse impact on Texas's minority students."[13]

## HIGH-STAKES GRADUATION TESTING IN NEW YORK

The New York State Board of Regents has adopted new, more demanding standards for high school graduation. The adoption of these standards did not occur in isolation; rather it is part of a broader movement
of educational reform guided at the state level by policies to develop,
articulate, and raise standards for schools and students and to promote
adherence to these standards by means of more comprehensive and challenging assessments. Linda Darling-Hammond and Beverly Falk describe
the New York effort, begun in the early 1990s under former commissioner Thomas Sobol and continued by current commissioner Richard
Mills, as "a comprehensive system of learning goals and standards, curriculum frameworks, new assessments, and support strategies."[14]

New York has long had statewide tests of student performance. In
one sense the state has a great deal of experience with such testing, which
might prove useful in its current endeavor. However, the approach to
assessment reflected in the new Regents graduation requirements is a
major departure from past practices in several ways.

First, although high school graduation in New York has long
involved statewide exams, the state has operated a dual-track system.
The current requirements for graduation were developed in the early
1980s as part of the Regents Action Plan; students seeking a local high
school diploma have been required to pass Regents Competency Tests
(RCTs), assessments with relatively low demand, and the corresponding course units of study. Only students seeking a Regents diploma have
been required to pass a minimum of eight of the more demanding
Regents examinations and course units of study.[15] The result of this
assessment policy has been the development of two quite different curricular tracks through high school, with local diploma students taking less
challenging classes that prepare them for less challenging examinations, and

students pursuing a Regents diploma taking more demanding Regents courses to prepare them for more demanding examinations. The new graduation requirements will maintain the distinction between the local diploma and the Regents diploma, but all students will have the opportunity to earn a Regents-endorsed diploma by earning a passing score of 65 on the Regents examinations. Students who do not earn a passing score on the Regents examinations may receive a local diploma if they meet a lower standard on the same examination. Standards for the local diploma will be set by the local district, but the standard can be no lower than 55.[16] Curricular arrangements designed to help students to succeed on the new Regents examinations will be decided at the local level; the state department of education is encouraging districts to provide appropriate instruction for students who learn in different ways and at different paces, while not locking any students into tracks with lower expectations.[17] Thus, the new policy calls for a single set of standards toward which all students should work, with the means to reach those standards to be determined locally.

A second way that the new graduation requirements and assessments depart from past practices is that they are tied less to particular courses and more to comprehensive state standards. In each curricular area the state has adopted learning standards to guide both the development of curricula at various grade levels and the development of statewide assessments. These standards include connections between grade levels and across subject areas.

A third way is that the new graduation requirements envision continual revision of the Regents examinations to bring them into line with state and national standards and practices for assessment. These revised assessments are intended to include more than content coverage; they will also probe higher-order thinking and require a broader range of activities from students. Hence, the current Regents examinations, although certainly more demanding than the Regents Competency Tests, may not be as demanding as the revised Regents examinations. Thus, an analysis that compares the RCTs to the current Regents examinations or one that examines current pass rates on the Regents examinations may underestimate the extent of the change required to prepare students to succeed on the revised Regents examinations.

The requirements for a high school diploma in New York will be substantially changed by the new examination requirements. This change will occur over several years as students are required to pass the Regents examinations in various fields instead of the current Regents Competency Tests.

The schedule for implementing the new testing standards is as follows:

| YEAR | REQUIREMENT FOR ENTERING NINTH-GRADERS |
|------|----------------------------------------|
| 1996 | Take the English Regents exam |
| 1997 | Take the English and mathematics Regents exams |
| 1998 | Take the English, mathematics, and social studies Regents exams |
| 1999 | Take the English, mathematics, social studies, and science Regents exams |
| 2000 | Achieve a score of 65 or above on the English and social studies exams |
| 2001 | Achieve a score of 65 or above on the English, social studies, mathematics, and science exams |

## EXEMPTIONS

Students with disabilities typically have legally mandated Individualized Education Programs (IEPs) or 504 plans (named after Section 504 of the Rehabilitation Act of 1973, a civil rights statute requiring that persons with disabilities be provided services that are as effective as those provided persons without disabilities; students identified as eligible for Section 504 need to be provided with services so they can participate fully in a regular classroom or basic program). Exemptions are allowed both for students with short-term disabilities and for those with ongoing disabilities whose IEPs or 504 plans contain test modification provisions.[18] Modifications in testing procedures may be made at the discretion of the principal for students with short-term disabilities who do not have an IEP or a 504 plan, but a full report must be made to the Office of State Assessment; if a student is expected to continue to need test modifications, a referral must be made for the development of an IEP or 504 plan. Modifications for students with short-term disabilities may include extending the time for the test, administering the test in a special location, allowing the answers to be recorded in any manner, and (except for tests of reading comprehension) reading the test to the student.

For students whose IEPs or 504 plans include test modifications, principals must provide modified testing procedures, including reading or signing questions to students, recording student answers in an alternative manner, the use of spell checking and grammar checking programs, or excusing students with severe spelling disabilities from spelling requirements. Large-type examinations, Braille examinations, and reader-administered examinations may also be provided where appropriate.

## RACIAL/ETHNIC DISPARITIES IN PERFORMANCE

Because the new Regents examinations have not been widely administered and because data on prior Regents examination results have not been available by racial/ethnic group membership, we are able to consider possible racial/ethnic disparities in performance only by examining school-level Regents pass rates in relationship to school-level student body characteristics. To do this, we examined data from the *Statistical Profiles of Public School Districts.*[19] This report contains data on the proportions of students who received Regents diplomas in 1994–95 and the proportions of racial and ethnic minority students in each school. The correlation between the proportion of Regents diplomas and the proportion of black students in a school is –0.33. Figure 2.1 (page 30) shows that, although there is a wide distribution of the proportion of Regents diplomas among schools whose student bodies are less than 20 percent black, among schools in which black students constitute more than 50 percent of the student body the proportion of Regents diplomas remains below 40 percent. This negative relationship between the proportion of black students in a school and the proportion of Regents diplomas awarded is reflected in the correlations involving the proportions of students passing individual Regents exams reported in Table 2.3 (page 30).

In a parallel set of analyses, we found that the correlation between the proportion of Regents diplomas and the proportion of Hispanic students in a school is –0.22. Figure 2.2 (page 31) shows that, although there is a wide distribution of Regents diploma rates among schools that are 15 percent Hispanic, the Regents diploma rate for such schools remains below 60 percent. When the proportion of Hispanic students exceeds 40 percent, the Regents diploma rate remains below 40 percent. The negative relationship between the proportion of Hispanic students in a school and the proportion of Regents diplomas awarded is reflected in the correlations involving the proportions of students passing individual Regents examinations, as noted in Table 2.4 (page 31).

These analyses involving the racial and ethnic minority status of students show that there is a negative relationship between the proportion of minority students in a school and the proportion of Regents diplomas awarded in that school. The negative relationship is stronger in the case of black students than in that of Hispanic students, but even for Hispanic

## FIGURE 2.1. RATE OF REGENTS DIPLOMAS BY PERCENTAGE OF BLACK STUDENTS

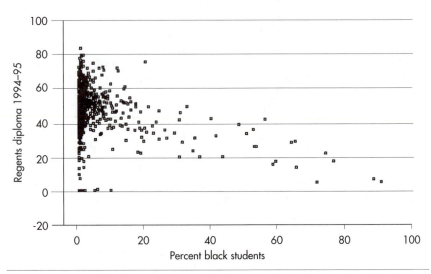

*Source:* Gary Natriello, *The New Regents High School Graduation Requirements: The Nature of the Change and the Demands Placed on Schools and School Districts* (New York: Community Service Society, 1997).

## TABLE 2.3. CORRELATIONS BETWEEN THE PROPORTION OF BLACK STUDENTS IN A SCHOOL AND THE PROPORTION OF STUDENTS PASSING INDIVIDUAL REGENTS EXAMINATIONS

| REGENTS EXAM | CORRELATION | NUMBER OF SCHOOLS |
|---|---|---|
| English | −0.28 | 690 |
| Math I | −0.33 | 685 |
| Math II | −0.31 | 692 |
| Math III | −0.27 | 680 |
| Biology | −0.33 | 665 |
| Chemistry | −0.25 | 679 |
| Earth science | −0.32 | 531 |
| Physics | −0.21 | 665 |
| U.S. history | −0.27 | 693 |
| Global studies | −0.33 | 676 |

*Source:* Gary Natriello, *The New Regents High School Graduation Requirements: The Nature of the Change and the Demands Placed on Schools and School Districts* (New York: Community Service Society, 1997).

## FIGURE 2.2. RATE OF REGENTS DIPLOMAS BY PERCENTAGE OF HISPANIC STUDENTS

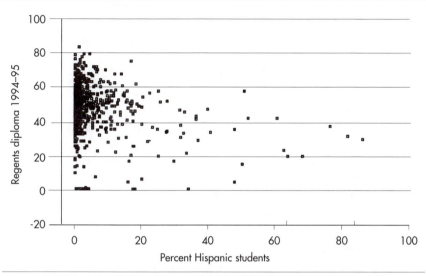

Source: Gary Natriello, *The New Regents High School Graduation Requirements: The Nature of the Change and the Demands Placed on Schools and School Districts* (New York: Community Service Society, 1997).

## TABLE 2.4. CORRELATIONS BETWEEN THE PROPORTION OF HISPANIC STUDENTS IN A SCHOOL AND THE PROPORTION OF STUDENTS PASSING INDIVIDUAL REGENTS EXAMINATIONS

| REGENTS EXAM | CORRELATION | NUMBER OF SCHOOLS |
| --- | --- | --- |
| English | −0.22 | 690 |
| Math I | −0.24 | 685 |
| Math II | −0.16 | 692 |
| Math III | −0.16 | 680 |
| Biology | −0.25 | 665 |
| Chemistry | −0.15 | 679 |
| Earth science | −0.23 | 531 |
| Physics | −0.12 | 665 |
| U.S. history | −0.19 | 693 |
| Global studies | −0.23 | 676 |

Source: Gary Natriello, *The New Regents High School Graduation Requirements: The Nature of the Change and the Demands Placed on Schools and School Districts* (New York: Community Service Society, 1997).

students the relationship is significant and extends across all of the individual Regents examinations.

To determine the relationship between performance on the Regents examinations and students' family resources, we examined the relationship between schools' rates for the awarding of Regents diplomas and their rates for participation in the free lunch program. The correlation between these two school-level measures is –0.62, indicating that as the percentage of students participating in the free lunch program increases, the percentage of students earning a Regents diploma decreases. As Figure 2.3 reveals, in schools in which half or more of the students participate in the free or reduced-price lunch program, fewer than 35 percent of the students earn a Regents diploma. Among schools in which less than half of the students participate in the free or reduced-price lunch program, there is more variability among schools in the Regents diploma rate, but the average is considerably higher than 35 percent.

We also examined the relationship between the percentage of students in a given school awarded a Regents diploma and the percentage of the student body classified as having limited English proficiency.[20] The correlation between these two school-level measures is –0.45, indicating that as the percentage of students with limited English proficiency in a school increases, the Regents diploma rate decreases. Figure 2.4 shows this relationship (page 34).

Clearly, the burden of responding to the change represented by the new standards will not fall on schools evenly. Schools with greater proportions of students from backgrounds of poverty and with limited English proficiency will face the greatest challenge in moving toward an all-Regents program. Even in the absence of pass rates for particular minority groups, these data clearly indicate that the new Regents standards will have a disparate impact on racial and ethnic minorities, the poor, and students with limited English proficiency.

## LEGAL CHALLENGES

With the new Regents standards and examinations not yet in effect, there are no active legal challenges to the testing program. However, attorneys for the Committee for Fiscal Equity, which is challenging the constitutionality of the state educational finance system, plan to incorporate the new Regents standards and examinations into arguments relating to the need for additional resources to provide a sound, basic education in numerous districts statewide. Other advocacy groups have indicated an interest in the performance of students with disabilities and those who have limited English proficiency.

**FIGURE 2.3. RATE OF REGENTS DIPLOMAS BY
PERCENTAGE OF STUDENTS RECEIVING FREE
OR REDUCED-PRICE LUNCH**

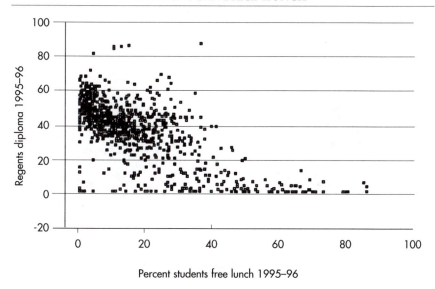

Percent students free lunch 1995–96

*Source:* Gary Natriello, *The New Regents High School Graduation Requirements: The Nature of the Change and the Demands Placed on Schools and School Districts* (New York: Community Service Society, 1997).

## HIGH-STAKES GRADUATION TESTING IN MINNESOTA

Minnesota's new graduation standards, which will pertain to students from the class of 2002 and later, have two elements: basic standards defining the basic skills needed to live and work in contemporary society, and high standards defining what a student should know, understand, and be able to do to demonstrate a high level of achievement. To satisfy the basic standards, students must pass tests in reading and mathematics first administered in the eighth grade and a test in written composition first administered in the tenth grade in order to graduate. To satisfy the high standards, students must meet twenty-four of forty-eight possible standards in ten learning areas by completing performance packages (sets of locally designed assignments) in the ten learning areas. In addition, the state requires testing for students in the third and fifth grades. These Minnesota Comprehensive Assessments are administered in reading and math in third grade and in reading, math, and written composition in fifth grade.

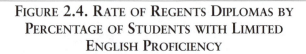

FIGURE 2.4. RATE OF REGENTS DIPLOMAS BY
PERCENTAGE OF STUDENTS WITH LIMITED
ENGLISH PROFICIENCY

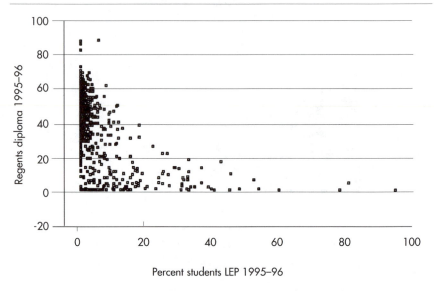

*Source:* Gary Natriello, *The New Regents High School Graduation Requirements: The Nature of the Change and the Demands Placed on Schools and School Districts* (New York: Community Service Society, 1997).

## EXEMPTIONS

There are exceptions to the standard testing procedures for both students with disabilities and students with limited English proficiency. Students with disabilities are eligible for accommodations or modifications as called for in their IEP or 504 plans. An accommodation involves the same test or assignment administered with a variation in time, format, setting and/or manner of presentation, such as a blind student taking a Braille version of a test. A modification is an adjustment in the test or assignment that involves a change in the standard for a particular student, such as a student completing work on only part of a standard. For students who pass the basic standards tests, with or without accommodations, the transcript shows the notation "Pass-State"; for students with IEPs or 504 plans who pass modified versions the transcript indicates "Pass-Individual." Students may be exempted from the tests if their cognitive ability is limited to the extent of prohibiting them from taking the test, if taking the test would be detrimental to the student beyond a reasonable level of stress or anxiety, or if the student's IEP or 504 plan did not expose him or her to the material covered by the test.[21]

Each school district is responsible for establishing a process to determine how students with limited English proficiency are to be included in basic standards testing. Such students are identified as those "whose first language is not English and whose test performance may be negatively impacted by lack of English language proficiency."[22] Students can be temporarily exempted from the tests only if they have spent less than three years in a school where the primary language of instruction is English. Accommodations for students with limited English proficiency can include adjustment in the time, location, and presentation format of the test. Districts also can determine the conditions under which students may take a translated or interpreted version of the mathematics test or the test of written composition. The notation "Pass-Translate" is recorded on the records of students who pass a translated test. For the test of written composition, local districts determine how, at the request of a student or parent, a composition can be reviewed to be eligible for a designation of "Pass-LEP," signifying that the student has limited proficiency in English and the composition, although written in English, meets a different standard. The reading test may not be translated.

## RACIAL/ETHNIC DISPARITIES IN PERFORMANCE

The first statewide administration of the Minnesota basic standards tests took place in 1996. Analyses of this data by researchers at the Roy Wilkins Center at the University of Minnesota revealed substantial differences in the test outcomes for students from different racial/ethnic groups.[23] Students in all minority groups performed less well on the test than majority students. As Figure 2.5 (page 36) indicates, white students averaged 80 percent correct on the math, Asian American students averaged 73 percent correct, Native American and Hispanic students averaged 65 percent correct, and African American students averaged 58 percent correct. For the reading test the pattern was much the same. There, white students averaged 70 percent correct, Asian students averaged 62 percent correct, Native American students averaged 57 percent correct, Hispanic students averaged 54 percent correct, and African American students averaged 50 percent correct. Figure 2.6 (page 37) displays these differences.

## LEGAL CHALLENGES

With Minnesota's new graduation standards yet to take effect fully, there are no ongoing legal cases pertaining to them. However, the results of the new state tests are likely to be used by lawyers for the St. Paul

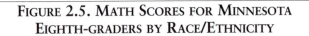

## FIGURE 2.5. MATH SCORES FOR MINNESOTA EIGHTH-GRADERS BY RACE/ETHNICITY

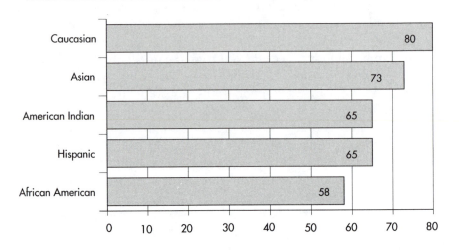

*Source:* Roy Wilkins Center for Human Relations and Social Justice, *Analysis of the 1996 Minnesota Basic Standards Test Data* (Minneapolis: University of Minnesota, 1997).

Public Schools in their case against the State of Minnesota challenging the adequacy of state funding.

## INTERPRETATIONS

Interpretations of the purpose and disparate impact of high-stakes testing are heavily dependent upon the perspective brought to the question. If we accept that high-stakes testing has a positive motivational effect on parents, students, teachers, and school administrators, then we can take comfort in the fact that policies that mandate challenging high-stakes testing for all students may in fact extend educational opportunities more broadly than earlier practices, which divided students into different educational tracks with different levels of quality, different challenges, and different educational and occupational trajectories. If we accept the legitimacy of high-stakes tests as devices that appropriately measure student performance and the effort that necessarily precedes that performance, then we can be satisfied that we are creating a system that justly rewards those who work hard to develop their talents. If managers of state educational systems employ high-stakes tests as only one element of a

## FIGURE 2.6. READING SCORES FOR MINNESOTA EIGHTH-GRADERS BY RACE/ETHNICITY

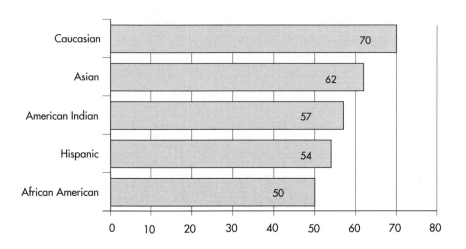

Source: Roy Wilkins Center for Human Relations and Social Justice, *Analysis of the 1996 Minnesota Basic Standards Test Data* (Minneapolis: University of Minnesota, 1997).

broader rational examination of the processes, opportunities, and outcomes of schooling and if they configure such systems to provide to all students processes and opportunities sufficient to lead to desired and mandated outcomes well in advance of the testing events, then we can view such tests as appropriate management tools. If advocates for the provision of equitable and adequate schooling resources for all students can use the results of high-stakes tests to reveal deficiencies in the current arrangements for the education of all children, including less-advantaged children, then we can be encouraged that such tests will have a positive impact on what is arguably the least equitable educational system among modern nation states.

There is, however, an equally plausible set of assumptions that is less satisfying to contemplate. If the motivational consequences of high-stakes tests are not positive or at least not uniformly positive across racial, ethnic, and social class lines, then we should be concerned about their potential to exacerbate already substantial inequities in schooling outcomes. Claude Steele's research, which shows that the threat of conforming to race-based stereotypes about academic ability may depress the academic performance of racial and ethnic minorities, suggests precisely this possibility.[24] If we have reason to question the legitimacy of current testing technologies to support the purposes to which they are being put, then we should be concerned that the "science" of testing and measurement is being abused to justify and achieve social purposes that would otherwise be indefensible. If managers of state educational systems deploy high-stakes tests in isolation from more comprehensive efforts to provide adequate and equitable educational resources, then we should question the true intent of such testing programs. If defenders of the current arrangements for schooling rely on the results of high-stakes tests to define any and all patterns of educational deficits as originating and residing in the backgrounds and individual capacities of students alone, then we should be concerned that these tests will be used to justify the maintenance of an educational system that only appears to provide fundamental educational rights, while denying those rights in defiance of state and federal constitutional provisions.

## RECOMMENDATIONS

Whatever interpretation one prefers to place on the high-stakes testing movement, there are a number of things that we can do to improve the use of such tests to enhance the educational rights of U.S. students. First, we can develop programs of research to allow us to understand more fully the consequences of high-stakes testing, and indeed of assessment processes more generally, on individuals and their performance. Second, we can explore more aggressively the capacity of high-stakes and other tests and assessments to reflect the full range of human capabilities. Third, we can continue to expand our conceptions of human capacity beyond those typically captured in mainstream tests. Fourth, we can continue to hold proponents of the rationality of high-stakes testing accountable for applying a correspondingly vigorous rational analysis to the educational processes and opportunities necessary to ensure student success on those tests. Finally, we can continue to use the results of high-stakes tests to reflect back on the system and its obligation to provide equal opportunity for learning, in effect making the stakes for policymakers no less high than we make them for eighteen-year-old high school students.

CHAPTER THREE

# High-Stakes Testing and Economic Productivity

HENRY M. LEVIN

Almost every major call for education reform argues that reform is needed to create and maintain a competitive labor force.[1] As stated by the National Education Goals Panel, "The nation's strength is rooted in its ability to compete economically, and its ability to perform economically is rooted in its education system."[2] These calls for reform also assert that high-stakes testing in schools—testing in which important consequences are premised on results[3]—will foster the economic competitiveness of the nation. The tests will improve the U.S. labor force and provide employers with useful information for selecting employees.

Yet, using tests to ascertain how well schools are doing in preparing a productive workforce and to determine who is likely to be a productive employee requires not only that such tests be valid predictors of workplace productivity, but also that the link between test criteria and worker productivity is large enough to make productivity predictions with great precision. In this chapter I will assert that this link is missing. Traditional tests, including those used for international comparisons, show only nominal statistical links to measures of worker productivity, and the new standards on which current tests are being constructed have not been validated at all. That being the case, if current high-stakes tests do no better at this task than the more traditional tests, they have the potential of resulting in massive unfairness and misallocation of resources.

Before proceeding to the substance of these arguments, it is important to avoid misunderstandings that may arise from this message. Let me state at the outset that I believe worker skills are important to productivity and that existing test instruments can measure them with partial success. Let me also state that nothing in this chapter should be interpreted as a rejection of testing when properly used or as a rejection of high standards, which are important for many reasons. Although I have some concern about who sets the standards and how they are used and assessed by schools, these are issues that are more generally debated among educators and policymakers. The specific concern that I address in this chapter is an improper use of testing, namely the use of test results as the primary determinant for employee selection.

There are two claims implied in the case for testing for workplace competencies; first, that those students who do well on the tests will be much better prepared for the workplace than those who do poorly, and second, that the overall workforce and economic productivity will be improved dramatically by increasing the number of labor force participants who do well on the tests. Yet, as I will demonstrate below, there is consistent evidence that test scores have only a small relation to workplace productivity when earnings or supervisory ratings are used as criteria. The link is so small that when test scores are used for employment selection, there is a high probability that many workers will be rejected for jobs that they could perform and many will be selected for jobs that they cannot perform.[4] The danger here is that the opposite of what was intended can arise. That is, the economy can be compromised by substantial "misallocation" of labor while injustices simultaneously will be done to many individuals in job placement. To the degree that the tests induce errors in placement that impact women or certain minorities more heavily than others, there can be systematic adverse effects on particular groups as well, not just on individuals.[5]

## TEST SCORES AND PRODUCTIVITY

Productivity of individual workers is not easy to measure because workers in different occupational positions and different firms often perform activities that are incommensurable. Although a few studies have compared worker productivity within narrow occupations or for piecework, typical measures of worker productivity are indirect and measured through a proxy. The two most common of these measures are earnings and supervisory ratings.

Using earnings as a measure of productivity assumes that wages are set in perfectly competitive markets and that both individuals and employers are "pricetakers," meaning that they must accept the prevailing wage established by the market to compensate workers for a given level of productivity. The theoretical model underlying these assumptions is grounded in neoclassical economics and can show rigorously the equivalence of wages and productivity. Although most markets deviate at least somewhat from the perfectly competitive, textbook assumptions, the prevailing view is that earnings are a good approximation of productivity in most situations.

Supervisory ratings of worker performance have long been used as a measure of productivity by industrial psychologists.[6] Supervisors may rate worker performance on different duties or dimensions of their jobs, which are then combined for overall ratings, or they may provide one summary rating of performance. Such ratings may be used to set compensation or promotions. They also may be used for selecting employees from among a pool of candidates. For a considerable period of time, the U.S. Employment Service recommended job applicants to prospective employers on the basis of applicant scores on the General Ability Test Battery.[7]

## TEST SCORES AND EARNINGS

Historically, a one-standard-deviation difference in test scores—controlling for race, gender, educational level, and experiences—has been associated with about a 3 to 4 percent difference in earnings.[8] However, reading scores are much poorer predictors of earnings than are mathematics scores or quantitative measures of literacy.[9] For example, in a recent paper, Richard Murnane and his colleagues reported that mathematics test results always demonstrated a statistically significant effect on estimations of earnings, while reading test results demonstrated a statistically insignificant or negative effect.[10] Paradoxically, it is common for school districts to place a greater stress on raising reading scores and give them a higher public visibility than mathematics scores. Although research on the effects of test scores on earnings usually uses the broader term *cognitive skills,* such research is often limited to the use of mathematics scores because these show the highest relation to earnings.[11]

The most recent findings show that, over the decade of the 1980s, the economic returns for cognitive skill as reflected in mathematics scores have increased.[12] However, the overall impact still seems relatively small, with one standard deviation of test score being associated with only about a 7 percent increase in wages for men and about twice that for women. We need to bear in mind that educational reforms rarely have been shown *consistently* to raise test scores in mathematics by more than 0.25 standard deviations. For males, an increase of about

0.25 standard deviations in test scores suggests an increase in earnings of about 2 percent, equivalent to working about thirty-two hours more per year. For women the improvement in earnings would be about twice this amount.

Yet, even an effect size of 0.25 (standard deviation units) is rare. In a highly publicized study, James Coleman and Thomas Hoffer found that students in private schools averaged about a 0.06 standard deviation advantage over similar students in public schools.[13] This advantage is roughly equivalent to about six points on the verbal or mathematics portions of the Scholastic Aptitude Test (SAT), where the mean score is 500 and the typical score for students in the most elite schools is about 700. A difference in an SAT score of six points, or twelve points on the combined test, is unlikely even to be noticed on a college application. Nor would such differences translate into large increases in earnings. Based on the 1986 earnings estimates from Murnane, John Willett, and Frank Levy and the 0.06 standard deviation of private school advantage noted by Coleman and Hoffer, male graduates of private schools would receive about four cents more per hour than male public school graduates, and female graduates of private schools would receive about six cents more per hour than female public school graduates.[14]

The largest relation between earnings and test scores is reported by Steven W. Raudenbush and Rafa M. Kasim.[15] They use data from the National Adult Literacy Survey (NALS) in 1992, which probably contains the most sophisticated measures of skills of any existing survey that gathers this type of information from adults. NALS conceptualizes literacy as the ability to comprehend prose, to extract and use information from documents, and to draw inferences from quantitative information.[16] Raudenbush and Kasim conclude that an increase of one standard deviation in literacy was associated with almost an 18 percent gain in wages in 1992.[17] However, this is surely an overstatement because their measure of test scores was derived at the same time as the income measure, rather than in a prior time period that could be used for prediction. This means that test performance is likely to be as much a consequence of occupational placement as a predictor of occupation and earnings.[18]

In addition, the causal relationship between literacy scores and occupation does not function in only one direction. People in more demanding and remunerative occupations will face more literacy challenges on a regular basis, which reinforces literacy and contributes to their test performances. Conversely, when people are in less demanding positions, their test performance suffers because of less exposure to the types of practices that the tests measure.[19] Direct evidence that supports this pattern is found in the International Adult Literacy Survey (IALS) undertaken by the Organisation for Economic Co-operation and Development (OECD) in 1994, which used the same literacy measures as NALS. It found that people with higher test performance had consistently greater practice in using specific literacy skills in the workplace in both the United States and other countries. Thus, their jobs enhanced or reinforced such skills.[20] For this reason, the higher test performances in higher-paying jobs are likely to be at least partially attributable to on-the-job practice and use of such skills rather than entirely to prior skill attainments. Any causal relationship is likely to go in both directions, from test score to earnings and from earnings (based on occupational placement) to test score. Both theory and empirical evidence predict a bidirectional impact, and the estimated earnings coefficient of test scores will be overstated in a single equation model. An unbiased estimate of the coefficient requires a simultaneous equations system.

Further, these equations explain only a small part of the variance in earnings. In *The Role of Cognitive Skills in Explaining Inequality in the Earnings of American Workers,* Richard Murnane and his colleagues were generally able to explain less than 20 percent of the total variance in earnings by using family background variables, race, educational attainment, work experience, and mathematics scores as explanatory variables.[21] This means that people with the same family background, race, educational attainment, work experience, and mathematics test score had widely different earnings, so that people with a given test score would have earnings that overlap substantially with people with much higher and much lower test scores. In short, the possession of considerable information on family background, race, educational attainment, work experience, and mathematics test scores does not permit precision in estimating earnings. Thus, limiting the information only to test scores provides predictions of earnings that are not much of an improvement on random predictions.

In a 1996 article, Derek A. Neal and William R. Johnson claimed that differences in cognitive skills explain from 50 to 90 percent of the gap in hourly wages between black and white male workers.[22] This is a surprising claim in itself because, although the test score gap between black and white males has narrowed by half since the mid-1960s according to the National Assessment of Educational Progress (NAEP),[23] the black-white wage gap for males narrowed primarily during the period of civil rights enforcement—from 1965 to about 1979—

and has grown slightly since that time, even among young black workers who should have benefited economically from reductions in the test score gap.

A closer examination of Neal and Johnson's findings reveals that their methods actually overstate the effects of reducing the test score gap on reducing the wage gap. Wages and earnings are linked statistically not only to test scores, but also to family background and education.[24] In turn, test scores are influenced by family background and education. However, because the Neal and Johnson study excludes family background and education from the equations that explain wages, test scores represent not only their own impact on wages but also their correlation with the two missing variables.[25] By excluding family background as measured by socioeconomic status and education from the equation, the test score variable substantially overstates the influence of differential cognitive skills on the wage gap between blacks and whites.

In a later study that uses the same methodology, Johnson and Neal explore the apparent role of test scores in explaining the gap in annual earnings between blacks and whites.[26] Earnings take account of both the wage rate and employment. They found that the earnings gap between black and white males is more than twice as large as the gap in wage rates. They also found that the part of the earnings gap that is explained statistically by test scores is much smaller than for wages. As with their earlier analysis of the wage gap, the explanatory power of test scores is overstated because they do not include individuals' socio-economic status and education in the equations.

One argument for eliminating number of years of education from the equation is that it is not a measure of what is learned, but rather is a means to an end—the end of cognitive knowledge. If test scores measure cognitive knowledge, then no educational variable is needed. This assumes that the only effect that education has on earnings is through its effect on test scores. But as Samuel Bowles and Herb Gintis have shown, adding a test score variable to an earnings equation in which educational attainment is already included reduces the coefficient for educational attainment by only 25 percent.[27] By inference, some three-quarters of the effect of schooling occurs through its *noncognitive* effect on earnings, which Bowles and Gintis argue is the effect that schools have of molding changes in personality and behavior that are functional in the workplace.[28] An alternative explanation is that the test instruments that are used measure only a small part of the overall skills that are required in the workplace. For example, Robert Sternberg has suggested that standardized tests measure only a portion of the knowledge and analytical skills, and almost none of the creative and practical skills, that are valued at work.[29]

In their 1998 article, Raudenbush and Kasim reported that the black males in their sample were earning about 75 percent of the wages of the white males. If test scores in all three areas of literacy were equalized, they estimated that this would rise to 85 percent. Yet, recall that their estimates of the impact of test scores are clearly biased upward, so that an unbiased estimate would surely be less than this.[30]

Even at the bottom of the educational distribution the relation between test scores and earnings holds, and it pales in relation to the impact of additional years of educational attainment. For example, Gordon Berlin and Andrew Sum found that each additional grade level completed was associated with four times as large a gain in earnings as that associated with the equivalent of an additional grade of basic skills as measured by test scores (Armed Forces Qualification Test). In addition, completion of the last year of high school was associated with ten times the increase in annual earnings associated with test score gain the equivalent of an additional grade.[31]

## TEST SCORES AND SUPERVISORY RATINGS

The other principal measure of worker productivity is supervisory ratings of worker performance. Industrial psychologists have a long history of assessing the productivity of workers through such measures. A variety of worker characteristics such as previous work experience, education, and test scores have been evaluated statistically for their links to such supervisory ratings to see how well they predict worker performance.[32] Of these, the test scores of workers have been among the most prominent predictors.

The most widespread attempt to use test scores to predict job performance has been based on the General Ability Test Battery (GATB), which the U.S. Employment Service has used to rank workers for prospective employers. GATB includes subtests of intelligence, verbal aptitude, and numerical aptitude, as well as a range of other measures. But according to a study by the National Research Council, the predictive validity of GATB with respect to supervisory ratings of workers is about 0.25.[33] This means that about 6 percent of the variance in supervisory ratings of worker productivity can be explained statistically by GATB test scores, leaving 94 percent to be explained by other factors. People with identical GATB scores are almost as likely to have very high or very low supervisory ratings as others drawn randomly from the labor force. Nevertheless, until recently, the U.S. Employment Service used GATB results to rank job candidates on predicted productivity in referring them to prospective employers.

Industrial psychologists have used GATB to assert that the allocation of available people to jobs according to test scores will raise economic output by very large amounts, as much as $153 billion annually according to estimates made about two decades ago.[34] These estimates, however, were based on grossly exaggerated assumptions that vastly inflate the apparent impacts. For example, they assume that for the economy as a whole there are ten applicants for each job opening (an implied unemployment rate of 90 percent) and that validity coefficients are 100 percent larger than those that are justifiable.[35]

The research on the validity of the effect of test scores on supervisory ratings shows remarkably similar results to those of the work on earnings. In both cases, there is a consistency of statistically significant results, but the estimated impacts are very small. Perhaps this is a source of confusion in the literature. Many interpreters forget that statistically significant results are simply an affirmation that the results were unlikely to be found by chance in repeated sampling of the population. This is a far cry from suggesting that the results are economically significant and that improving the test results will have a dramatic impact on the economy and on individual productivity, which has not been demonstrated in the literature. Even the claim that most of the gap between black and white earnings would be eliminated if test scores between the races were equalized is vulnerable; first, the statistical estimates are flawed, and second, the black-white test score gap of one standard deviation is about four times what even the most successful replicable school reforms, such as the Tennessee Class Size study,[36] have been able to achieve.

## NEW STANDARDS

Although traditional tests seem to have low validity coefficients, one could argue that new standards and their associated tests now are predicated on testing in new domains and with more authentic means of performance. Certainly the new standards are attempting to focus more closely on the types of worker characteristics for which the Department of Labor has argued in its SCANS report.[37] This is especially true of the new standards produced by the National Center on Education and the Economy and the University of Pittsburgh,[38] which I find to be rich and challenging. However, a major obstacle to those who would use cognitive tests to validate student performance for future workplaces is the fact that few of the worker characteristics identified by standards are based upon "knowledge." Most encompass work behaviors and habits such as teamwork, collaboration, initiative, and forms of problem solving that require adaptability and spontaneous responses. These characteristics are hardly measured by existing test instruments.[39]

Despite the claims that the new educational standards movement has established criteria that are closely related to the needs of modern workplaces and will improve productivity if they are met in the workforce, there is very little validation. Instead, the best that can be said is that this body of work is often thoughtful and provocative.[40] Robert L. Linn has raised a large number of cautionary points about using the new standards for predicting worker productivity, including the fact that most of the competencies and skills emphasized in workplace reports "differ in important ways from descriptions of traditional academic outcomes," which are still the basis for high-stakes testing.[41] There is a lack of empirical studies that link newer standards and tests to workplace productivity, and at this moment there is no evidence that the new high-stakes tests that have been adopted, or are in the process of being adopted, are more highly predictive of worker productivity than the more traditional measures. A healthy skepticism is called for until the evidence is produced.

## POTENTIAL CONSEQUENCES

Since the publication of *A Nation at Risk* in 1983, a conventional wisdom has emerged that the performance of the U.S. economy is largely predicated on the test score performance of our students and their relative standing among students from other nations. If anything, the direct evidence challenges this simplistic view. At the time that *A Nation at Risk* was produced, the U.S. economy—in recession and with a high unemployment rate—was languishing in contrast to our international competitors. The report asserted that our poor economic performance was mirrored in and probably caused by our poor test score performance relative to those of our competitors. Since that time the schools have been subjected to wave after wave of reforms aimed at enhancing curricula, instructional strategies, and educational standards.

Even under the most optimistic conditions, the lag in implementing reforms, coupled with the fact that the labor force contains relatively small numbers of recent graduates of these reformed systems, suggests that the labor force has yet to be affected. Moreover, there is little evidence of any dramatic improvement in test scores among seventeen-year-old U.S. students on either the NAEP or on international comparisons such as the Third International Mathematics and Science Survey (TIMSS). Yet, despite the lack of evidence of a resuscitated education system, the U.S. economy has become the most competitive in the world. Japan and the Western European nations are languishing with what are record-high and stubborn unemployment rates and without the sustained economic growth record that the United States has experienced. Further, our Asian competitors such as Korea and Hong Kong, which have some of the highest test scores in international studies, have been mired in serious economic malaise. Also, recent econometric studies have found that there is little evidence that education was the driving force of the previous Asian economic miracles, with vast investments in capital and expansion of the labor force explaining almost all of their economic growth.[42]

Microeconomic evidence also challenges the test-score explanation. When Honda, Toyota, and Nissan established operations in the United States, using local workers from areas that were hardly known for the quality of their education, they found that they could produce automobiles as efficiently and with the same high quality as in Japan.[43] BMW and Mercedes have invested hundreds of millions of dollars to establish automobile assembly plants in relatively rural areas of South Carolina and Alabama, respectively, states at the bottom of the U.S. educational hierarchy in test scores and educational investment. Both are producing vehicles that have been rated highly in quality.

What is probably more important than their workers' test scores is the fact that these firms are effectively organized and managed and have high capital investments using modern technologies, team production, job security, and substantial training of workers.[44] The organization and management place special emphasis on incentives for working productively in teams and for rewarding quality in production. Training is intensive and continuous, constantly updating the skills of workers, which not only increases the value of the workers to the firm but also increases the attachment of the workers through job-specific skills that may not be directly transferable to other firms.

The real danger of applying high-stakes testing to employment and economic decisions lies in how the test scores are used. For example, if employers believe that workers who attain a score at or above a certain level have a high probability of being more productive, they will feel it is appropriate to adopt that "cut score" for making employment decisions. Certainly, this is the goal in many states that are considering or promoting high-stakes testing, both as an incentive for students to excel and as a signal to employers of productive workers. The New York State Regents diploma has been discussed as having the potential to become such a signal at several meetings that I have attended on the subject.

However, consider the following. Assume that a job applicant needs to be in the upper-half of the job productivity distribution to be considered for the most productive jobs. We can ask, What proportion of job applicants who are one standard deviation below the mean score is likely to be above the mean in job productivity? Bear in mind that workers who are one standard deviation below the mean are at the sixteenth percentile on the test criterion. With a predictive validity of 0.2 (very much in the range of existing studies), some 42 percent of those with scores one standard deviation below the mean would be expected to have job productivity levels above the mean, and about one-third of those with test scores *two standard deviations* below the mean (the bottom 3 percent of the test population) would be expected to have job productivity levels above the mean.[45] This means that using test scores as predictors of job performance would generate huge numbers of false negatives (those who can be good performers, but are rejected) and false positives (those who are poor performers, but are accepted).

Thus, the exclusive or primary use of test scores for employment selection will lead to massive unfairness as well as great potential for misallocation of human resources, with deleterious consequences for the economy. This should not be a surprising outcome when we consider that both the SCANS competencies and those proposed by Sternberg are not measured on existing test instruments.[46] Of course, future tests based upon new standards might have higher predictive validities. However, no validation studies have been done on the new standards that would support such a claim.

In conclusion, high standards may be important goals for a variety of reasons. Certainly, the educational reform movement to which I am attached, Accelerated Schools, has placed this goal in the forefront.[47] However, when it is argued that the primary reason for high standards and high-stakes testing is to create a productive workforce for the economy, we should be cautious. Paradoxically, if decisionmakers believe such a claim and act accordingly in making employment decisions, both equity and economic efficiency may be sacrificed. Such decisionmaking is also likely to have particularly pernicious and unjustified effects for blacks and Hispanics, who score substantially lower than whites on virtually all academic tests.[48]

# CHAPTER FOUR

# The Impacts of Minimum Competency Exam Graduation Requirements on College Attendance and Early Labor Market Success of Disadvantaged Students

## JOHN H. BISHOP AND FERRAN MANE

*Let us send a signal out to the world that the days of underedu-
cating our young people, the days of underestimating our young
people are over.*
    —Hugh Price, President of the National Urban League[1]

Educational reformers and most of the American public believe that
teachers ask too little of their pupils. Leaders of the African American
and Hispanic communities have criticized the low expectations and goals
that teachers and school administrators often set for their children. These
low expectations, they believe, result in watered down curricula and a
tolerance of mediocre teaching and inappropriate student behavior. The
result is that the prophecy of low achievement becomes self-fulfilling.

Although research has shown that learning gains are substantially
larger when students take more-demanding courses,[2] few students—
minority or majority—enroll in these courses. There are several reasons
for this. The first is that guidance counselors in some schools allow only
a select few into the most challenging courses. While most schools give
students and parents the authority to overturn counselor recommendations, many families are unaware they have that power or are intimidated

by the counselor's prediction of failure in the tougher class. As one student put it, "African-American parents, they settle for less, not knowing they can get more for their students."[3]

A second source of the problem is that most students prefer courses that have the reputation of being fun and not requiring much work to get a good grade. As one student put it, "My counselor wanted me to take Regents history and I did for a while. But it was pretty hard and the teacher moved fast. I switched to the other history and I'm getting better grades. So my average will be better for college. Unless you are going to college in the state, it doesn't really matter whether you get a Regent's diploma."[4]

Many parents support their children's preference for easier courses. Even in wealthy communities they often demand that their children switch to easier courses where good grades are easier to get. Describing the situation prior to his school's shift to an all-Regents curriculum, one guidance counselor told us:

> A lot of . . . parents were in a "feel good" mode. "If my kids are not happy, I'm not happy. . . ." Probably . . . 25 percent . . . were going for top colleges. They were pushing their kids hard. The rest—75 percent (I'm guessing at the numbers)—said "No, that's too hard, they don't have to do that. . . ." If they [the students] felt it was too tough, they would back off. I had to hold people in classes, hold the parents back. [I would say,] "Let the kid get C's. It's OK. Then they'll get C+'s and then B's." [But they would demand,] "No! I want my kid out of that class!"[5]

Teachers are aware of student preferences and adjust their style of teaching and their homework assignments with an eye to maintaining enrollment levels. Attempts to get students to volunteer for tough courses often fail: "An angry math teacher [who remembered] the elimination of a carefully planned program in technical mathematics for vocational students simply because not enough signed up for it . . . [said], 'It's easy to see who really makes decisions about what schools teach: the kids do.'"[6]

Guidance counselors, students, and parents avoid rigorous courses largely because the rewards for the extra work are small for most students. Employers hardly ever consider the rigor of high school courses when making hiring decisions. While selective colleges evaluate grades in light of course demands, historically most colleges have not factored the rigor of high school courses into their admissions decisions.[7] Consequently, the bulk of students who do not aspire to attend selective colleges quite rationally avoid rigorous courses and demanding teachers.

State-level political and educational leaders have been concerned about this problem for decades. Since traditional policy instruments—budgetary support for schools and school construction, teacher certification rules, and so forth—did not address learning standards, other instruments were sought. Many states increased the number of courses required to graduate. This appears to have helped, but it does not ensure that the courses taken are challenging or that students work up to their potential. Another approach has been to require that schools give students achievement tests and publish the results. The hope is that publicly identifying low–performing schools will spur school administrators into taking remedial action. Some states and cities have developed interventions, such as reconstitution for poorly performing schools. Other jurisdictions have rewarded schools for year-to-year gains in achievement test scores.

One of the most common responses to problems of low expectations and low achievement has been to define standards for learning, test students against these standards, and require that students pass exams assessing the achievement of these standards before graduating. Table 4.1 (page 54) presents data from 1980 and 1992 on the proportion of high school students who are required to pass minimum competency examinations (MCEs) to graduate from high school. School principals were the source of the information on graduation requirements. In most cases, MCEs have been mandated by state legislatures. In other cases, local school districts established the requirement. In 1980, 49 percent of the nation's high school students faced an MCE requirement; in 1992, 56 percent faced MCE requirements. The increase appears to have been concentrated in states and school districts with large minority populations: in 1992, 79 percent of Hispanic and African American students faced such requirements.

Surveys of public opinion about MCEs suggest that the policy is supported not only by voters and teachers but by students as well (see Table 4.2, page 55). In 1997, representative samples of adults, teachers, and students were asked the following question: "Suppose your school required students to learn more and tested them before they were allowed to graduate. Do you think that most kids would pay more attention to their school work and study harder or not?" "Yes" answers were given by 71 percent of adults, 75 percent of teachers, 74 percent of white high school students, 82 percent of Hispanic students, and 80 percent of African American students.[8] Similar proportions agreed that in addition, "most kids would actually learn more."

This survey also asked, "Do you think: Schools should expect inner-city kids to learn as much and achieve at the same standards as kids

TABLE **4.1.** HIGH SCHOOLS REQUIRING PASSAGE OF A MINIMUM
COMPETENCY EXAM TO GRADUATE: PROPORTION OF
SENIORS WHO ATTEND BY SOCIOECONOMIC STATUS,
READING AND MATH SCORES, AND ETHNICITY

|  | 1980 | 1992 |
|---|---|---|
| *Socioeconomic status* |  |  |
| Low | 0.560 | 0.647 |
| Medium | 0.503 | 0.557 |
| High | 0.487 | 0.442 |
| *Reading and math scores* |  |  |
| Low | 0.547 | 0.643 |
| Medium | 0.515 | 0.565 |
| High | 0.466 | 0.457 |
| *Ethnicity* |  |  |
| White/Asian | 0.466 | 0.479 |
| Black | 0.567 | 0.790 |
| Hispanic | 0.568 | 0.790 |
| Total[a] | 0.49 | 0.56 |

[a] Averages of the ethnicity-specific rates in low, medium, and high columns using national proportions of high school students from each ethnic group as weights.

*Source:* Tabulations of High School and Beyond (HSB) and National Education Longitudinal Study-88 (NELS-88) principal survey responses weighted by the number of seniors sampled at the high school. The High School and Beyond (HSB) survey oversampled schools with large minority populations. HSB and NELS-88, U.S. Department of Education, National Center for Education Statistics, Washington, D.C.

from middle-class backgrounds? Or, Should schools make things easier for inner-city kids because they come from poor backgrounds?" As Table 4.2 shows, the first option was selected by 60 percent of the adults, 73 percent of the teachers, 86 percent of the white students, 78 percent of the Hispanic students and 84 percent of the African American students.

The students' responses to these questions suggest that they do not perceive themselves to be working very hard and that they would try harder if more were required of them. Also noteworthy is the opposition of minority students to making "things easier for inner-city kids because they come from poor backgrounds." Many survey respondents, however, thought that tougher graduation tests also would have some negative consequences. A little more than half of students agreed that "more kids will drop out" and "more kids will dislike education and resist learning."

TABLE 4.2. STUDENT OPINION ABOUT THE EFFECTS OF MINIMUM COMPETENCY TESTS

*"SUPPOSE YOUR SCHOOL REQUIRED STUDENTS TO LEARN MORE AND TESTED THEM BEFORE THEY WERE ALLOWED TO GRADUATE."*

| | PERCENT RESPONDING YES | | | | |
| | HIGH SCHOOL STUDENTS | | | ADULTS | TEACHERS |
| | BLACK | HISPANIC | WHITE | | |
|---|---|---|---|---|---|
| Do you think that most kids would pay more attention to their school work and study harder or not? | 80 | 82 | 74 | 71 | 75 |
| Do you think that most kids would actually learn more or not? | 79 | 75 | 72 | 72 | 75 |
| Do you think that more kids will drop out or not? | 55 | 53 | 54 | 45 | 49 |
| Do you think that more kids will dislike education and resist learning or not? | 55 | 56 | 51 | 38 | 27 |
| Do you think: Schools should expect inner-city kids to learn as much and achieve at the same standards as kids from middle-class backgrounds? | 84 | 78 | 86 | 60 | 73 |
| or | | | | | |
| Should schools make things easier for inner-city kids because they come from poor backgrounds? | 13 | 19 | 10 | 32 | 22 |

*Source:* Jean Johnson and Steve Farkas, *Getting By: What American Teenagers Think about Their Schools* (New York: Public Agenda, 1997), 1–54, Table 8.

Are they correct? What effects have minimum competency exams had on high school dropout rates, college entrance rates, and college dropout rates? If students develop the skills assessed by minimum competency exams, will the labor market reward them for it? What effects have MCEs had on the quality of the jobs obtained by high school graduates? Are these effects different for students from less-advantaged or minority backgrounds? New York was one of the first states to make graduation contingent on passing a series of minimum competency exams. How are New York's policies evolving, and what impacts are they likely to have? These are the questions to be addressed in this chapter.

## THE EFFECTS OF MINIMUM COMPETENCY EXAM GRADUATION REQUIREMENTS ON DROPOUT RATES

A number of studies have examined the effect across states of minimum competency exam graduation requirements on enrollment rates and high school graduation rates. Dean Lillard and Phillip DeCicca found that dropout rate increases were associated with increases in the number of courses necessary to graduate, but not with the use of MCEs.[9]

In order to study this issue in greater depth, we analyzed state-level data on enrollment rates and high school graduation rates. The dependent variables were the enrollment rate of seventeen-year-olds (taken from the 1990 Census and from National Center for Education Statistics, *Education in States and Nations*)[10] and the high school graduation rate (the ratio of the number of high school diplomas awarded in the state to the number of seventeen-year-olds).[11] Data on each state's high school graduation requirements—minimum competency exams and the number of Carnegie units required to graduate—were taken from the 1992 and 1996 issues of the *Digest of Educational Statistics*.[12] (A Carnegie unit is a measurement applied to those high school courses that colleges traditionally counted, or gave credit for, in their admissions process.) To take into account the differences in states' demographic features, the analysis controlled for key factors associated with educational outcomes.[13] Subanalyses for New York data also were conducted to detect any specific effects for their Regent examinations.[14] (Results are presented in Appendix Table 4.5, pages 78–79.)

Our conclusion is that there is no evidence in these data that MCEs of the type that existed at the beginning of the 1990s lower enrollment rates or graduation rates.[15] New York State's voluntary Regents exams also appear to have no significant effects on dropout rates or graduation rates. However, the number of Carnegie units required to graduate does have significant negative effects on enrollment rates of seventeen-year-olds, but not on graduation rates.[16]

Many states have increased their graduation requirements by three or four Carnegie units over the past few decades. Our analysis implies that these increases in Carnegie units required for graduation, *ceteris paribus*, should have decreased enrollment rates of seventeen-year-olds by about one percentage point. Yet, despite the policy shifts making high school graduation more difficult to achieve, high school completion rates have climbed during this period. Table 4.3 (page 58) presents data on dropout rate trends. The table shows that the high school completion rates (including GEDs) of nineteen- to twenty-year-old African Americans rose from 67.2 percent in 1972–73 to 70.6 percent in 1981–82 and then to 75.2 percent in 1990–92. Hispanic completion rates also increased. During the 1970s, high school completion rates of white nineteen- to twenty-year-olds fell slightly, from 85.3 percent in 1972–73 to 84.7 percent in 1981–82. They then rose to 87.7 percent in 1990–92. Dropout rates—whether indicated by nonenrollment status for grades 10 to 12 (event dropout rates) or by non–high school graduate, nonenrollment status for sixteen- to twenty-four-year-olds (status dropout rates)—also declined during the period when MCEs were being introduced and graduation requirements were being increased. Clearly, if tougher graduation standards do tend to increase dropout rates, their effects were counterbalanced and indeed overwhelmed by other forces that reduced dropout rates, such as growing incomes and the rising payoff to high school completion and college attendance.

# THE EFFECTS OF MINIMUM COMPETENCY EXAMINATION GRADUATION REQUIREMENTS ON LABOR MARKET SUCCESS

## HOW IMPORTANT IS IT TO IMPROVE THE SKILLS THAT MINIMUM COMPETENCY EXAMINATIONS ASSESS?

Opponents of MCEs sometimes dismiss findings in support of such exams—such as Barbara Lerner's report that test scores were raised by the introduction of MCEs in many southern states[17]—by arguing that the tests used to track student performance over time and the MCEs themselves assess low-level literacy skills that are not very important in the economy. The MCE graduation requirement, some argue, distorts teaching because teachers focus on developing low-level literacy skills rather

TABLE 4.3. TRENDS IN DROPOUT RATES BY ETHNICITY

|  | Event dropout rate:[a] % grades 10–12 | | | Status dropout rate:[b] % sixteen- to twenty-four-year-olds | | | Completed high school:[c] % nineteen- to twenty-year-olds | | |
|---|---|---|---|---|---|---|---|---|---|
|  | White | Black | Hispanic | White | Black | Hispanic | White | Black | Hispanic |
| 1972–73 average | 5.4 | 9.8 | 10.6 | 11.9 | 21.8 | 33.8 | 85.3 | 67.2 | 55.0 |
| 1981–82 average | 4.8 | 8.7 | 9.9 | 11.4 | 18.5 | 32.4 | 84.7 | 70.6 | 57.8 |
| 1990–92 average | 3.4 | 5.3 | 7.9 | 8.5 | 14.0 | 32.3 | 87.7 | 75.2 | 58.1 |
| 1995–96 average | 4.3 | 6.6 | 10.7 | 7.95 | 12.55 | 29.7 |  |  |  |

a The percentage of students in grades 10 to 12 in October of a given year who are not enrolled in high school or graduated the following October.
b The percentage of sixteen- to twenty-four-year-olds that have not graduated from high school and are not attending high school currently.
c The percentage of nineteen- to twenty-year-olds who have a high school diploma or GED.

*Note:* Changes in Current Population Survey interviewing and editing procedures may make data on event dropout rates in the late 1990s inconsistent with previous data.
*Source: Dropout Rates in the United States 1992,* Tables A32, A38, A50; and Marilyn McMillen, *Dropout Rates in the United States, 1996,* National Center for Education Statistics, Washington, D.C., December 1997, Tables A20 and A23.

than higher-order problem-solving skills, writing skills, computer skills, occupation-specific skills, or affective competencies that are presumed more important. They argue that tests similar to the MCEs used by many states have weak relationships with wages and youth labor market success. Where is the sense, they ask, in threatening to deny a credential that employers reward very handsomely—the high school diploma—in order to induce teachers to teach and students to learn basic reading and math literacy skills that employers do not reward by paying higher wages. The problem with this argument is that it is not consistent with employer behavior during the 1990s and mistakes form (a diploma) for substance (the skills and knowledge diplomas signal).

When literacy, schooling, and earnings are all measured from the same period, simple tests assessing literacy have at least as strong a relationship with unemployment and earnings of adults as years of schooling. Table 4.4 presents evidence for this assertion from the National Adult Literacy Survey. Adults in the top prose literacy group earn roughly 3 times as much as those in the bottom literacy group and have one-fifth the chance of being unemployed. College graduates, by contrast, earn 2.35 times as much as high school dropouts and have two-fifths the chance of being unemployed.

### TABLE 4.4. RELATIONSHIP OF PROSE LITERACY AND SCHOOLING TO EARNINGS AND UNEMPLOYMENT OF MALES

|  | EARNINGS ($) | UNEMPLOYMENT (%) |
|---|---|---|
| **Literacy** | | |
| Level 1 | 48,965 | 2.3 |
| Level 2 | 39,941 | 4.1 |
| Level 3 | 29,610 | 6.4 |
| Level 4 | 22,046 | 11.5 |
| Level 5 | 15,755 | 14.9 |
| **Schooling** | | |
| BA or more | 38,115 | 4.8 |
| Associate degree | 31,855 | 5.5 |
| 13–15 years | 27,279 | 7.4 |
| 12 years | 22,494 | 8.2 |
| 9–11 years | 16,194 | 12.4 |

*Source:* Andrew Sum, *Literacy in the Labor Force: Results from the National Adult Literacy Survey* (Washington, D.C.: National Center for Education Statistics, 1999).

## PROSPECTIVE STUDIES OF THE LONG-TERM EFFECTS
## OF ACADEMIC ACHIEVEMENT IN HIGH SCHOOL

Simple tabulations of earnings against literacy or schooling such as those in Table 4.4 yield estimates that are biased upward of the effects of learning and schooling attainments during one's youth.[18] To measure the effects of learning during the first twelve years of school, prospective studies are needed that examine the effects of competencies measured toward the end of high school on labor market success ten, twenty, and thirty years later. Studies of this type have found that tests measuring basic skills at the end of high school have large effects on wages ten, fifteen, and twenty years later, but only small effects in the years immediately after high school.[19] Effects are small for recent high school graduates because few employers use tests assessing basic literacy as an aid in screening job applicants, and most do not ask for information on high school grades. Over time, however, they learn which employees are the most competent by observing job performance. Those judged most competent are more likely to get further training, promotions, and good recommendations when they move on. Poor performers are encouraged to leave. Since academic achievement in high school is correlated with job performance,[20] the sorting process results in basic skills assessed during high school having a much larger effect on the labor market success of thirty-year-olds than of nineteen-year-olds, even when contemporaneous measures of completed schooling are held constant.

The labor market rewards for learning increased substantially during the 1980s. Thus, recent studies find larger test score effects than did studies done during the 1970s.[21] Joseph Altonji and Charles Pierret's 1997 prospective study of how scores on the Armed Forces Qualification Test (AFQT) taken while a teenager affect subsequent labor market success provides estimates of the magnitude of these effects in the late 1980s and early 1990s.[22] Controlling for a contemporaneous measure of completed schooling, they found that an increase of one standard deviation on the AFQT was associated with only a 2.8 percent increase in wage rates the first year out of school but a 16 percent increase eleven years later. By contrast, the impact of a year of schooling decreased with time out of school, from 9.2 percent for those out just one year to 3 percent for those out twelve years.

Large as it is, this 16 percent figure substantially understates the total effect of improved K–12 learning on earnings as an adult. First, test scores influence hours of work and the risk of unemployment, not just wage rates. Second, compared to the MCEs of many states, the

AFQT is an incomplete measure of what students are learning in high school.[23] If reliable measures of other skills learned in school (such as science, social studies, writing, and technical and computer skills) were included in the model, the total effect of test scores would be larger. The third and most important source of bias comes from using a contemporaneous measure of schooling as a control. Much of the benefit of learning in the first twelve years of school comes from the assistance it provides in continuing schooling beyond high school. Yet, this benefit is not reflected in the effects of the AFQT because it is captured by the contemporaneous measure of schooling. If a prospective measure of schooling (completed schooling at the time of the AFQT test) were substituted for the contemporaneous measure, the AFQT's effects on earnings would be much larger.

In sum, the skills assessed by MCEs clearly have large effects on labor market outcomes ten, twenty, and thirty years after high school graduation. Students who are stimulated by an MCE graduation requirement to learn more in high school will be rewarded by the labor market.

## HOW DO MINIMUM COMPETENCY EXAMINATION GRADUATION REQUIREMENTS IMPACT COLLEGE ATTENDANCE, WAGE RATES, AND ANNUAL EARNINGS?

Proponents of MCEs argue that they force teachers to set higher standards for all students, not just for middle-class white students or for students in honors or college prep classes. All students (and students from lower-income backgrounds in particular) will have to take tougher courses and study harder. The students who are at risk of failing the minimum competency test will get more attention and tutoring from school staff. They will learn more, and that will result in (1) more of them entering, staying in, and completing college, and (2) assuming school completion, them getting better jobs.

MCEs are hypothesized to improve job opportunities in two ways. First, by improving student achievement they raise worker productivity.[24] Even when this does not immediately raise workers' earnings, the effect of academic achievement on wages grows with time and eventually becomes very large.

Second, MCEs send a signal to employers that "*all* the graduates of this high school meet or exceed your hiring standards." The fact that they have passed the MCE is the proof. In most communities, competencies developed in the local high school are poorly signaled to employers.

The lack of signals makes the employers with the best jobs reluctant to risk hiring recent high school graduates. Indeed, they often carry in their heads very negative stereotypes regarding recent high school graduates. A black personnel director interviewed for a CBS special on educational reform proudly stated, "We don't hire high school graduates any more, we need *skilled workers.*"[25] They prefer, instead, to hire workers with many years of work experience because the applicants' work records serve as signals of competence and reliability that help employers identify the most qualified.

Establishing a minimum competency exam, therefore, is one way a school district or state education system can try to overcome this signaling problem and help its graduates get good jobs. The existence of the MCE graduation requirement is well known to local employers. With the MCE requirement, the school's diploma now signals more than just "seat time"; it signals meeting or exceeding certain minimum standards in reading, writing, and mathematics. This should make local employers more willing to hire the school's recent graduates. Because of the negative stereotypes that many employers have regarding minority youth, the MCE graduation requirement should be particularly helpful to these graduates.

The foregoing logic generates a number of testable predictions regarding the graduates of high schools with an MCE graduation requirement. Holding constant socioeconomic status, test scores, grades, types of courses taken, paid employment during senior year, current and past college attendance, and a complete set of other individual and school characteristics:

1.  Graduates of MCE high schools:

    *   Will be more likely to go to college. This will be particularly true for black and Hispanic students, for those from low-income backgrounds, and for those with low scores on other sorts of tests.

    *   Will be less likely to drop out of college.

    *   Will be more likely to complete a bachelor's degree within five years.

    *   Will be offered higher-paying jobs. This will be particularly true for Hispanic and African American students and for those from low-income backgrounds.

2. The tendency of employers to reward graduates of schools with MCEs will be visible in data on wage rates in the first year after high school graduation.

These hypotheses were tested in the two nationally representative longitudinal data sets—High School and Beyond (HSB) seniors of 1980 and the National Educational Longitudinal Study (NELS) students graduating in 1992—that contain information on MCEs mandated by state law or local school boards. The analysis sample is composed of the students in the two longitudinal studies who graduated from high school between January and September of their scheduled year of graduation. The HSB seniors were interviewed two, four, and six years after graduating from high school about continued schooling, employment, earnings, and changes in family status. Thus, we are able to assess both short-term and intermediate effects of school characteristics. NELS 1992 graduates were interviewed two years after graduation. Again, we controlled for other factors that were likely to be related to the outcomes of interest so that they were not confused with MCE's unique effects in our findings (see Tables 4.6 and 4.7 in the appendix to this chapter, pages 80–83).[26]

*College Attendance.* The analysis of HSB data found that MCEs had significant positive effects on the probability of being in college for a majority of student subgroups during the four-year period immediately following high school graduation. Effects were largest for students in the middle and bottom of the test score distribution and tended to be greater in the second and third years out than in the first, fourth, and subsequent years out.

Socioeconomic status also interacts with MCEs in the way hypothesized. MCEs have an immediate and significant effect on the college enrollment of students of low socioeconomic status. Students of middle and high socioeconomic status are affected, but not until the second and third year out of high school. For 1992 graduates the same pattern appears to be developing. Combining full- and part-time enrollment, the results suggest that MCEs raise enrollment rates of students from low socioeconomic backgrounds by 4.4 percentage points, students of middle socioeconomic status by 2.4 percentage points, and students of high socioeconomic status not at all.

Women graduating from MCE high schools are significantly more likely to go to college full-time and men are significantly more likely to go part-time. When results are broken down by ethnicity, MCEs are found to have effects for all groups, but effects are somewhat larger (though not significantly so) for minority students. Effects were significant in the first year following graduation only for Hispanics, and significant for almost all subgroups in the second and third year following graduation.

*Wage Rates.* For graduates in 1980, MCEs had significant effects on wage rates of those who were in the low and middle test score groups, as hypothesized. They had no effect on wages of students with high test scores. Students from backgrounds of low and moderate socioeconomic status had significantly higher wage rates when they attended MCE high schools; students from high socioeconomic backgrounds did not. Finally, MCEs were associated with higher wage rates for minority youths but not white youths. Black youths from MCE high schools were paid a significant 4.2 percent more in the first year after graduating, but the effect diminished in later years. Hispanic youths graduating from MCE high schools in 1980 were paid consistently (between 3.7 and 4.6 percent) more at one year, three years, and five years following graduation.

The wage rate benefit of graduating from an MCE high school in 1992 was considerably larger than it was for 1980 graduates. MCE graduates in 1992 were paid 4.1 percent more if they were male and 3.2 percent more if they were female. This compares to average effects of from 1.6 in 1980 to 1.7 percent for 1990 graduates.[27] Who benefited also changed. MCEs are related to an astonishing 5.2 to 6.3 percent higher wage rate for students with medium and high test scores, and possibly to a 4.9 percent lower wage rate for students with low test scores.[28] Another difference is that 1992 graduates who attend high schools with MCEs are paid more, without regard to their socioeconomic background. White students, who did not benefit in the early 1980s, were benefiting in 1992. Minority students, who in 1980 were the sole beneficiaries of attending an MCE high school, no longer benefited in 1992.

*Annual Earnings.* The analyses of earnings demonstrate the effects of MCEs on both time spent working and wage rates. Except for Hispanics, 1980 graduates of MCE high schools did not earn more than graduates of non–MCE high schools in the years immediately following graduation. Earnings effects grew over time, however, so that by 1985 annual earnings were $484 higher for whites, $808 higher for blacks, and $703 higher for Hispanics. For 1992 graduates, a number of the subgroups appear to have received statistically significant earnings benefits in the first calendar year after graduating from an MCE high school. Students from low socioeconomic backgrounds who graduated from an MCE high school earned $694 extra, an increase in earnings of more than 10 percent. Students from the middle of the test score distribution earned $424 extra (a 7.5 percent increase) when they graduated from an MCE high school.

Remember that all these findings are from analyses that control for the quality of the high school and the individual's academic achievement through test scores, grade point average, participation in extracurricular activities, and an indicator for taking remedial courses in either math or English. Apparently, the existence of MCEs is associated with higher achievement in ways not captured by the individual tests given as part of the HSB and NELS 1992 surveys. This unmeasured gain in achievement apparently has long-range effects on a student's ability to complete college and get a higher paying job.

To summarize, the MCEs that existed in the 1980s and early 1990s did not lower high school completion rates as some had feared. Instead they are associated with higher college attendance and college retention rates. Students who graduated from MCE high schools immediately obtained significantly higher paying jobs and kept their pay advantage for the next five years. In addition, large earnings benefits appeared five years after high school graduation. The immediate wage rate benefits of graduating from an MCE high school were larger for the students graduating in 1992 than in 1980, although white students got the higher payoff, suggesting a less egalitarian bias in 1992 than in the early 1980s.

MCEs are changing. Additional states and cities such as Chicago, Ohio, and Massachusetts have introduced them. Other states such as New Jersey and New York are improving their exams by adding essays and open-response questions and raising the standard that must be achieved to graduate. While MCEs of the past have not increased dropout rates, that does not guarantee that MCEs that set much higher minimum standards will not have that effect.

## THE NEW YORK STATE REGENTS EXAMINATIONS

The most dramatic increase in graduation standards is in New York State. This section of the chapter provides background on New York's Regents examination system and plans to reform it by requiring *all* students to take and pass Regents exams in five core subjects. It reports on the high schools that "jumped the gun" on this reform by eliminating bottom track classes in the early 1990s and requiring instead that all students take demanding Regents courses in five core subjects. The primary change has been a massive redirection of energy and attention to struggling students.

## THE REGENTS SYSTEM

New York State has been administering curriculum-based Regents examinations to high school students since June 1878. As Sherman Tinkelman, assistant commissioner for examinations and scholarships, described it in a 1966 report:

> The Regents examinations are closely related to the curriculum in New York State. They are, as you can see, inseparably intertwined. One supports and reinforces the other. . . . These instruments presuppose and define standards. . . . They are a strong supervisory and instructional tool—and deliberately so. They are effective in stimulating good teaching and good learning practices.[29]

Sponsorship by the state Board of Regents is crucial to the role these examinations have played in setting and maintaining high standards and promoting reform. On occasion, examinations have been deliberately revised to induce changes in curriculum and teaching.

> For years our foreign language specialists went up and down the State beating the drums for curriculum reform in modern language teaching, for change in emphasis from formal grammar to conversation skills and reading skills. There was not very great impact until we introduced, after notice and with numerous sample exercises, oral comprehension and reading comprehension into our Regents examinations. Promptly thereafter, most schools adopted the new curricular objectives.[30]

The examinations are taken throughout one's high school career. A typical student taking a full schedule of college preparatory Regents courses would take Regents exams in mathematics and earth science at the end of grade 9; mathematics, biology, and global studies exams at the end of grade 10; mathematics, chemistry, English, American history, and foreign language exams at the end of grade 11; and a physics exam at the end of grade 12. Students who want to take advanced placement (AP) classes in their junior and senior years often start taking Regents courses and exams in grade 8.

In 1996, the ratio of the number of students taking the mathematics course 1 exam to average enrollment in a high school grade was 89 percent; of the students taking the course, 28 percent scored below the 65 percent passing grade. Participation percentages were in the sixties for the global studies, American history, biology, and English exams; failure rates were 25 percent in global studies, 19 percent in American history, 25 percent in biology, and 20 percent in English. Those not taking Regents exams were typically in "local" courses that are considerably less challenging than Regents courses. A system of Regents competency tests (RCTs) in reading, writing, math, science, global studies, and U.S. history and government set a minimum standard for those not taking Regents courses.

For students, the stakes attached to Regents exams have not been high.[31] Exam grades counted for less than an eighth of the final grade in the course and influenced only the type of diploma received. College admissions decisions depended primarily on grades and SAT scores, not Regents exam scores. Indeed, the modest payoff to taking Regents exams may have been one of the reasons why many students were not taking Regents courses. In the 1996–97 school year, only 42 percent of graduating seniors got a Regents diploma, signifying that they took eight or more Regents-level academic courses and passed the associated exams.

## The Statewide Shift to an All-Regents Curriculum

The shift to an all-Regents curriculum began in New York City. On May 1, 1994, the New York City Board of Education announced that starting with those entering grade 9 in the fall of 1994, all students would have to take three Regents-level math and three Regents-level science courses before graduating. Ramon Cortines, chancellor of the New York City school system, declared: "The easy way out is the road to nowhere. If achievement in our schools is to improve, we must raise our expectations for students and staff. Our system will fail in its obligation to this community unless we equalize educational opportunity and raise standards in all of our schools."[32] With this step, New York City abolished the bottom track.

Two years later, the state Board of Regents decided to raise the bar for the entire state. Students would be required not only to take Regents-level courses, but also to pass the Regents exams for these courses. Specifically, students entering grade 9 in 1996 or later were required to take a new six-hour Regents English examination and pass it at the 55 percent level. The class of 2001 has the additional requirement of passing an examination in algebra and geometry. The class of 2002 must also pass Regents examinations in global studies and American history. When laboratory science exams are added for the graduating class of 2003, the phase-in of all five new and required Regents exams will be complete. The new requirements have effectively abolished the bottom track. Everyone, including those pursuing vocational programs at area vocational-technical schools, will be required to achieve the standard in the five core subjects that previously had been expected only of those going to four-year colleges.

The Regents examinations are being revised in a number of subjects. The revised exams are, if anything, more demanding than the exams they replace.[33] Once schools have adjusted to the revised exams and the requirement that all students take them, the Board of Regents intends to raise the scores necessary to pass from the 55 percent to 60 percent and then to 65 percent. New York State has embarked on establishing the first high-stakes, curriculum-based, external exit examination system in United States history.

## ALL-REGENTS HIGH SCHOOLS: HOW DID THEY DO IT?

What kinds of changes in school policies and resource allocation will be necessary to move to an all-Regents curriculum in the five core subjects? This question was addressed by interviewing teachers, administrators, and school board members at ten high schools that had already moved to an all-Regents curriculum and had significantly increased the number of students taking and passing Regents exams.[34]

*Generating Support.* The districts that increased their participation in Regents exams to high levels did not accomplish the goal quickly and easily. The key to success was not getting a tax rate increase through the school board or introducing some new teaching system. In most cases the formal and structural changes were modest. It was the school's culture— both the teacher culture and the student peer culture—that had to and did change.

The initiative generally came from a new district superintendent who then recruited or promoted people into key jobs who would support his vision for the elimination of the bottom or local track. Staff and community support for eliminating local or basic classes in core subjects was cultivated carefully. In many cases, the goal of shifting to an all-Regents curriculum was not announced until many years after important initial steps had been taken and some early successes had been achieved. The new superintendent had to deal with the fact that teachers and the community felt that the school was already doing a great job. They took pride in the accomplishments of the honors students. How could they be convinced to end the low-expectations basic or local track into which struggling and lazy students were fleeing? The Regents exams and the report card outlining district-level results provided the benchmark that the superintendent was able to use to shame and inspire teachers into setting high standards for all students. As one superintendent put it, "External validation of what you're doing and forcing teachers, administrators and the community to look at yourself as reflected in the eyes of people outside of you and matching a standard that exists outside your school district was critical!"[35]

The long history and prestige of Regents exams helped in selling the reform to parents. As the school board president of an all-Regents school district said, "All-Regents was . . . helpful for us. It was very concrete. It was something the parents could relate to. When parents thought of a Regents program in their own experience, they thought about students who were college bound."[36] Outside recognition was sought and excellence awards were frequently received. According to another school board president of an all-Regents school district, "The whole community is walking around with their chests out. Which really helps out. There is a pride that this is what _____ is today."[37] The president of the teachers union local in an All-Regents school district remarked that: "[All-Regents] put us up on a new standard. It made a change in the high school and [brought] the recognition of this high school as a place where positive things are happening."[38]

The outside recognition increased teacher and community support for the initiative. Praise for past accomplishments spurred teachers to raise standards even higher and work harder still. The focus on the external standard meant that the professional pride of the teachers became invested in getting marginal students "through the Regents." The visibility of each success made the extra work seem worthwhile.

Eliminating the local or basic track and the general increase in standards persuaded more students to take honors, AP, and International Baccalaureate classes. "Every level of kid in that classroom is getting a new challenge. Because we are an All-Regents high school, we are offering more AP classes. Kids are ready for that next challenge."[39]

*A Focus on Struggling Students.* All the districts substantially increased the time and resources devoted to teaching and tutoring struggling students. Since they had initiated the raising of the bar, school administrators felt a moral obligation to do everything in their power to help students succeed. As one school board president in an all-Regents district said, "You need to . . . provide the remedial and tutorial support that every individual kid needs. It's a terrible thing to put in a tough program that kids are going to fail. Every one of these kids can do it—they take a different amount of time to do it."[40]

In this school, the guidance counselor met with incoming freshmen and developed a plan, the goal of which was to obtain a Regents diploma. Milestones were tracked, and if a student started having difficulties the counselor arranged tutoring. The extra time was obtained in a variety of ways:

- Assigning more homework, especially for students formerly in local courses.

- Assigning struggling students to "stretch" Regents courses, taking one and a half or two years to cover the material of a standard, one-year Regents course.

- Assigning struggling students to classes with more than five periods a week. A number of the schools that settled on this option had tried two-year-stretch Regents courses and felt that spending extra time in a one-year period worked better.

- Increasing summer school attendance, especially for struggling primary and middle school students.

- Reducing the number of study halls (because most students "do not use study halls productively") and providing regular tutoring sessions instead.

- Adding extra periods at the beginning or end of the school day, during which struggling students received extra help.

- Having students in the National Honors Society and the International Baccalaureate program provide peer tutoring.

*Teachers Were Inspired to Work Harder.* The new focus was inspiring to teachers and it encouraged them to work harder. For example, the principal of an all-Regents high school commented, "[Teachers] worked above and beyond the contract. Nobody asks them to do it. . . . I've never worked in a place like this before!" The school secretary at the same school said, "The [teachers] were willing to give their every effort and time above and beyond the school day. They would stay for hours on end late in the . . . evening. . . . She [the principal] presented it so well. She's just a motivator!"[41]

In many schools, the increase in teacher time devoted to tutoring was also accomplished by relieving teachers of hall duties and supervision of study halls and lunch duties. In one school, the position of department chair was eliminated, and the release time formerly given to department chairs was reallocated to teaching and tutoring. In some schools, teaching assignments were no longer allocated by seniority. The best teachers were reassigned to classes with many struggling students. In some schools, teaching assistants who were fully qualified teachers were hired to provide tutoring. Evening review sessions were offered in the months preceding the Regents exams. Teacher contracts were not renegotiated, but local union leaders sometimes chose not to make an issue of things that in the past might have led to grievances.

In one district, many teachers could not adapt to the new way of doing things and left. Young teachers who believed the all-Regents goal was both desirable and feasible were hired in their stead.

## IMPLICATIONS FOR STATE AND LOCAL EDUCATIONAL POLICIES

Requiring that all students reach the Regents standard in five core subjects will significantly increase student achievement, college attendance and completion, and the quality of jobs that students get after high school. The biggest beneficiaries of the policy are likely to be the students, often from disadvantaged backgrounds, who have been encouraged or allowed to avoid rigorous courses in the past. In the all-Regents high schools there was a major reallocation of teachers' time and resources toward struggling students; it was their achievement that increased the most. Administrators reported that college enrollment rates went up after they shifted to the all-Regents program.

It is not clear, however, that the parents of students struggling under the new requirements will see it that way. When the principal of an all-Regents high school was asked who opposed the elimination of the easier, local courses, she said:

> Parents of children . . . who . . . felt [their kids] couldn't do
> it. . . . [One parent approached her in the school parking lot.] She

started yelling at me. She told me she hated the all-Regents high school. Her kids were not as successful. If you sit in a consumer math class you get a 90. If you sit in a sequential math class, you have to struggle to get a 65. . . . She was very angry about it. . . . Parents are a big obstacle. . . . Your kids don't want to do this. They're going to complain about it. Which means you are going to work harder as a parent.[42]

Once students start failing Regents exams and having to repeat courses in order to graduate, there will be a crescendo of complaints. Claims will be made that schools have not done enough to help students succeed on the new exams.

What can the Board of Regents and the state legislature do to help local schools meet their obligation to help students meet the new, higher standards? How can the number of dropouts and graduation delays be minimized? The most important change is to increase the amount of time that struggling students spend on the task of learning. This was the central recommendation to the Board of Regents from a representative group of teachers, school administrators, and parents convened by New York State's commissioner of education to consider how to minimize the number of students failing to meet the new, higher learning standards. This group, inelegantly named the "Safety Net Study Group," recommended a radical increase in the amount of instruction that struggling and disadvantaged students receive. The following is an extensive excerpt from their recommendations.

The success of this upgrading of standards will depend on a systemic program of prevention and intervention strategies that each district and, in turn, each school must provide. These strategies include, but are not limited to:

- Providing extra learning opportunities through extended time for students in need of this service.

- Providing clear direction to students and their parents of what is expected of the student, what is the student's current academic status and what the student still needs to do to earn a Regents diploma.

- Providing a transitional program from elementary to middle school and from middle school to high school.

- Providing a clearly defined promotional policy so that all students and their parents understand the criteria from grade to grade.

*Recommendation 1—Grade Specific Curriculum:* Each school district and, in turn, each school should be required to have grade specific curriculum consistent with State standards. . . . If a district does not meet the learning standards, then State intervention procedures will be implemented. "Schools under registration review" is the state's intervention program.

*Recommendation 2—Extra Help/Extra Time:* . . . Enrichment and remediation programs should be provided as additions to and to reinforce core courses of study as opposed to "pullout" programs. [Pullout programs take struggling students out of their regular class to give them small group instruction by a resource teacher.] The state should revise the commissioner's Regulations on remediation . . . to require that students receive the extra help/extra time they may need to meet the standards. These students' enrichment and remedial activities will be provided within the school year, including after school instruction, evening instruction, Saturday instruction, etc.

*Recommendation 3—Mandatory Summer School:* When a student fails to meet academic expectations, based on grade-level assessments, then that student would be required to attend summer school. . . . Since the State is responsible for summer school, it would need both to revise the current summer school requirements and procedures to accommodate this expansion and to review and revise the current assessments provided during the summer sessions. . . . In addition the State would provide the necessary financial assistance to support the extra cost of mandatory summer school.

*Recommendation 4—Professional Development:* . . . Each district should provide professional development to all staff, kindergarten through grade 12, to enable them to assist students to meet the new graduation requirements. . . .

*Recommendation 5—Student Promotional Guidelines:*[43] Each school district should have a plan that explains the movement of students from grade to grade (especially when they move between different school buildings) and identifies the ways that schools engage parents, students and other community members to help students understand and achieve higher standards.[44]

The all-Regents schools studied obtained large increases in the time teachers spend with students by reorganizing teachers' schedules and getting teachers to work above and beyond their contracted hours. Inspiring leadership that induces teachers to work far beyond the contract for no additional pay will not be available in most districts. Consequently, teachers will have to be paid extra for working longer hours. The costs of tutoring, longer school days, review sessions, and staff development that are associated with preparing students for Regents exams should not be subject to caps in state funding formulas. Districts with large numbers of disadvantaged pupils and low first grade test scores should get large increases in state aid.

Schools with large numbers of struggling students probably should lengthen the school day and school year for all students, not just for a targeted minority who are behind the rest. The Edison schools have been successful with this approach. The New York City public schools and its teacher union have recently announced a move in this direction as well. Forty schools will be reorganized and reopened with forty minutes added to the school day and new math and reading programs (Success for All). To help attract talent and compensate for the extra work, teachers selected for these schools will receive a 15 percent wage increase and an additional week of professional development.

One of the most effective forms of professional development is having teachers serve on the committees that grade essays, multistep mathematics problems, and extended answer questions. Canadian teachers who have served on grading committees for their provincial exams describe it as "a wonderful professional development activity."[45] Having to agree on what constituted excellent, good, poor, and failing responses to essay questions or open-response science and math problems resulted in a sharing of perspectives and teaching tips that most found very helpful. Therefore, teachers should grade the Regents exams in centralized regional locations under the guidance of well-trained leaders. Scoring rubrics, however, should be developed centrally to maintain consistent standards across the state.

## What Will Happen to Dropout Rates?

Anticipating the new requirements, many school districts have already started shifting to an all-Regents curriculum, and the number of students taking Regents-level courses and passing Regents exams is rising. Between 1995 and 1997, the proportion of the student enrollment taking and passing (having a score of 65 percent or higher) Regents exams rose from 50.3 percent to 56.3 percent in English, from 53 percent to 59 percent in sequential mathematics I, and from 41 percent to 44 percent in biology.

Nevertheless, we predict very high failure rates—between 25 and 40 percent in some subjects—the first time Regents exams are administered to all students. Even if the reforms proposed above were implemented immediately, they would not have been in operation long enough to prevent this from happening. Many students will have to retake examinations after taking additional academic courses or special summer make-up courses. Will this generate a large increase in dropout rates as students despair of ever passing all five exams? We think not. Our prediction is that New York students will respond the same way that European students respond to tough graduation requirements: they will study harder and stay in high school longer. The tougher graduation requirements are not fully phased in until the class of 2003. We predict that four years later, in 2007, dropout rates will be at or below current levels and this will be accomplished without making the Regents exams easier than they are right now. We base this forecast on the following:

- When they discover how difficult the standards are, students will react by studying harder. Teachers will gain experience with teaching to the new standards and will get better at it. Teachers who are unable to teach to the higher standards will leave the profession and be replaced by teachers who can. The firestorm that may result from the high failure rates in the first year to generate a large infusion of state aid directed specifically at helping struggling students and schools serving disadvantaged populations. The impending rise in graduation standards helped convince the legislature to increase school aid in the most recent budget cycle, and much of it was targeted on expanding after-school programs and summer schools. The Board of Regents has proposed an even bigger increase next year and again used the rising standards as a rationale.[46]

- The high-stakes exams will make having quality teachers more critical than in the past. The resulting competition for quality teachers will drive salaries up. Nations with high-stakes, curriculum-based exams pay their secondary school teachers more than nations without such exams.[47] Parental support of more school spending will increase. Better teachers will ensure a better education, thus keeping failure rates down.

- We expect (and recommend) that the plan to increase the 55 percent passing standard on the Regents exams to 60 and then 65 percent be postponed indefinitely.

- The Regents examination graduation requirement replaces a Regents Competency Test graduation requirement that already sets a fairly high minimum. Thus, the change in failure rates will not be as dramatic as many expect. In 1996, the ratio of the number of students failing an RCT to average enrollment per grade in the state was 21 percent in mathematics and global studies and 20 percent in science. In New York City, failure ratios on the RCT were above 40 percent in these three subjects.

- The Regents exam graduation requirement does not apply to all high school students in the state. The 10 percent of students who are in private schools are not covered. Special education students with an Individualized Education Plan are exempted, and Regents exams are not required to earn a GED. Many of the students who are unable to pass all five Regents exams at the 55 percent level will complete high school by transferring to a private high school or a GED program. A transfer to a GED program is considered a switch to another kind of school, not dropping out of school.

Let us imagine, however, that our prediction of stable or rising high school completion rates is wrong. Would a 2 to 4 percent decline in completion rates imply that increasing graduation requirements was a mistake? No. Focusing solely on graduation rates mistakes symbol for substance. What counts is how much students learn, not what proportion of them have a specific paper credential. It is the competencies developed in high school that enable a student to survive and thrive in college, not the diploma. Many community colleges admit students without diplomas. Higher standards will result in all students learning more on average.[48] Those who graduate will be more competent and will be able to command a better wage in the labor market. As demonstrated earlier, this effect is quite large; MCEs are related to a 3 to 4 percent increase in average wage rates. The average high school dropout will also be more competent, and this too will result in higher pay. College attendance rates will be higher, and those affected in this way are big gainers.

There will be losers—the hypothesized 2 to 4 percent of the age cohort that would have graduated under the old standards but do not under the new, higher-standards regime. Joseph Altonji and Charles Pierret's analysis predicts that dropping out generates about an 18 percent reduction in earnings in the first year out of school and a 6 percent loss in the twelfth year out (assuming no change in test scores).[49] However, these losses pale in comparison to wage rate gains of over 3 percent experienced by the 96 to 98 percent of young people whose years of completed schooling are not changed or are increased by the higher standards.

## APPENDIX TO CHAPTER 4

TABLE 4.5: DETERMINANTS OF SCHOOL ENROLLMENT AND HIGH SCHOOL GRADUATION RATES

TABLE 4.6: EFFECTS OF REQUIRING PASSAGE OF A MINIMUM COMPETENCY TEST TO GRADUATE FROM HIGH SCHOOL: READING AND MATH TEST SCORES, GENDER

TABLE 4.7: EFFECTS OF REQUIRING PASSAGE OF A MINIMUM COMPETENCY TEST TO GRADUATE FROM HIGH SCHOOL: SOCIOECONOMIC STATUS, RACE/ETHNICITY

### TABLE 4.5. DETERMINANTS OF SCHOOL ENROLLMENT AND HIGH SCHOOL GRADUATION RATES

| MINIMUM-COMPETENCY-TEST VARIABLE | Percentage of seventeen-year-olds enrolled in high school 1990 Census[a] | | Education in States and Nations (1991)[b] | | Secondary school graduates per 100 persons seventeen years old[b] | |
|---|---|---|---|---|---|---|
| | 1992[c] | 1996[d] | 1992[c] | 1996[d] | 1992[c] | 1996[d] |
| State minimum competency exam | −0.76 (1.10) | 1.05 (1.41) | −0.17 (0.37) | 0.87[e] (1.81) | −1.19 (0.64) | −0.08 (0.04) |
| New York State | 1.78 (0.98) | 1.80 (0.98) | 0.33 (0.27) | 0.05 (0.04) | −0.83 (0.17) | −0.88 (0.18) |
| Number of Carnegie units required to graduate | −0.27[f] (2.59) | −0.34[g] (3.22) | −0.15[f] (2.26) | −0.19[g] (2.88) | −0.20 (0.73) | −0.24 (0.82) |
| No Carnegie unit graduation requirement | −4.79[f] (2.84) | −5.96[g] (2.80) | −3.05[f] (2.22) | −3.73[g] (2.73) | −1.46 (0.26) | −1.97 (0.34) |
| Parents' education index[h] | 0.29[f] (3.22) | 0.34[g] (3.19) | 0.11 (1.55) | 0.13[e] (1.97) | 0.81[g] (2.76) | 0.87[g] (3.04) |
| Percentage in poverty (people 18 years or less)[i] | 0.043 (0.55) | 0.063 (0.84) | −0.02 (0.40) | −0.014 (0.30) | −0.04 (0.19) | −0.01 (0.07) |
| Percentage foreign born[j] | −0.15[e] (1.74) | −0.22[f] (2.69) | −0.19[g] (3.27) | −0.22[g] (4.18) | −0.11 (0.44) | −0.17 (0.77) |
| Percentage of public school students black[k] | −0.037[f] (1.40) | −0.071[f] (2.45) | −0.040[f] (2.33) | −0.061[g] (3.33) | −0.215[g] (3.04) | −0.231[g] (2.93) |

| Percentage public school students Hispanic[k] | -0.036 (0.97) | -0.046 (1.26) | -0.006 (0.26) | -0.014 (0.59) | -0.236[f] (2.40) | -0.239[f] (2.39) |
|---|---|---|---|---|---|---|
| Adj R Squared | 0.4922 | 0.5010 | 0.5405 | 0.5708 | 0.6496 | 0.6460 |
| RMSE | 1.657 | 1.642 | 1.087 | 1.050 | 4.463 | 4.486 |
| Mean of dependent variable | 88.9 | 88.9 | 84.2 | 84.2 | 75.8 | 75.8 |

[a] Data on enrollment rates from *1990 Census of the Population* (Washington, D.C.: U.S. Census Bureau, 1991).

[b] Data on enrollment and graduation rates from Richard P. Phelps, Thomas M. Smith, and Nabeel Alsalam, *Education in States and Nations* (Washington, D.C.: U.S. Department of Education, National Center for Education Statistics, 1991), pp. 73, 149.

[c] Regressions using a competency-test variable based on a 1985 study by the Education Commission of the States in the National Center for Education Statistics, U.S. Department of Education, *Digest of Educational Statistics, 1992* (Washington, D.C.: U.S. Government Printing Office, 1992), p. 148.

[d] Regressions using the 1996 minimum-competency-test variable are based on National Center for Education Statistics, U.S. Department of Education, *Digest of Educational Statistics, 1996* (Washington, D.C.: U.S. Government Printing Office, 1996), p. 149.

[e] Statistically significant at 10 percent level.

[f] Statistically significant at 5 percent level.

[g] Statistically significant at 1 percent level.

[h] Average of the percentage of parents obtaining a secondary high school diploma and the percentage of parents obtaining a university degree. Richard P. Phelps, Thomas M. Smith, and Nabeel Alsalam, *Education in States and Nations* (Washington, D.C.: U.S. Department of Education, National Center for Education Statistics, 1991), p. 139.

[i] Richard P. Phelps, Thomas M. Smith, and Nabeel Alsalam, *Education in States and Nations* (Washington, D.C.: U.S. Department of Education, National Center for Education Statistics, 1991), p. 49.

[j] "Social and Economic Characteristics U.S.," *1990 Census of the Population* (Washington, D.C.: U.S. Census Bureau, 1991), p. 174, n. 79.

[k] National Center for Education Statistics, U.S. Department of Education, *Digest of Education Statistics, 1993* (Washington, D.C.: U.S. Government Printing Office, 1993), p. 61.

TABLE 4.6. EFFECTS OF REQUIRING PASSAGE OF A MINIMUM COMPETENCY TEST TO GRADUATE FROM HIGH SCHOOL

| | READING AND MATH TEST SCORES | | | GENDER | |
| --- | --- | --- | --- | --- | --- |
| | Low | Middle | High | Male | Female |
| *Log average wage rate* | | | | | |
| Class of 1980 in 1981 | 0.025 (1.45) | 0.020[a] (1.74) | 0.005 (0.40) | 0.017 (1.45) | 0.016 (1.63) |
| Class of 1980 in 1984 | 0.041[a] (1.85) | −0.025 (−1.57) | −0.010 (−0.56) | −0.012 (0.75) | 0.007 (0.52) |
| Class of 1980 in 1986 | 0.021 (1.02) | 0.029[a] (1.85) | 0.010 (0.53) | 0.017 (1.05) | 0.034[b] (2.45) |
| Class of 1992 in 1992–94 | −0.049 (1.46) | 0.052[c] (2.63) | 0.063[c] (2.65) | 0.041[c] (2.18) | 0.032[a] (1.69) |
| *Earnings (1992 $)* | | | | | |
| Class of 1980 in 1981 | 460[a] (1.60) | −207 (0.99) | −151 (0.72) | −12 (0.05) | 161 (0.96) |
| Class of 1980 in 1982 | −41 (0.11) | −89 (0.32) | −80 (0.30) | −148 (0.53) | 193 (0.82) |
| Class of 1980 in 1983 | −240 (0.63) | 40 (0.13) | −163 (0.54) | −302 (1.01) | 227 (0.95) |
| Class of 1980 in 1984 | 77 (0.17) | 380 (1.59) | 291 (0.77) | 473 (1.40) | 320 (1.16) |
| Class of 1980 in 1985 | 474 (1.01) | 1077[c] (2.89) | 368 (0.79) | 979[b] (2.52) | 758[b] (2.33) |

| | 60 | 424[b] | 158 | 269 | 208 |
|---|---|---|---|---|---|
| Class of 1992 in 1993 | (0.16) | (2.21) | (0.93) | (1.28) | (1.40) |
| *College attendance* | | | | | |
| Class of 1980 in 1981–82 | 0.043[c] (3.19) | 0.011 (0.83) | -0.009 (-0.59) | 0.017 (1.43) | -0.000 (-0.07) |
| Class of 1980 in 1982–83 | 0.038[c] (2.51) | 0.043[c] (2.99) | -0.006 (-0.33) | 0.018 (1.39) | 0.024[b] (1.88) |
| Class of 1980 in 1983–84 | 0.041[c] (2.95) | 0.045[c] (3.15) | 0.007 (0.38) | 0.026[b] (1.93) | 0.026[b] (2.06) |
| Class of 1980 in 1984 | 0.011 (0.857) | 0.022[a] (1.62) | 0.018 (0.94) | 0.021 (1.59) | 0.008 (0.65) |
| Class of 1980 in 1985 | -0.001 (0.069) | 0.003 (0.21) | 0.02 (1.16) | -0.013 (0.92) | 0.002 (0.16) |
| Class of 1980 in 1986 | 0.015 (0.91) | -0.017 (-1.09) | -0.01 (0.85) | -0.011 (0.97) | -0.002 (-0.16) |
| Class of 1992 in 1992–94 full-time | 0.011 (0.52) | 0.017 (1.04) | -0.004 (0.24) | -0.009 (0.57) | 0.029[b] (1.99) |
| Class of 1992 in 1992–94 part-time | -0.001 (0.06) | 0.008 (0.90) | 0.005 (0.58) | 0.016[b] (2.09) | 0.002 (0.26) |

[a] Statistically significant at the 10 percent level.
[b] Statistically significant at the 5 percent level.
[c] Statistically significant at the 1 percent level.

*Source:* Analysis of follow-up data for High School and Beyond—Senior Cohort and NELS-88. HSB and NELS-88, U.S. Department of Education, National Center for Education Statistics, Washington, D.C. Sample is all students who graduated from high school during calendar year 1980 or 1992. All models contain a full set of background variables including test scores and grades. In addition, models predicting earnings and wage rates contain controls for the number of months spent attending college full-time and months spent attending part-time.

TABLE 4.7: EFFECTS OF REQUIRING PASSAGE OF A MINIMUM COMPETENCY TEST TO GRADUATE FROM HIGH SCHOOL

| | Socioeconomic Status | | | Race/Ethnicity | | |
|---|---|---|---|---|---|---|
| | Low | Middle | High | White | Black | Hispanic |
| *Log wage rate* | | | | | | |
| Class of 1980 in 1981 | 0.036[b] (2.08) | 0.017[a] (1.69) | -0.012 (0.78) | -0.005 (0.56) | 0.042[b] (2.20) | 0.037[b] (2.17) |
| Class of 1980 in 1983 | -0.017 (0.73) | -0.006 (0.42) | 0.005 (0.25) | -0.015 (1.10) | -0.014 (-0.54) | 0.045[a] (1.85) |
| Class of 1980 in 1985 | 0.019 (0.83) | 0.025[a] (1.79) | 0.011 (0.52) | 0.008 (0.61) | 0.031 (1.28) | 0.046[b] (1.98) |
| Class of 1992 in 1992–94 | 0.039 (1.27) | 0.037[b] (2.11) | 0.049 (1.61) | 0.047[c] (3.09) | -0.007 (0.22) | -0.007 (0.22) |
| *Earnings (in current $)* | | | | | | |
| Class of 1980 in 1981 | 194 (1.09) | 113 (0.93) | -286[a] (1.74) | -161 (1.45) | 93 (0.54) | 500[b] (2.37) |
| Class of 1980 in 1982 | -86 (0.34) | 69 (0.40) | -113 (0.51) | -227 (1.46) | 111 (0.44) | 402 (1.42) |
| Class of 1980 in 1983 | -220 (0.83) | 64 (0.33) | -149 (0.39) | -208 (1.16) | 5 (0.02) | 477 (1.56) |
| Class of 1980 in 1984 | 0 (0.00) | 264 (1.21) | 103 (0.32) | 117 (0.56) | 470 (1.39) | 330 (0.91) |
| Class of 1980 in 1985 | 377 (1.02) | 620[b] (2.27) | 286 (0.72) | 484[a] (1.88) | 808[b] (2.05) | 703[a] (1.67) |

| Class of 1992 in 1993 | 694[b] (2.22) | 171 (0.94) | 107 (0.54) | 318[b] (2.31) | 59 (0.18) | 59 (0.18) |
|---|---|---|---|---|---|---|
| *College attendance* | | | | | | |
| Class of 1980 in 1981–82 | 0.027[a] (1.72) | 0.008 (0.70) | −0.008 (0.49) | 0.000 (0.01) | 0.011 (0.59) | 0.031[a] (1.77) |
| Class of 1980 in 1982–83 | 0.022 (1.26) | 0.018 (1.37) | 0.032[a] (1.66) | 0.018 (1.41) | 0.032 (1.56) | 0.039[b] (2.04) |
| Class of 1980 in 1983–84 | 0.024 (1.42) | 0.027[b] (2.12) | 0.030 (1.52) | 0.032[b] (2.49) | 0.038[a] (1.89) | 0.011 (0.62) |
| Class of 1980 in 1984 | 0.004 (0.28) | 0.013 (1.02) | 0.029 (1.32) | 0.022[a] (1.66) | −0.002 (0.09) | 0.002 (0.09) |
| Class of 1980 in 1985 | −0.009 (0.53) | 0.013 (0.98) | 0.004 (0.16) | 0.009 (0.64) | −0.014 (0.070) | 0.022 (1.10) |
| Class of 1980 in 1986 | −0.012 (0.59) | −0.011 (0.77) | 0.005 (0.24) | −0.009 (0.64) | −0.007 (0.32) | 0.007 (0.34) |
| Class of 1992 in 1992–94 full-time | 0.032 (1.49) | 0.011 (0.72) | −0.003 (0.18) | 0.011 (0.93) | 0.018 (0.69) | 0.018 (0.69) |
| Class of 1992 in 1992–94 part-time | 0.012 (1.11) | 0.013 (1.60) | 0.001 (0.07) | 0.010[a] (1.71) | 0.010 (0.73) | 0.010 (0.73) |

[a] Statistically significant at the 10 percent level.
[b] Statistically significant at the 5 percent level.
[c] Statistically significant at the 1 percent level.

*Source:* Analysis of follow-up data for High School and Beyond-Senior Cohort of 1980 and NELS-88. HSB and NELS-88, U.S. Department of Education, National Center for Education Statistics, Washington, D.C. Sample is all students who graduated from high school during calendar year 1980 or 1992. All models contain a full set of background variables including test scores and grades. In addition, models predicting earnings and wage rates contain controls for the number of months spent attending college full-time and months spent attending part-time. The 1992 Hispanic and black graduates were merged because of an insufficient number of observations for separate analysis.

# CHAPTER FIVE

# The Adverse Impact of High-Stakes Testing on Minority Students
## Evidence from One Hundred Years of Test Data

GEORGE MADAUS AND MARGUERITE CLARKE

It's a bull market for high-stakes testing programs in education, far surpassing the bull market days of minimum competency testing of the early 1970s. Now they are called assessments, not tests. However, while their look and feel may have changed, deep down the underlying technology has not, and the same issues about their impact and effects persist. The range of high-stakes testing programs is expansive: from readiness testing for entrance to kindergarten; to tests required for promotion and graduation; to accountability testing for teachers, schools, and districts; to testing teachers for certification. These high-stakes testing programs will not go away; if anything, they will become more important as policy tools and societal signaling devices. For example, policymakers in several states are setting high standards on state exams to deliver a "wake-up call" to students, teachers, parents, and the public to what they portray as a generalized crisis, deterioration, and failure of public education.[1]

Advocates of the standards movement that is now sweeping the country take for granted that high standards on high-stakes assessments—in current parlance, assessments "worth teaching to"—can reduce adverse impacts in test performance by influencing what is taught and learned. Paradoxically, they are both right and wrong. They are right because high-stakes tests do influence which and how things are taught and learned. The history of high-stakes testing over the last five centuries is testimony to that truism: test scores will go up. However, as teaching turns into test preparation, test results cease to reflect what examinees really know or can do. Therefore, it is wrong to believe that we can test our way out of our educational problems. Quite the opposite is true: our fixation on test results deflects attention from fundamental educational problems and thus hinders reform.[2]

In this chapter, we examine four aspects of current high-stakes testing that impact minority students and others who are traditionally poorly served by the educational system. Our analysis is based primarily on research done at Boston College over the past thirty years. After reviewing the available evidence, we come to the following conclusions:

- high-stakes, high-standards tests do not have a markedly positive effect on teaching and learning in the classroom;

- high-stakes tests do not motivate the unmotivated;

- contrary to popular belief, "authentic" forms of high-stakes assessments are not a more equitable way to assess the progress of students who differ by race, culture, native language, or gender;[3]

- high-stakes testing programs have been shown to increase high school dropout rates, particularly among minority student populations.

## EXPLORING THE ACHIEVEMENT GAP

Before developing these points, it is worth looking at some of the trend data available on the test performance of minority students since the 1970s. Results from several studies, including the National Assessment of Educational Progress (NAEP), the National Education Longitudinal Study (NELS), and the SAT-I (formerly known as the Scholastic Assessment Test), indicate that while the achievement gap between black and Hispanic students and their white counterparts has been generally narrowing over the years, it is still "a substantial" one.[4]

For example, results from the 1996 trend NAEP provide evidence that averages for nine-, thirteen-, and seventeen-year-old black and Hispanic students in mathematics were generally higher than those for their counterparts in 1973 (see Figures 5.1–5.3, pages 87–89). In addition,

## FIGURE 5.1. TRENDS IN RACIAL/ETHNIC GROUP DIFFERENCES ON THE NAEP MATHEMATICS TEST: NINE-YEAR-OLDS

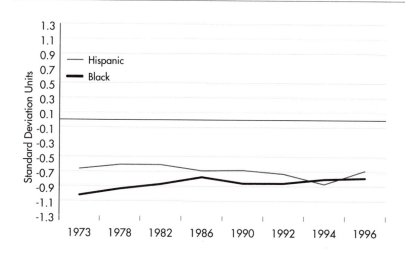

*Note:* The performance of white students for each year is taken to be the zero point of the scale. Groups above the zero line perform better, groups below perform worse.

*Sources:* "Weighted Means, Standard Deviations, and Percentiles of Mathematics Distributions with Jackknifed Standard Errors," Educational Testing Service, Princeton, N.J., undated and unpublished tabulations; John Mazzeo, Educational Testing Service, personal communication, September 1997; Jay R. Campbell, Kristin E. Voelkl, and Patricia L. Donahue, *NAEP 1996 Trends in Academic Progress* (Washington, D.C.: National Center for Education Statistics, 1997).

gains made by these groups were generally larger than those made by white students.[5] However, tempering this positive trend is the realization that the average proficiency for white thirteen-year-olds as measured on the 1996 NAEP scale was around the level achieved by black seventeen-year-olds.[6] In addition, data from the main NAEP for 1996 indicate that at grades 4, 8, and 12, achievement gaps between white students and their black and Hispanic counterparts ranged from 0.8 to 1.1 standard deviation units. To put this in context, a difference of 1 standard deviation implies that just 16 percent of the low-achieving group perform at levels exceeded by 50 percent of the higher achieving group.

## FIGURE 5.2. TRENDS IN RACIAL/ETHNIC GROUP DIFFERENCES ON THE NAEP MATHEMATICS TEST: THIRTEEN-YEAR-OLDS

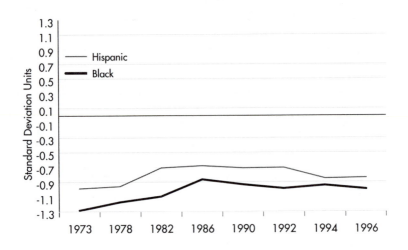

*Note:* The performance of white students for each year is taken to be the zero point of the scale. Groups above the zero line perform better, groups below perform worse.

*Sources:* "Weighted Means, Standard Deviations, and Percentiles of Mathematics Distributions with Jackknifed Standard Errors," Educational Testing Service, Princeton, N.J., undated and unpublished tabulations; John Mazzeo, Educational Testing Service, personal communication, September 1997; Jay R. Campbell, Kristin E. Voelkl, and Patricia L. Donahue, *NAEP 1996 Trends in Academic Progress* (Washington, D.C.: National Center for Education Statistics, 1997).

Similar outcomes for racial differences in mathematics scores are found on longitudinal studies such as the NELS and High School and Beyond (see Figure 5.4, page 90) and on college admissions tests such as the ACT (formerly known as the American College Test) and the SAT-I. As the trend lines in Figures 5.5 and 5.6 indicate (pages 91–92), Asian American students were the highest performers on both the ACT assessment and the SAT-I from 1977 to 1997. White students, the second-highest performers, achieved at average levels that were about 0.3 of a standard deviation unit lower than Asian students. The average performance of black students was consistently lower than those of all other groups and stood well below those of Asian and white students in 1997. Nevertheless, it is important to emphasize that

## FIGURE 5.3. TRENDS IN RACIAL/ETHNIC GROUP DIFFERENCES ON THE NAEP MATHEMATICS TEST: SEVENTEEN-YEAR-OLDS

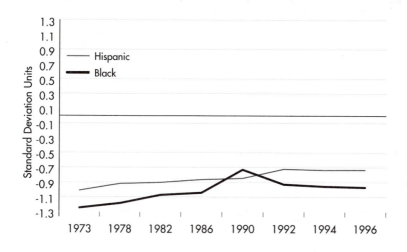

*Note:* The performance of white students for each year is taken to be the zero point of the scale. Groups above the zero line perform better, groups below perform worse.

*Sources:* "Weighted Means, Standard Deviations, and Percentiles of Mathematics Distributions with Jackknifed Standard Errors," Educational Testing Service, Princeton, N.J., undated and unpublished tabulations; John Mazzeo, Educational Testing Service, personal communication, September 1997; Jay R. Campbell, Kristin E. Voelkl, and Patricia L. Donahue, *NAEP 1996 Trends in Academic Progress* (Washington, D.C.: National Center for Education Statistics, 1997).

while all groups improved their performances from the mid-1970s on, some of the largest improvements on average were made by blacks. The improved performance of Mexican American students, especially on the ACT assessment, is also notable. An important finding in a study by Gail T. McLure, Anji Sun, and Michael J. Valiga of ACT scores between 1987 and 1996 was that the improved performance of minority groups in general on the ACT mathematics test coincided with a pattern of increases in the number of courses taken by students from these groups.[7]

Explanations for these achievement gaps have run the full gamut. A lot of attention has been given to the tests themselves and possible flaws therein. However, in today's high-stakes testing context, it is becoming

## FIGURE 5.4. TRENDS IN RACIAL/ETHNIC GROUP DIFFERENCES ON THE NATIONAL LONGITUNDINAL STUDY, HIGH SCHOOL AND BEYOND, AND NATIONAL EDUCATION LONGITUDINAL STUDY MATHEMATICS TESTS: HIGH SCHOOL SENIORS

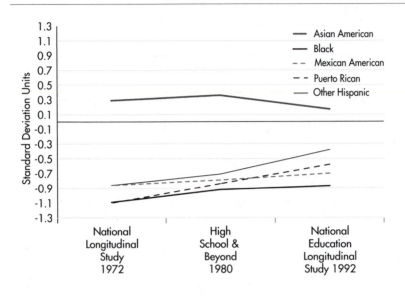

*Note:* The performance of white students for each year is taken to be the zero point of the scale. Groups above the zero line perform better, groups below perform worse.

*Source:* U.S. Department of Education, National Center for Education Statistics, "Trends among High School Seniors, 1972–1992," NCES 95-380 (Washington, D.C.: U.S. Government Printing Office, 1995).

harder and harder to blame the tests for large performance differences among groups—what the courts call "adverse impact." Today, there is a realization that differential results can reflect genuine group differences in whatever trait is being assessed.[8] These tests—even when faulty— are signaling that something is wrong. Sturm and Guinier's analogy of test results being the miner's canary is apt.[9] Further, there will be no breakthrough in the technology of testing to ameliorate the adverse impact we see on cognitive measures. Technically we can only tinker at the margins.

One caveat about the malleability of testing technology: a major weakness of the high-stakes, high-standards assessment movement is that the standard-setting process increasingly results in cut scores—the scores

## FIGURE 5.5. TRENDS IN RACIAL/ETHNIC GROUP DIFFERENCES ON THE ACT MATHEMATICS TEST: HIGH SCHOOL SENIORS

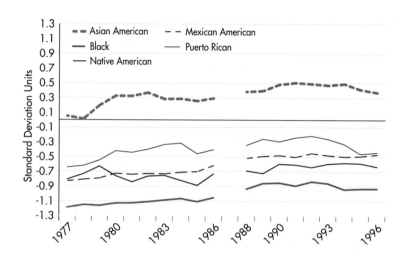

*Note:* The performance of white students for each year is taken to be the zero point of the scale. Groups above the zero line perform better, groups below perform worse. Data were not available for 1987.

*Sources:* "ACT Math Scores and ACT Score Means and SDs for Successive Years of ACT-Tested College-Bound Seniors 10 percent National Sample," American College Testing, Iowa City, Iowa, undated and unpublished tabulations; James Maxey, American College Testing, personal communications, August–September 1997.

that serve to demarcate passing from failing, or from one achievement level to the next—that are very high relative to current distributions of scores on standardized achievement tests. For example, according to the four cut scores used by the NAEP, the percentages of students at the advanced mathematics level never exceed 4 percent. Yet, independent achievement data from the SAT-I, ACT, and advanced placement tests in mathematics call into question the NAEP percentages.[10] Thus, the NAEP's description of national math attainment is a classic *ipse dixit.* The bleak picture is valid only so long as one accepts the cut scores as definitive. Another example is the Massachusetts Comprehensive Assessment System (MCAS), which results in large numbers of students falling into the "failure" and "needs improvement" categories

## FIGURE 5.6. TRENDS IN RACIAL/ETHNIC GROUP DIFFERENCES ON THE SAT-I MATHEMATICS TEST: HIGH SCHOOL SENIORS

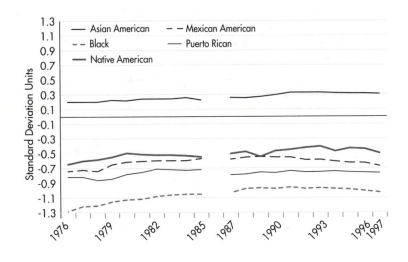

*Note:* The performance of white students for each year is taken to be the zero point of the scale. Groups above the zero line perform better, groups below perform worse. Data were not available for 1986.
*Source: College Bound Seniors: National Report* (New York: College Entrance and Examination Board, 1972–1997).

despite contradictory, standardized, norm-referenced data. In short, many policymakers fail to recognize that the arbitrary nature of cut-score methodologies cries out for the external validation of the categories produced and used to label students.

There are three additional problems with very high cut scores.[11] First, they result in schools and parents getting essentially no information other than "failure," "inadequate," or "needs improvement" for large numbers of children. Second, they provide a misleading view of change. Large changes that stay within one of the levels go unnoticed, and trivial changes that cross a cut-score boundary are treated as important. Finally, the school systems often set goals for overall or annual improvement that are simply not possible to meet by legitimate means. This gives teachers an additional incentive to teach to the test in inappropriate ways.

# THE IMPACT OF HIGH-STAKES TESTING
## ON TEACHING AND LEARNING

Contemporary policymakers who advocate the use of tests as levers of educational reform certainly recognize the historical role of testing in controlling what is taught and learned. There seems to be little argument that tests affect the curriculum. Indeed, the power of an examination to shape what is taught and learned was noted at least as far back as the sixteenth century, when Philip Melanchthon, a Protestant, German teacher, wrote in *De Studiis Adolescentum*, "no academical exercise can be more useful than that of examination. It whets the desire for learning, it enhances the solicitude of study while it animates the attention to whatever is taught."[12]

The concept of the power of an important test is beautifully captured by Chief Inspector of Schools Edmond Holmes, writing about nineteenth-century school examinations in Great Britain. Victorian style apart, Holmes' observation remains true today for the United States:

> Whenever the outward standard of reality (examination results) has established itself at the expense of the inward, the ease with which worth (or what passes for such) can be measured is ever tending to become in itself the chief, if not sole, measure of worth. And in proportion, as we tend to value the results of education for their measurableness, so we tend to undervalue and at last ignore those results which are too intrinsically valuable to be measured.[13]

How do important tests exert such an influence? What are the mechanisms that vest high-stakes tests with their power to change instruction and learning? Four principles explain the importance of such tests on what is taught and learned; the latter three are special cases of the first as played out in education.[14]

1.  The more any quantitative social indicator is used for social decisionmaking, the more likely it will be to distort and corrupt the social process it is intended to monitor. This very general principle comes from the work of Don Campbell and is a social version of Heisenberg's uncertainty principle.[15]

2.  One of the necessary conditions for measurement-driven instruction to work is that valued rewards or serious sanctions are perceived to

be triggered by test performance. If teachers perceive that important decisions are related to the test results, they will teach to the test.[16]

3.  When test stakes are high, past exams come to define the curriculum. Once a high-stakes testing program has been in place for several years, teachers see the kind of intellectual activity required by the previous test questions and prepare students to meet these demands.[17]

4.  When teaching to the test, teachers pay attention to the form of the test as well as the content. When this occurs, the form of the questions can narrow the focus of instruction, study, and learning to the detriment of other skills.[18]

Today, advocates of "authentic" assessment (that is, assessment that requires active engagement, such as producing extended responses, generating material for portfolios, or carrying out experiments) presume that such assessments are somehow outside the purview of the latter three principles. Not so. A powerful illustration that these supply-type exams—exams that require students to produce their own answers to a question rather than choose from a set of possible answers—are also likely to distort instruction comes from samples of student essays from an Irish examination of the mid-1940s, the Primary Leaving Certificate.[19]

Box 5.1 illustrates how students learned to memorize stock responses that would be adaptable to any writing prompt. Note the similarity between the answers to three different writing prompts from three different students across three different years. Scores from such tests said more about students' memories and test-taking strategies than they did about students' ability to write.[20]

How do the four principles about the impact of tests on curriculum specifically affect minority students? A 1992 national study, sponsored by the National Science Foundation, of the effects of high-stakes tests—primarily standardized, multiple-choice tests—on math and science instruction found that students in classrooms with a high percentage of minority students are affected significantly more by such tests than are their peers in classrooms with few minority students.[21] Teachers with more than 60 percent minority students in their class, compared to teachers with less than 10 percent minority students, reported more reliance on mandated standardized tests for various uses, more test pressure, and more test preparation and influence on instruction. They more often reported that test scores were "very important" or "extremely important" either to themselves or

## BOX 5.1.

### A BICYCLE RIDE (1946)

I awakened early, jumped out of bed and had a quick breakfast. My friend, Mary Quant, was coming to our house at nine o'clock as we were going for a long bicycle ride together.

It was a lovely morning. White fleecy clouds floated in the clear blue sky and the sun was shining. As we cycled over Castlemore bridge we could hear the babble of the clear stream beneath us. Away to our right we could see the brilliant flowers in Mrs. Casey's garden. Early summer roses grew all over the pergola which stood in the middle of the garden.

### A DAY IN THE BOG (1947)

I awakened early and jumped out of bed. I wanted to be ready at nine o'clock when my friend, Sadie, was coming to our house. Daddy said he would take us with him to the bog if the day was good.

It was a lovely morning. White fleecy clouds floated in the clear blue sky. As we were going over Castlemore bridge in the horse and cart, we could hear the babble of the clear stream beneath us. Away to our right we could see the brilliant flowers in Mrs. Casey's garden. Early summer roses grew all over the pergola which stood in the middle of the garden.

### A BUS TOUR (1948)

I awakened early and sprang out of bed. I wanted to be ready in good time for our bus tour from the school. My friend, Nora Greene, was going to call for me at half-past eight as the tour was starting at nine.

It was a lovely morning. White fleecy clouds floated in the clear blue sky and the sun was shining. As we drive over Castlemore bridge we could hear the babble of the clear stream beneath us. From the bus window we could see Mrs. Casey's garden. Early summer roses grew all over the pergola which stood in the middle of the garden.

*Source:* Primary Leaving Certificate, Irish examination answer papers, Department of Education, Dublin, Ireland.

to administrators for placing students in special services, determining graduation, recommending textbooks, planning curriculum and instruction, evaluating student progress, and giving feedback to students.

About 75 percent of both math and science teachers with classes that had high percentages of minority students reported pressure from their district to improve standardized test scores, in comparison to about 60 percent of teachers with classes that had low percentages. Teachers in classrooms with high percentages of minority students significantly more often reported teaching test-taking skills, teaching topics known to be on the test, increasing emphasis on tested topics, beginning preparation more than a month before the test, and including topics not otherwise taught. Case studies conducted in six urban districts with large minority enrollments confirmed the finding of the national survey that instruction by teachers facing high-stakes testing pressure is often heavily oriented toward test preparation. There is little question that high-stakes tests have greater consequences for minority and poor children than they do for majority and more affluent students, although the latter also feel the impact of these tests.[21]

## THE IMPACT OF HIGH-STAKES TESTING ON STUDENT MOTIVATION

The idea that mandating a high-stakes assessment will improve students' motivation to learn is one that goes back at least to the eighteenth century.[22] A recent monograph sponsored by the American Educational Research Association examined the claim that high-stakes assessments will move obstinate, dispirited, lazy, or recalcitrant students to try harder in school.[23] Three corollaries associated with contemporary assertions about the motivational force of high-stakes testing emerged.[24] First, the greater the reward offered (or the more noxious the consequences of not complying), the harder students will try. Second, the meaning of rewards and punishments is essentially the same for all students (including poor, middle class, and minority). Third, student arousal is maximized when rewards are distributed on a competitive basis.[25]

Unfortunately, these assumptions about motivation are flawed. The concept of motivation used in claims about the power of examinations lacks definition and clarity.[26] The complexity of the construct, its variety of meanings, and the different mechanisms that elicit it are ignored in blanket claims about the examinations' motivational power. Investigators in cognitive psychology, while identifying goals as central to the motivational process, point to the complexity of the relationships and processes involved, the idiosyncrasy of individuals' choices of goals and subgoals, and differences between students in their assessment of their ability and self-efficacy.[27] There seems to be little appreciation among reformers that motivation may be even more complex in the context of external (that is, imposed from outside the school), high-stakes, national examinations, embedded as they are in complex school, cultural, and social networks. In other words, advocates of the motivational potential of examinations have not paid enough attention to who will be motivated and who will not. This point is particularly relevant when the examinations are referenced to "world-class" standards that all students, regardless of grade level, circumstances, context, and individual differences, are expected to attain.

Furthermore, to become motivated students must first see that striving for the rewards attached to examination performance is not only important in their lives but also realistic.[28] In practice, however, some students immediately dismiss the examination because they feel they lack the ability to do what is necessary to pass. Others, while believing they may have the ability to pass, are not motivated to work toward examination success because they do not see the test credential necessarily resulting in jobs or college because of scarcity, competition, or lack of relevance in their social setting. Still others perceive not only that they lack the ability, but that the rewards in reality are illusory even for many who might pass.

In addition, there is no reason to believe that the motivational power of examinations will be the same at all grade levels. Since present reform proposals call for testing at elementary and middle grades, we need to consider how examinations over the course of many years will influence the behavior of students at these age levels.

There can be no doubt that some students in other countries do indeed work hard to pass high-stakes external examinations. Further, many pay considerable sums of money to attend test-preparation schools, and some, no doubt, internalize the competitive values embedded in the examinations. It may even be true that some students develop genuine, intrinsically motivated behavior or, at any rate, relatively autonomous forms of extrinsic motivation. However, experience with external examinations indicates that all too many students focus their efforts on mastering strategies to help them over the examination hurdle rather than on developing mastery of subject matter and honing lasting competencies.

This consequence does not seem to have been anticipated by some testing proponents in the United States. For example, a laudable objective

of the Learning Research and Development Center and the National Center
on Education and the Economy is that their proposed examination system
would lead students to see that school is a place to learn and not just a
place to be labeled as smarter or slower than other students.[29] While implic-
itly recognizing the distinction between competence and performance,
there does not seem to be an appreciation that high-stakes external examinations are likely to thwart rather than support the attainment of this
objective. In his description of a cramming (or test preparation) school,
Wilfred Sheed offers an amusing insight into the effects of focusing on
performance rather than on learning in the context of external examinations. The crammer, Jenkins Tutorial Establishment in London, offered

> successful examination results as it might a forged passport
> [bypassing] education altogether. Their only texts were exami-
> nation papers—all the relevant ones set in the last fifty years,
> with odds of repetition calculated and noted as in the Racing
> Form. Within six months, I was able to pass London matricu-
> lation without knowing any of the subjects involved; and by
> applying Jenkins' method later, to pass every exam that ever
> came my way afterwards. Hence I remain a profoundly unedu-
> cated man.[30]

There are further consequences of external examinations.[31] For
example, many teachers, under pressure to help students secure good
examination results, will be more controlling in their teaching. In fact, the
"rhetoric from Washington continues to advocate greater accountability,
greater discipline, and increased use of standardized testing, all of which
are means of exerting greater pressure and control on the educational
process."[32] The fact that examinations are bureaucratically controlled
from the top down, rather than under the control of practitioners, parents, and the local community moving from the bottom up, has implications for adopting and pursuing goals. Further, insofar as it involves
increased control of teacher and student behavior through the imposition
of rewards and sanctions associated with test performance, other
undesirable consequences are possible. When controlling events are
perceived to determine behavior, students' need for competence, self-
determination, conceptual learning, and creativity will not be met, but
rather diminished.[33]

Examinations also can increase competition and cheating on the part
of some students. We argued above that situations that emphasize test
performance rather than learning per se narrow the curriculum to what

is embodied in the tradition of past examinations. We therefore expect the pursuit of high-stakes examination performance in time to corrupt the examination, resulting in invalid inferences about achievement based on performance.

Another important consideration is that students who may not be motivated to pursue examination success for sociocultural reasons or on the basis of estimates of their present levels of achievement or ability are likely to become alienated from both the examinations and the whole educational process.[34] The fact that around 10 percent of students, mostly from disadvantaged backgrounds, avoid taking any public examination before leaving school is regarded as a serious problem in several European countries. In America, research on dropouts also shows that many, while fully appreciating the importance of educational credentials, do not believe that such credentials are of much help in their social milieu. The motivational argument of proponents of high-stakes national examinations does not address these realities. We will examine the dropout issue later in this chapter. Suffice it to say here that motivation and dropout issues are intertwined.

Many of the reform arguments relating to motivation in education have their origins in the world of industry. However, the use of external motivation techniques in industry has little relevance to the high-stakes assessment situation in education. In industry, skills have already been acquired, and rewards are tangible and immediate and serve to reinforce and direct behavior. The feedback mechanisms in industry are also well developed and more immediate. None of these conditions hold for high-standards, high-stakes assessments. Other high-stakes exam situations—no-pass no-play or no-pass no-drive programs, for example—do not seem to motivate very well, despite the fact that they are more immediate and real for many students than are high-stakes school assessments.[35]

These considerations lead to the conclusion that it is incumbent on reformers to weigh more carefully the costs and benefits that are likely to be associated with the variety of outcomes of examination-induced motivation.[36] While there are possible positive aspects, such as the specification of clear goals and standards for teachers and students, greater consideration needs to be given to the nature of those goals and standards and how they might need to vary for different students. Other important issues also should be addressed, including the probability that many students will not be motivated at all. Moreover, for many who are motivated, the high stakes associated with the assessment may work toward focusing their efforts on improving their test performance rather than on the more demanding job of developing general competence, higher-order thinking skills, problem-solving ability, and creativity. It is these latter traits that reformers claim will be the eventual outcome of standards-based reform. Yet, until such issues are addressed, we can have little confidence in high-stakes assessments as a panacea for the ills of American education.

## THE IMPACT OF AUTHENTIC ASSESSMENTS ON THE PERFORMANCE OF STUDENTS WHO DIFFER IN RACE, CULTURE, NATIVE LANGUAGE, OR GENDER

An outgrowth of the high-stakes, high-standards movement is the belief that authentic assessments are more equitable for assessing the progress of students who differ in race, culture, native language, or gender.[37] This assumption, however, is questionable in light of data from a high-stakes authentic assessment implemented by the United Kingdom in 1992.[38]

These data permitted an examination of the relative performance of gender, linguistic, low-income, and special needs groups on the authentic assessments administered to seven-year-olds as part of the national curriculum.[39] No matter what the method of authentic assessment, once all other factors had been taken into account there were substantial differences between particular groups of students. Low-income students, students whose first language was not English, and special needs students performed at significantly lower levels than other students on English, mathematics, and science assessments. Gender was the only factor that varied in impact across the three subjects. In English and mathematics, girls performed at a significantly higher level than boys, although the difference in mathematics was small. However, in science there was no significant difference between boys and girls.

As would be expected, older students performed better than younger students on the United Kingdom exams. The United Kingdom data appear to validate the trend recognized by the United States in the 1980s—that improved high-stakes test performance was related to age. However, this fact, along with concerns about improving upper-level grade performance, created controversial incentives and practices at the school level in the United States during this period (see Chapter 8 by Robert Hauser in this volume). For example, one tactic used by schools to improve reading scores in upper primary grades was to put pressure on teachers to emphasize reading skills more strongly. This emphasis, however, came at the expense of other, more traditional goals for children in kindergarten through third grade. A related tactic to improve upper-level performance was that of "red shirting" kindergarten students, or holding them back a grade. Educators realized that retaining children in kindergarten, or not letting them enter in the first place if they did not have the necessary "readiness," would ultimately contribute to higher test scores. If for no other reason, students would perform better because they would be a year older when they took the tests.[40]

The United Kingdom results are from the early stages of a new program, from a different country and educational system, and from seven-year-olds only. Nonetheless, at the very least, they point to the need to monitor carefully group differences in light of positive equity claims made about authentic assessment technology. These results are cautionary to those making such claims.

## THE IMPACT OF HIGH-STAKES ASSESSMENTS ON HIGH SCHOOL DROPOUT RATES

One aspect of high-standards, high-stakes assessments that needs considerably more attention is the relationship between such assessments and dropping out of high school. Five suggestive lines of evidence argue for a careful examination of this relationship.

The first intriguing data come from the minimum competency testing (MCT) era. An overall, albeit quite crude, view of the relationship between MCT and dropout rates comes from examining the ten states with the highest dropout rates in 1986 and the ten states with the lowest dropout rates that year.[41] Correlational data indicate a strong relationship between attrition, or dropout, rates and the existence of MCT programs in these states.[42] Five of the ten states with the lowest dropout rates had no minimum competency testing programs. The other five states with low dropout rates had MCT programs that could be characterized as involving relatively low stakes: four used the tests for decisions about remediation, and only one used them for accountability; none required the tests for critical decisions about graduation or grade promotion. Furthermore, in three of these five states, local, not state, education agencies set the standards.

States with the highest dropout rates, on the other hand, had MCT programs for which standards were set, at least in part, at the state level. Nine of the ten used the tests in decisions about high school graduation; four used them in decisions about promotion. In sum, the ten states with the highest dropout rates employed minimum competency tests with higher stakes and less flexible standards than the states with the lowest dropout rates.

These data are not evidence of a causal relationship between high-stakes MCT programs and dropout rates. The states with the highest dropout rates differed in other important ways from the states with the lowest dropout rates. The latter were largely in the West and Midwest, and they had a relatively low proportion of minority and poor students among their school-age populations. Perhaps high dropout rates are symptoms of the educational system's failure, which spurred legislators to mandate MCT programs in the first place, or perhaps MCT does contribute in some way to the dropout problem.[43] In any case, crude as these data may have been, they underscore the need to explore further competing hypotheses about the connection, or lack of connection, between high-stakes testing and dropping out.

A second line of evidence comes from a correlational study that examined the relationship between MCT in eighth grade and early high school dropout patterns.[44] The results suggest that in schools with high proportions of students from families with low socioeconomic status, MCTs are linked to higher dropout rates. The dropout rates from these schools are two to six percentage points higher, on average, than from similar schools with no such requirement. The overall conclusion is, "It is the concentrated poverty of these schools and their communities, and their concomitant lack of resources, that link MCT policies to higher dropout rates, rather than other risk factors, such as student grades, age, attendance, and minority group membership."[45]

A third, more recent line of evidence on the connection between dropping out and high-stakes assessments, especially for minorities, comes from an analysis of data from the Texas Assessment of Academic Skills (TAAS).[46] One study suggested that the TAAS requirement was related to over 25,344 black and Hispanic students of Texas's 1993 sophomore cohort dropping out of school. For white students, the dropout figure was 14,809. Black and Hispanic students dropped out at a significantly higher rate than did white students even when accounting for socioeconomic status,[47] academic track, language program participation, and school quality.

While these data apply to one particular cohort, they fit well with patterns Walt Haney observed for Texas enrollment rates over a twenty-year period. After breaking down enrollment rates by ethnicity, Haney found that the grade 12/grade 9 enrollment ratio has dipped considerably for both black and Hispanic students since about 1990 but has remained quite stable for white students. For example, in 1989 (the year prior to implementation of the TAAS), the grade 12/grade 9 enrollment ratio for whites was around 0.76. Even after the TAAS was implemented in the 1990–91 school year, this ratio never dipped below 0.73. In 1989, the grade 12/grade 9 enrollment ratio for blacks was quite close to that for whites, at around 0.74. However, since the implementation of the TAAS this ratio has dipped dramatically, falling to a low of about 0.55 in 1994 and hovering around 0.57 in 1997. Hispanic students also experienced a similar drop in their enrollment ratio during this period. Again, we cannot argue causation from these correlational data, but these findings call out for more detailed interviews with a carefully chosen, random selection of dropouts to gauge the actual impact of the TAAS on their decisions to leave school.

A fourth line of evidence on the association between high-stakes tests and dropping out comes from work on the relationship between grade retention, being overage for one's grade, and dropout rates. Research on the effects of grade retention—whether or not it is coupled with high-stakes testing—has generally concluded that its detrimental effects outweigh any purported benefits.[48] In particular, research has found that being overage for their grade as a result of having been retained in an earlier grade eats away at students' sense of efficacy, with the impact especially severe for black students. Compared to on-grade students, these overage students are twice as likely to be retained again.[49] Many of these students ultimately become disengaged and drop out; and many, under the pressure of high-stakes testing, drop out earlier in their school careers than otherwise would be expected. In fact, being overage for one's grade is a better predictor of dropping out than below-average test scores.[50]

These findings were played out fifty years ago in Ireland in response to a mandatory primary school leaving certificate examination that was administered to all sixth-grade pupils between 1943 and 1967.[51] Teachers were employing a policy of not promoting weaker pupils in order to control the potential failure rate on the examination. This policy tended to take place at two points in the system—moving from grade 3 to grade 4, and from grade 5 to grade 6. A pupil that was held back at one or both points would be eligible to leave school before he or she reached the sixth grade—reducing the number of these overage students who ever sat for the primary examination.

A final piece of related—but little known—evidence about dropouts in the United States comes from data from the Third International Mathematics and Science Study (TIMSS). The data indicate that about 35 percent of the senior cohort was no longer enrolled in school when the

TIMSS tests were administered in the spring of 1995.[52] Further, a post hoc check revealed that the NAEP data on dropouts are quite consistent with the TIMSS data.[53] The "no longer enrolled" figure for TIMSS is quite a bit higher than the National Center for Education Statistics (NCES) dropout rate of 12 percent for the United States for 1995, but one possible explanation is that many students who are enrolled in October, the month used in calculating the NCES rate, were no longer in school by April/May when the TIMSS tests were administered. The higher rate of missing seniors revealed by the TIMSS and NAEP data comes at a time when all but one state has a state testing program, and when the state tests are increasingly tied to graduation. The TAAS results discussed above are a case in point. Once again, this conjecture is correlational, not causal, but it points to the need for a more carefully designed study to gauge the impact of high-standards, high-stakes assessments on decisions to drop out of school.

## CONCLUSION

Testing is a powerful, but often blunt, tool. Like a medication, it may fail or have diverse, unintended negative consequences. A testing program, for example, may unfairly or unreasonably deny opportunities to certain classes of people. It may reward or punish the wrong individuals or institutions, or it may undermine the performance of institutions it is intended to strengthen. Further, the four issues described above—the impact of testing on teaching and learning, the motivational power of high-stakes assessments, claims that authentic assessments are fairer to minority students than traditional standardized multiple-choice testing, and the role of high-stakes assessments in decisions to drop out of school—all need to be carefully monitored. Policymakers and test users have been able to turn to extensive commercial, not-for-profit, and governmental infrastructures that have evolved over the past ninety years to assist them in test development, administration, scoring, and reporting. However, there has been no analogous infrastructure for independently evaluating a testing program before or after implementation or for monitoring test use and impact.

In its 1990 report *From Gatekeeper to Gateway: Transforming Testing in America*, the National Commission on Testing and Public Policy recognized "the need for sound, fair, and reasonably efficient mechanisms to help make difficult decisions about individuals and institutions."[54] It also noted that "although tests have become important instruments of public accountability, there are few mechanisms to *audit* or *appraise* the quality of publicly sponsored tests, to monitor their use as instruments of social policy, and to assess their impact on individuals, groups, and institutions."[55] To remedy this, the commission called for "the development of *additional institutional means* to examine the quality of tests and assessment instruments and to provide oversight of test use."[56]

Since 1990, a variety of factors, including changes in statute and case law, national and state policy initiatives, and plebiscites, have both transformed educational testing and increased the need for oversight. All have altered the uses of tests, in some cases fundamentally, and all have the potential to affect profoundly both educational systems and individuals, particularly students currently ill-served by the educational system. These changes also raise difficult equity and technical questions, placing policymakers, educators, and even researchers in uncharted territory. Perhaps at no time in the past half century have questions and consequences surrounding educational testing been as widespread and as serious.

In many other areas where technology and policy intersect, the public insists on oversight to protect individuals from unintended negative effects. For example, faced with the policy decision to introduce a major new, untried medical technology to millions of children, the public would ask about the safety, efficacy, quality, and social and economic effects of the new technology or treatment. Public agencies have been established to address such concerns systematically. The effects of testing are now so diverse, widespread, and serious that it is necessary to establish similar mechanisms for catalyzing inquiry about, and systematic independent scrutiny of, them.

In response to the need for monitoring high-stakes educational testing, in September 1998 the Ford Foundation provided start-up funding for an independent, institutional oversight agency called the National Board on Educational Testing and Public Policy. Housed in the Lynch School of Education at Boston College, the board will review testing programs and encourage close consideration of the diverse uses of testing in education. It will be a permanent institutional entity, as opposed to a transitory commission that studies a situation and then issues a report and recommendations that are easily ignored and then soon forgotten.[57]

Few would disagree with the objectives of raising educational standards and improving the general quality of American education. It seems clear, however, that efforts to foster academic achievement should involve more than simply setting demanding standards and mandating examinations. The task remains of identifying strategies to achieve efficiently and effectively the desirable reform objectives—without having a negative impact on any subpopulation of students. Those strategies will, among other things, need to address the issue of restructuring the academic experiences of students in ways that will help them appreciate the value of academic achievement, increase their expectations and aspirations, and enhance their sense of academic efficacy.[58] This is a much more difficult and, we dare say, expensive task than mandating tougher standards and a high-stakes examination referenced to them.

# CHAPTER SIX

# Do High-Stakes Graduation Tests Improve Learning Outcomes?
## Using State-level NAEP Data to Evaluate the Effects of Mandatory Graduation Tests

MONTY NEILL, WITH KEITH GAYLER

The test-driven approach to school reform is sweeping the nation. More and more states are adopting high-stakes testing for graduation and grade promotion, and they are using test results to impose sanctions on schools, districts, teachers, and students.[1] Texas and North Carolina have been widely cited recently as examples for other states to follow as they reform elementary and secondary education.[2] Both states are praised for their rising scores on the National Assessment of Educational Progress (NAEP). Supporters of test-driven reform maintain that NAEP scores in Texas and North Carolina have risen because those states have implemented extensive testing coupled with strong accountability sanctions.[3]

Should the testing and accountability practices of these two states be held out as an example to other states? We conclude they should not. Our nationwide comparison of states with and without high-stakes graduation tests shows there is no clear relationship between high-stakes tests and gains on the NAEP. Indeed, at grade 8 the relationship is the inverse: states *without* high-stakes graduation tests have been more likely to show progress. Rather than rely on test-driven reform, states should support alternative means for improving education that have been developed and proved in practice at exemplary schools. These schools use alternate methods of assessment and model better approaches to accountability.

In this chapter, first we will consider the advantages and limitations of using the NAEP for the purpose of studying the impact of mandatory high school graduation exams on student learning outcomes. Next, we will analyze and interpret available NAEP data on state-level achievement. Finally, we will discuss some fundamental questions about the limits of test-driven school reform and offer some alternative approaches to assessment that both improve student learning and provide accountability.

## STRENGTHS AND LIMITATIONS OF USING THE NAEP TO EVALUATE STATE PROGRESS ON STUDENT LEARNING

Test advocates often claim or imply that instituting tests to determine who obtains a high school diploma will produce improvements in student learning. In support of this argument, advocates primarily cite rising scores on state tests that are used as graduation requirements. Yet this evidence of improvement in student learning is inherently unpersuasive because of the test-score inflation that often results from teaching to the test.[4] Progress on an independent measure would be a far stronger assurance of real improvement. If the high-stakes testing of students really induces teachers to upgrade curricula and instruction or leads students to study harder or better, then scores should also increase on other independent assessments.

To provide a strong measure of student learning, such an independent assessment would have to be a fair and balanced representation of the domains that are assessed. It would have to sample in a balanced manner all the areas of each domain, including factual content, skills, and higher-order thinking. The difficulty, and at times impossibility, of assessing all the needed aspects of a domain with a paper-and-pencil test or within a relatively limited time span inevitably means that some areas of learning defined as important by content and learning standards will not be assessed. Still, a strong assessment within those limits would be one that gets closest to balanced coverage of each domain.

Convincing evidence of the effects of high-stakes tests could be derived from comparing scores on state exams with those on commercial tests used by districts. For example, while Houston city schools demonstrated strong gains on the Texas Assessment of Academic Skills (TAAS), student scores were quite low on the district-administered Stanford 9 (a nationally normed, commercial standardized test), thus casting doubt on the validity of the TAAS gains.[5] However, only a patch-work of commercial exams is in use across the nation, and recent research suggests that these exams cannot readily be equated since their content varies substantially.[6] Moreover, these tests vary in importance from district to district, and thus some may be the focus of instruction, which would lead to score inflation. Therefore, comparisons might be flawed even if they could be made. Furthermore, assessment experts have found that these tests measure primarily lower-level thinking skills within the subjects and thus cannot show the learning of higher-level problem solving.[7]

The National Assessment of Educational Progress provides a means for comparing states, though not districts, as most states now participate in the voluntary state-level NAEP assessments. The NAEP is a set of assessments—exams and surveys—given periodically to a national sam-ple of students at grades 4, 8, and 12 in a variety of subjects, including reading and math. Since 1990, many states have voluntarily participated in additional NAEP exams that provide state-level data at some grade lev-els in some subjects.

The NAEP appears to be the best available measure for evaluating whether students in a state have made significant gains in learning, at least in the tested subjects. The assessment frameworks are fairly well accepted by practitioners in the tested disciplines and by policymakers. Through the combination of multiple-choice questions and items that require students to construct responses, NAEP exams are likely to assess more complex knowledge and cognitive processes than do most com-mercial or state exams. That is, using the NAEP has the advantage of measuring at least some of the more advanced skills and knowledge called for by many state standards and by Title I of the Federal Elementary and Secondary Education Act.[8]

As they are administered only to samples of students every few years, the NAEP tests cannot readily be taught to, though the frameworks on which they are based could be. Since the tests have relatively low stakes, there is no reason why teachers should try to "beat the test." However, the assumption that the NAEP is a neutral measure across the states may not be true. For example, an NAEP exam in any particular subject might be far more similar to some states' tests than to others'. North Carolina deliberately aligned its standards and tests to NAEP frameworks,[9] and we have heard anecdotally from researchers working in Texas that the state has made a similar substantial alignment. It is also possible that the exclusion of students with special needs will affect a state's scores; and if a state changes the proportion of those excluded, the state's score could rise or fall and the extent of any improvement in scores could be diminished or magnified.[10]

State-level NAEP results are available for math from 1992 and 1996 at grades 4 and 8 as well as from 1990 at grade 8.[11] Results for reading are available from 1994 at grade 4[12] and 1998 at grades 4 and 8.[13] Since state comparisons of score gains can be made at both grades 4 and 8 in math, but only grade 4 in reading, we focus on math. At grade 8, thirty-seven states participated in both 1992 and 1996, and thirty-five participated at grade 4 in both years.

In this chapter we explore whether having a high-stakes exam, such as a mandatory high school graduation test, leads to learning gains that can be generalized to results on something other than the exam itself. A substantial minority of states (sixteen or more in 1992, 1994, and 1996) required that students pass a high school graduation exam to obtain a standard diploma.[14] All states with high school graduation exams also had tests at both the elementary and middle school levels (as did most other states), although not necessarily at grades 4 and 8.[15] In the period under discussion, no states mandated the use of exams for grade promotion.

The NAEP does not produce state-level data at grade 12. It would be reasonable to hypothesize that high school graduation tests exert an influence at the lower grades and that states with high school graduation tests put a greater emphasis on test scores in general, but we have no direct evidence to support these hypotheses.

The National Center for Fair & Open Testing (FairTest), a national assessment reform advocacy organization, has found in several studies that testing is more prevalent in southern states: they test more and are more likely to have high stakes.[16] Indeed, most states with high school graduation exams are in the South. These states historically have had a more centralized education system, including a state curriculum, and were generally the first states to adopt minimum competency tests and high school graduation tests.[17] Arguably, therefore, the weight given to testing is generally greater in the southern states.

It has been well demonstrated that high-stakes testing programs strongly influence curricula and instruction[18] and are more likely to have a strong impact when the proportion of minority students is larger.[19] Thus, it is plausible that southern states, which include most of the states with high school graduation exams and have higher proportions of African American students than states elsewhere, are more likely to have test-driven curricula and instruction across the grades. If this is true, then high school graduation exams should have an impact on earlier grades, even if somewhat indirectly; and if the impact is positive and generalizable, their NAEP scores should rise more than those of states without high school graduation tests. However, as shown below, this has not been the case.

Many states, with or without high school graduation exams, attach other forms of high stakes to tests, particularly rewards or sanctions for schools or districts, which might have an impact on teacher behavior toward the tests. However, the nature of these sanctions and rewards varies enormously from state to state, making any systematic comparison highly problematic. The one regular source of information about such test use, the annual Council of Chief State School Officers surveys, varies from year to year in how it asks for this information and in the quality of the information it receives from the states.[20]

We think it is plausible, then, to conclude that states with high school graduation exams place more emphasis on testing throughout the system, and that this emphasis has a strong impact on curricula and instruction. It is therefore reasonable to use NAEP results at grades 4 and 8 to see if states with high school graduation exams are more likely to show progress on this somewhat independent measure than are states without high school graduation exams. This will shed relevant light on whether high-stakes exams produce real learning gains or only inflated results on specific tests to which students are taught. Thus, we reviewed state NAEP math data[21] and conducted some basic analyses on gains in state NAEP math results at grades 4 and 8.

## FINDINGS

The essential finding from our analyses is that high-stakes graduation tests do not appear to be associated with gains in the NAEP at grade 8 and have an uneven association with gains at grade 4. In fact, states without high-stakes tests were more likely to show NAEP gains at grade 8 than were states with high school graduation tests.

Table 6.1 (page 112) shows states that had high-stakes high school graduation tests between 1992 and 1996.[22] The first block looks at gains in grade 4 math scores from 1992, and the second block presents gains in grade 8 math scores. Reading across the columns within each block, a check in a box indicates that the state made a gain (1) on the mean scale score that was statistically significant at the 5 percent level,[23] (2) in the percentage of students who moved from "below-basic" to "basic" or higher ("percent basic or above"), (3) in the percentage who moved from "below-basic" or "basic" to "proficient" or "advanced" ("percent proficient or

### TABLE 6.1. STATES WITH HIGH-STAKES GRADUATION TESTING: GAINS IN NAEP MEAN SCORES AND ACHIEVEMENT LEVELS

NAEP MATHEMATICS STATISTICALLY SIGNIFICANT GAIN FROM 1992 TO 1996

| | GRADE 4 | | | | GRADE 8 | | | |
|---|---|---|---|---|---|---|---|---|
| | MEAN SCALE SCORE | PERCENT BASIC OR ABOVE | PERCENT PROFICIENT OR ABOVE | PERCENT ADVANCED | MEAN SCALE SCORE | PERCENT BASIC OR ABOVE | PERCENT PROFICIENT OR ABOVE | PERCENT ADVANCED |
| Alabama | | | | | | | | |
| Florida | | | | | | | | |
| Georgia | | | | | | | | |
| Hawaii | | | | | ✓ | ✓ | | |
| Louisiana | ✓ | | | | | | | |
| Maryland | | | | | | | | |
| Mississippi | ✓ | ✓ | | | ✓ | | | |
| New Jersey | | | | | × | × | × | × |
| New Mexico | | | | | | | | |
| New York | ✓ | ✓ | | | | | | |
| North Carolina | ✓ | ✓ | ✓ | | ✓ | ✓ | ✓ | ✓ |
| South Carolina | | | | | | | | |
| Tennessee | ✓ | ✓ | ✓ | | ✓ | | | |
| Texas | ✓ | ✓ | ✓ | ✓ | ✓ | ✓ | | |
| Virginia | | | | | | | | |
| Total[a] | 6 | 5 | 3 | 1 | 5 | 3 | 1 | 1 |

[a] n = 15 for grade 4 NAEP assessment and n = 14 for grade 8 NAEP assessment.

*Note:* x indicates that the state did not participate in grade 8 NAEP mathematics testing.
*Source:* Clyde M. Reese et al., *NAEP 1996 Mathematics Report Card for the Nation and the States* (Washington, D.C.: National Center for Education Statistics, Office of Educational Research and Improvement, U.S. Department of Education, 1997).

above"), and (4) in the percentage who moved into the "advanced" category from one of the lower levels ("percent advanced").

Note that grade 8 from 1996 is not compared with grade 4 from 1992. In other words, these results are not for the same students across test administrations that are four years apart. Instead, "movement" refers to the status of different cohorts of students. That is, grade 4 in 1996 is compared with grade 4 in 1992 to see how well grade 4 students are doing on NAEP math tests. (See below for a summary of the cohort analysis by Paul Barton and Richard Coley.)

The mean scale score is the average numerical score attained by students at the grade level. The other three categories are levels developed by the NAEP to describe student achievement: "basic," "proficient," and "advanced," with a default level of "below basic." A statistically significant mean scale score gain may not appear as movement upward from one level to another because a wide range of scores is captured within each level. Among states with high-stakes tests, this phenomenon occurs in Louisiana at grade 4 and Tennessee at grade 8. No state moved statistically significant numbers of students up into "proficient" or "advanced" without also moving a statistically significant portion of students into "basic" from "below basic." North Carolina and Texas (particularly at grade 4) made the most sweeping gains.

Table 6.2 (page 114) presents states that did not have high-stakes exit tests from 1992 to 1996 and that participated in NAEP math assessments. At grade 8, Rhode Island and Delaware raised their mean scale score and showed movement into higher levels ("proficient and above") without increasing the percentage of students at the "basic" level to a statistically significant degree.[24] At grade 4, Colorado, Connecticut, Indiana, and West Virginia made the most sweeping gains; at grade 8, Connecticut, Maine, Michigan, Nebraska, and West Virginia did.

Table 6.3 (page 115) compares states with high school graduation tests and states without such tests on four measures at both grade levels. At grade 4, the percentages of states with statistically significant gains in mean scale scores are nearly identical. The one statistically significant gain was for students reaching the "basic or above" level, where just over one-quarter of the states without high school graduation tests showed statistically significant gains, and one-third of the states with tests showed such gains. The percentage point difference at the "advanced" category is similar to that at the "basic and above" category (six), but an analysis could not be conducted because no states without high-stakes tests made statistically significant gains in this category. Since there are fifteen states with high school graduation tests, the 6.7 percent gain represents just one state. In other words, only one state that requires a high school graduation exam showed statistically significant gains of students into the "advanced" group in mathematics at the grade 4 level.

At grade 8, states *without* high school graduation exams were more likely than states with exams to make gains in each category, and in each case the result was statistically significant. Three-fifths of the states without an exam made significant gains in mean scale scores, compared with one-third of the states with high school graduation tests. The difference at the "advanced" level represents two states without high school graduation

## TABLE 6.2. STATES WITHOUT HIGH-STAKES GRADUATION TESTING: GAINS IN NAEP MEAN SCORES AND ACHIEVEMENT LEVELS

NAEP MATHEMATICS STATISTICALLY SIGNIFICANT GAIN
FROM 1992 TO 1996

| | GRADE 4 | | | | GRADE 8 | | | |
|---|---|---|---|---|---|---|---|---|
| | MEAN SCALE SCORE | PERCENT BASIC OR ABOVE | PERCENT PROFICIENT OR ABOVE | PERCENT ADVANCED | MEAN SCALE SCORE | PERCENT BASIC OR ABOVE | PERCENT PROFICIENT OR ABOVE | PERCENT ADVANCED |
| Arizona | | | | | | | | |
| Arkansas | ✓ | | | | ✓ | ✓ | | |
| California | | | | | | | | |
| Colorado | ✓ | ✓ | ✓ | | ✓ | | | |
| Connecticut | ✓ | ✓ | ✓ | | ✓ | ✓ | ✓ | |
| Delaware | ↓ | | | | ✓ | | ✓ | |
| Indiana | ✓ | ✓ | ✓ | | ✓ | ✓ | | |
| Iowa | | | | | | | | |
| Kentucky | ✓ | ✓ | | | ✓ | | | |
| Maine | | | | | ✓ | ✓ | ✓ | ✓ |
| Massachusetts | | | | | ✓ | | | |
| Michigan | ✓ | ✓ | | | ✓ | ✓ | ✓ | |
| Minnesota | ✓ | | | | | | | |
| Missouri | | | | | | | | |
| Nebraska | | | | | ✓ | ✓ | | ✓ |
| North Dakota | | | | | | | | |
| Pennsylvania | | | | | × | × | × | × |
| Rhode Island | ✓ | | | | ✓ | | ✓ | |
| Utah | | | | | | | | |
| West Virginia | ✓ | ✓ | ✓ | | ✓ | ✓ | ✓ | |
| Wisconsin | | | | | ✓ | | | |
| Wyoming | | | | | | | | |
| Total[a] | 9 | 6 | 4 | 0 | 13 | 7 | 6 | 2 |

[a] n = 22 for grade 4 NAEP assessment and n = 21 for grade 8 NAEP assessment.

*Note:* ↓ indicates that the state saw a significant loss at this level; x indicates that the state did not participate in grade 8 NAEP mathematics testing.

*Source:* Clyde M. Reese et al., *NAEP 1996 Mathematics Report Card for the Nation and the States* (Washington, D.C.: National Center for Education Statistics, Office of Educational Research and Improvement, U.S. Department of Education, 1997).

TABLE 6.3: COMPARISONS OF NAEP ACHIEVEMENT SCORES IN STATES WITH AND WITHOUT HIGH SCHOOL GRADUATION TESTS

PERCENTAGE SEEING A SIGNIFICANT POSITIVE GAIN ON NAEP MATHEMATICS

| | GRADE 4 | | | | GRADE 8 | | | |
| --- | --- | --- | --- | --- | --- | --- | --- | --- |
| | MEAN SCALE SCORE | PERCENT BASIC OR ABOVE | PERCENT PROFICIENT OR ABOVE | PERCENT ADVANCED | MEAN SCALE SCORE | PERCENT BASIC OR ABOVE | PERCENT PROFICIENT OR ABOVE | PERCENT ADVANCED |
| States *without* high-stakes graduation tests | 40.9 | 27.3 | 18.2 | 0 | 61.9 | 33.3 | 28.6 | 9.5 |
| States *with* high-stakes graduation tests | 40.0 | 33.3 | 20 | 6.7 | 35.7 | 21.4 | 7.1 | 7.1 |
| Statistically significant difference at 0.005 level | none | HSG states significantly higher | none | cannot run tests since one percentage is 0 | Non-HSG states significantly higher | Non-HSG states significantly higher | Non-HSG states significantly higher | Non-HSG states significantly higher |

*Note:* HSG = states with high school graduation tests; Non-HSG = states without high school graduation tests.
*Source:* Clyde M. Reese et al., *NAEP 1996 Mathematics Report Card for the Nation and the States* (Washington, D.C.: National Center for Education Statistics, Office of Educational Research and Improvement, U.S. Department of Education, 1997).

tests and one state with such tests; although statistically significant, these results do not suggest great movement into the "advanced" level for either type of state. The move to "proficient or above" is more sizable for the states with high school graduation tests (six states) than for the states without them (only one) and is statistically significant.

The NAEP also enables comparisons of gains from 1990 to 1996 at grade 8, the only grade with state-level data for 1990.[25] Of thirty-two jurisdictions participating in both years, all but four (Alabama and Georgia with high school graduation tests and Montana and the District of Columbia without) showed statistically significant gains in scale scores.

## DISCUSSION

Given the long list of caveats, mixed results at grade 4, and clear evidence of better educational outcomes at grade 8 in states without high school graduation tests, it would be a mistake to read too much into these findings. Yet they do suggest that a good deal more research is needed before assuming that high-stakes testing will have a positive impact on student learning. In particular, NAEP state results at grade 12 might be useful (though here it also would be essential to know each state's dropout rate). Nonetheless, discussion of these results can help shed light on test-driven school reform.

Historically, the South has always lagged behind other regions on NAEP scores, as it did in 1992 and 1996 in math. The South historically has had lower incomes as well, so directly comparing regional levels of attainment on the NAEP simply reasserts the finding that NAEP results correlate highly with traditional indicators of test performance such as income.[26] This does not mean, however, that these states should be less able to show increases in NAEP scores. In fact, it may well be easier to move from "below basic" to "basic" (due to the simpler level of knowledge required) than from "basic" to "proficient" or "advanced," and southern states tend to have a far larger proportion of students at "below basic" in both math and reading than do states in other regions.[27] In order to better understand score gains, this issue should be researched.

Those concerned with the educational fate of low-income or minority students might look in particular at the proportion of students reaching "basic," since students from these demographic groups are disproportionately likely to score "below basic."[28] That is, given the class and racial distribution of test scores, gains by those at the bottom could be considered most important. (This is not an argument that such groups should settle for "basic," but that moving up to "basic" indicates important progress.) On this issue, at grade 4 states with high school graduation exams performed better than those without such exams, while the reverse was true at grade 8, and both relationships were statistically significant.

It is difficult to think of any reason why high school graduation tests should have a greater impact on grade 4 NAEP tests than on grade 8 NAEP tests. If high school graduation exams had a positive impact it seems more likely to see such results at grade 8, but in fact states without high school graduation exams tend to perform better at that grade. Critics of high-stakes testing could point to the tendency to teach to the test and the typical inability of most state tests to examine higher-order thinking skills in the subject areas and suggest that test-driven instruction in states with more visible emphasis on high-stakes test results has narrowed and limited curricula more stringently at grade 8. As a result, students in those states would tend not to make gains on the NAEP exam, which includes more higher-order components than do most state tests.

Of the states without high school graduation tests that showed gains in three or more categories at grade 8, Maine, Connecticut, and Michigan have state exams with a substantial proportion of constructed-response items, making these states' tests more like the NAEP in format and perhaps in the cognitive skills assessed.[29] West Virginia has had extensive testing using an all-multiple-choice, norm-referenced test, and it reported making a particular effort, using on-site reviews, to ensure that curriculum areas that are not tested are in fact taught.[30] Nebraska had no state test, but it required districts to use commercial exams of their own choice. It also requires districts to develop criterion-referenced assessments,[31] and it could be that those assessments make a difference in what is taught.

Among participating states without high school graduation tests but with state tests that are predominantly made up of constructed-response items, only Kentucky did not make sweeping improvements (gains in three or four categories, see Table 6.2) on the NAEP. Maine and Connecticut did make such improvements; Vermont did not participate in the NAEP; and California used an exam that included some constructed-response items, but used it only for a very brief time. Among states with a high school graduation exam (Table 6.1), only Maryland has tests with mostly constructed-response items (for grades 3, 5, and 8, not for high school), yet it showed no significant gains on the NAEP.

It is difficult to conclude from this that the kind of assessment used by a state strongly influences its likelihood of improvement on the NAEP. However, since the states using tests with more extended constructed-response items introduced their new assessments between

1992 and 1996, it may be that their effect was not yet felt at the time of our analysis.

We do know about the three states with high school graduation tests that showed significant gains at either grade in three or more categories—North Carolina, Texas, and Tennessee (see Table 6.1). Each state has received some prominence for its overall reform efforts; in North Carolina and Texas exams were part of a wider set of reforms,[32] and Tennessee has attracted some notice with its "value-added" testing program.[33] Arguably, multiple factors, not just high-stakes testing, have led to the gains in these states. Looking a bit more closely, only North Carolina showed gains across three or more of the levels at grade 8, while all three states did so at grade 4. There may be something in the nature of the exams in those states (as discussed above) or in other aspects of school reform (for example, ensuring more qualified teachers or an emphasis on improving education in the early grades by reducing class size) that made gains at grade 4 from 1992 to 1996 easier to attain than at grade 8.

Thus it may be that in the midst of many actions taken to improve schooling, the use of high school graduation exams is not the cause of any gains on NAEP exams. For example, when Monty Neill presented some preliminary information regarding NAEP gains to a conference of state educators in February 1998,[34] an employee of the North Carolina Department of Public Instruction responded that in his opinion the score gains had nothing to do with the tests but were caused by other elements of school reform, particularly improvements in the teaching force. Of course, he might be wrong. Our point is simpler: with multiple, intertwined factors of school reform, it is very difficult to attribute improvements on the NAEP to the high-stakes use of state tests.

David Grissmer and Ann Flanagan, however, conclude that in Texas and North Carolina, test score gains on the NAEP were due to accountability testing.[35] After analyzing the results of all seven NAEP state-level math and reading exams through 1996, they conclude that these two states had the highest average gains among states taking at least six tests. However, analyses conducted after Grissmer and Flanagan's 1998 study indicate that in Texas from 1992 to 1998 there was a drop of three points in NAEP reading scores for black students at grade 4, a very small gain for Latinos, and widening gaps in scores achieved by white students as compared with black and with Hispanic students.[36] Without replicating Grissmer and Flanagan's procedures, including their analysis of the other participating states, we cannot be sure how these 1998 test results would affect their conclusions. However, the 1998 reading results should raise further questions about the meaning of short-term test-score gains and the impact of high-stakes accountability programs. Tennessee, for example, which also showed sweeping gains at grade 4 in math from 1992 to 1996, failed to show any gains in reading at grade 4 from 1992 to 1998.[37] Grissmer and Flanagan also offer no evidence as to why other states with extensive high-stakes testing programs have not made significant gains.[38]

Paul E. Barton and Richard S. Coley's 1998 study of cohort growth in math from grade 4 in 1992 to grade 8 in 1996 also could challenge the findings of Grissmer and Flanagan.[39] Barton and Coley used NAEP scale scores in which all grade levels are placed on one scale. Of the thirty-seven states for which there is data, twenty-one cluster from +55 to +50 points of cohort growth, a five-point spread "equivalent to what is learned in about four months of school."[40] Nebraska, Michigan, North Dakota, Minnesota, North Carolina, and Colorado are the only states to have statistically outperformed any other jurisdiction other than Guam and the District of Columbia in terms of statistically significant cohort growth.[41] Of those six, only North Carolina has a high school graduation exam, and the only jurisdiction other than Guam and the District of Columbia over which it showed statistically significant growth was Georgia, giving North Carolina the weakest performance of the six high-scoring states. Not counting Guam and the District of Columbia, eleven states were outperformed at a statistically significant level of growth by one or more of the six high-scoring states. Of those eleven, seven had a high school graduation exam between 1992 and 1996. This evidence is consistent with our finding that states without high school graduation exams have been more likely to improve than states with such exams.

Finally, we should consider data by demographic category: do low-income or minority students gain more or less under a regime of high-stakes testing? Recent research on Texas finds, among other things, two important consequences from high-stakes testing in the 1990s:

1. On the 1998 NAEP reading test the score gap in Texas between whites and African Americans has widened, the opposite of what has happened on the state's own test.[42] It would seem then that the result that has been most touted about the Texas experiment—the improvement among minority groups—is an artifact of teaching to the test that has not been independently confirmed.

2. The graduation rate for all students declined by ten percentage points when the state made passing the test a condition of graduation.[43]

Within two years, the rate for whites returned to its original level of 70 percent. For African Americans and Latinos, the rate never rebounded and remains at 50 percent. The high-stakes use of the test, Walt Haney and Albert H. Kauffman conclude, is the only feasible explanation for the decreased graduation rate, a decrease that reduced the number of graduates by about 100,000 in the 1990s.[44]

Texas officials have maintained that the pass rate on the TAAS has increased for African Americans and Latinos and has narrowed relative to whites. This is true, Haney and Kauffman conclude, because large numbers of students are retained in grade 9 and leave school before taking the grade 10 high school exit exam.[45] That test is also used to hold schools accountable, so schools have a vested interest in lowering the number of students who receive low scores. That is, the gains in passing the test are due to pushing out large numbers of African American and Latino students before they take the grade 10 exam.

The preceding evidence thus does not support the conclusion that high school graduation exams are a useful way to improve learning outcomes on measures other than the state's own tests. Indeed, at grade 8 the evidence suggests that states are better-off without such tests. Since high-stakes tests often have been shown to have negative consequences,[46] the absence of positive results on the NAEP in states with high school graduation tests suggests the balance of using the tests is negative. This supports the views of test critics who charge that high-stakes tests are actually harmful.

## LIMITATIONS OF TESTING IN MEASURING AND SPURRING IMPROVEMENTS IN LEARNING

To this point, this discussion has assumed the validity of the NAEP as an independent measure of student learning. As noted above, it is generally respected, and it measures some higher-order thinking skills within subject areas better than do most standardized exams. Arguably, however, the NAEP itself is too limited a measure to stand for the full range of learning that society might expect students to acquire in school. Other than for a few experimental assessments, NAEP tests involve only paper and pencil, and the constructed-response items are fairly short. Extended tasks and projects are not included. Thus, some areas typically included in state standards are not assessed either by NAEP or by most of the state exams because of the testing methodology.[47]

The effective control over curricula and instruction exerted by the state tests makes it less likely that unmeasured content areas will be taught, particularly to students who historically have not done well on the tests. That is, children from low-income families and children of color will be less likely to receive high-level, cognitively rich instruction because the outcomes of such instruction are not measured and those children are in schools most "under the gun" to show improvements on the state tests. One conclusion that can be drawn from this is that there is a pressing need to use assessments and evaluations to demonstrate learning in the currently unmeasured areas (provided this can be done in ways that do not undermine teaching that which is to be measured). It is also possible that, in some states, NAEP gains are due to gains on cognitively less complex items.

Parenthetically, there are those who would argue for a "basics-first" approach in which students would be taught basic skills before moving on to more cognitively complex learning. Instead, we believe that learning both lower- and higher-order skills together is preferred, and that because the tests reinforce the so-called basics, they inhibit curricula and instruction that emphasize learning on multiple levels of cognitive complexity.[48] This debate also makes clear that tests are not neutral with regard to instructional approaches but inevitably favor some approaches over others.

It is possible that improvements in state exams may induce parallel improvements in schools where instruction in some important areas had not occurred because these areas were not measured previously. However, truly superior curricula and instruction could be crowded out. For example, the authors of the "Facing History and Ourselves" curriculum fear that Massachusetts's schools will have to drop the program in order to ensure coverage of the material included on the state test.[49] In Boston, Superintendent Thomas Payzant noted at a community summit that the highly respected Latin School, which focuses heavily on classical and modern languages, faces the prospect of having to drop a language at grade 8 in order to introduce a science course in that grade to prepare students to take the state test.[50] In New York, as discussed below, the new Regents exam requirements could destroy highly successful alternative programs that have different approaches to curriculum and instruction.

It seems unlikely that state assessment programs that require the standardized testing of every child in certain grades will be able to become rich, deep, and flexible enough to avoid crowding out the best curricula and instruction. If this is true, and if it is true that students deserve curricula and instruction far superior to those that can be induced or coerced through testing programs, then alternative approaches to accountability—assuming, as we do, that accountability is desired—are needed.

## ALTERNATIVES TO ACCOUNTABILITY TESTING

Test critics tend to argue not only that testing will narrow and undermine high-quality curricula and instruction, but that these can be better supported in all schools through means other than testing. That is, if the goal is to improve learning outcomes for all students, particularly for students of color and those from low-income backgrounds, other methods besides test-driven reform can succeed where test-driven reform cannot, or can succeed better with fewer negative consequences.[51]

Paul Black and Dylan Wiliam conducted an analysis of 250 reports and articles on formative assessment to show that improving formative assessment raises learning outcomes.[52] (Formative assessment is used to shape, or "form," instruction for individuals or groups.) The effect size on standardized tests ranged from 0.4 to 0.7, "larger than those found for most educational innovations."[53] (To illustrate, the lower effect size of 0.4 indicates that the "average" student involved in a formative assessment program would match the achievement of a student in the top 35 percent of students not engaged in a formative assessment program.)[54] Further, while all students showed improvement, low-scoring students showed the most improvement, thereby closing the score gap. Raising standardized test scores is not usually the objective of formative assessments, so the results do not stem from "teaching to the test."

The assessment practices discussed by Black and Wiliam involve eliciting regular feedback from teachers, tailoring assessments to individual needs, and teaching students how to assess their own progress.[55] These are integrated with modes of instruction that differ from the didactic, "frontal," or "chalk and talk" modes of instruction commonly associated with efforts to raise test scores.[56] As Black and Wiliam point out, the changes in instruction involve changes in *the nature of each teacher's beliefs about learning.*[57] One implication is that policymakers need to change perspective from educational "inputs" and "outputs" to the "inside [of] the black box"[58]—that is, to what happens in classrooms among teachers and students.

Mano Singham uses research by Claude Steele, John Ogbu, and Signithia Fordham to illustrate that the cultural divide between schools and many African American youths hinders those students' willingness to become engaged in their schooling.[59] Singham then cites research by Uri Triesman to show that students who study together in workshops do much better in their college courses. The benefits appear for all students, but especially for groups that historically have not done well. Singham concludes that the underlying problem is less how schools educate black students than "in the way we teach *all* students." He points to the low-level, fact-heavy, boring curriculum that turns off many students to learning, particularly those students with less-immediate reasons to become invested in schools. Such an approach is typically reinforced by state tests.

Neither Black and Wiliam's nor Singham's approaches, which are complementary, lead to easy policy changes or fast implementation. Rather, they both require profound alterations in teacher and student behaviors, substantial professional development, changes in school culture and in the organization of time in schools, and public support. These cannot be mandated, but they can be supported. Rather than top-down, test-driven reforms controlled by high-stakes state tests, they are bottom-up, horizontal reforms that rely strongly on classroom-based assessments.

While substantial research supports the claim that these kinds of educational changes will produce improvements in learning outcomes, even those measured by rather narrow tests, "scaling up" their implementation from the local level to the level of states or large districts will take time and might not succeed. If states and districts implement such changes, it will be necessary to undertake larger studies to examine whether or how well such efforts succeed, or what aspects of implementation really contribute to success when implemented in particular contexts.[60]

While NAEP data do not show effect sizes, there is no reason to believe that any state has shown gains of the sort associated with the studies reported by Black and Wiliam.[61] However, no state, with the partial exceptions of Vermont and Kentucky, has even attempted to devise assessments that have substantial classroom and formative uses and to then provide professional development to train teachers to use them.[62] Thus, data from large-scale efforts to improve teachers' assessment practices do not exist because the efforts themselves do not exist. Therefore, we must begin by learning from smaller efforts in order to think about how to create very different kinds of accountability programs.

One example of such an experiment may result from a proposal by the New York Performance Standards Consortium to develop an alternative to the state's Regents exams.[63] All students in New York State will soon be required to pass the Regents exams in order to graduate from a public high school.[64] The Consortium is a network of public alternative secondary schools, many of which had exemptions from previous state testing programs. Some of the high schools have produced remarkable results in terms of graduation rates, college attendance, and college completion, when compared with New York City as a whole.[65] A recent study found widespread success among the schools in the New York Networks for School Renewal, which includes many Consortium schools.[66]

However, these schools generally have educational programs that do not mesh well with the Regents exams. The schools typically place a premium on formative assessment, and they rely on portfolios and exhibitions as measures of student learning. The state indicated that it was willing to consider an alternative from the Consortium, but the alternative would probably have to take the form of an exam.[67] The Consortium worked to develop performance exams based on the sorts of projects and tasks used in its member schools. They argued that these exams will better match the state's standards than will the Regents exams, while being more faithful to the educational visions of the participating schools. Their proposal, however, was not limited to exams and the state ultimately rejected it.

In another experiment, the Bureau of Indian Affairs (BIA) has contracted with the Center for Language in Learning to use the *Learning Record*[68] in BIA schools as a formative and summative assessment.[69] The *Learning Record* is based on the *Primary Language Record* developed in London, England, to support and assess literacy growth among low-income and racially, culturally, and linguistically diverse populations.[70] It has been adapted and used somewhat extensively in New York City and California.[71] Its use involves literacy interviews with parents and students, extensive teacher observations and documentation, summary evaluations, placing students on scales of literacy development (reading and writing scales) that can be used as numerical indicators of the level of student literacy, and moderations (sessions in which trained outsiders rescore samples of records) among users. The moderations have attained high levels of agreement among raters, suggesting the results could be used as part of a more comprehensive accountability program.[72] Schools are also piloting math forms and scales. Over the past two years, the BIA project has begun to implement the *Learning Record* in the hope that it will provide valuable information about the use of classroom-based assessments to improve, document, and measure student learning on an increasingly large scale.[73]

To evaluate fully the sorts of changes discussed in this section will require some different measures. The major claim of improvement in these classroom-based efforts will rest not merely on the traditional or slightly expanded standardized tests (such as the NAEP), but on more sophisticated measures, most of which will have to be rooted in classroom work, not in on-demand assessments. The development of this capacity lags.[74]

However, the performance assessments being developed in New York City and the BIA's use of the *Learning Record* might prove themselves to be useful measures of student learning outcomes for such purposes.

Finally, the issue of "what works" cannot be divorced from the question, "works for what?" If the goal is relatively routine skill improvements that can be measured with standardized tests, it may be that measurement-driven reforms will have some impact, though the NAEP results discussed in this chapter bring even that into question. If the goal is to help all students become critical, reflective thinkers and learners in and across traditional and other subject areas, allowing both for human diversity of interest and talent and for the need to provide all students with rich opportunities to engage in all the subject areas, there is simply no reason to conclude that measurement-driven reforms such as high school graduation exams will facilitate reaching that goal.[75] Historically, at least some middle- and upper-class students have had such an opportunity, while very few children from low-income families or from minority groups have. Measurement-driven reform will not facilitate such opportunity. It likely will contribute to its denial.

As we have discussed, there are alternatives. They should be explored and developed. The road of high-stakes exams appears not to lead even to its limited goals, and there is no evidence it can lead to the richer goals all students deserve. Multiple paths routed through classrooms, as discussed briefly in the examples above, may appear initially to be more difficult, but that approach promises much more and is more likely to enable students to reach the goals.

# CHAPTER SEVEN

# The Harmful Impact of the TAAS System of Testing in Texas
## Beneath the Accountability Rhetoric

### LINDA McNEIL AND ANGELA VALENZUELA

Those who promote state systems of standardized testing claim that these systems raise the quality of education and do so in ways that are measurable and can be generalized. They attribute low test scores to management's failure to direct its "lowest-level" employees (that is, the teachers) to induce achievement in students. In Texas, the remedy to this situation has been to create a management system that will change behavior, particularly the behavior of teachers, through increased accountability. The means of holding teachers and administrators accountable is the average scores of each school's children on the state's standardized test, the Texas Assessment of Academic Skills (TAAS). As our report will show, this overreliance on test scores has caused a decline in educational quality for those students who have the greatest educational need.

Texas, a state with a history of low educational achievement and low investment in public education, has put into place an accountability system that hinges on the testing of children. The test has high-stakes consequences for the children: not passing the high school–level test is a bar to graduation (regardless of the student's accomplishments and courses passed), and soon scores on the reading section of the test will determine whether a child can be promoted from third to fourth grade.[1] The scores on the test also are used as the chief means of monitoring the performance of teachers, principals, and schools. School-level aggregations of children's scores are used to rate principals, schools, and even superintendents.

The rhetoric surrounding this accountability system is that it is raising educational quality. Politicians claim that this testing system is "saving" the Texas schools. The system is gaining national recognition as an exemplary accountability system because scores on the state test have, in most districts, been rising. The system's popularity is further bolstered by the idea that it must be improving the education of Latino and African American children since, in many parts of the state, their test scores also are rising.

Before other states rush to copy the Texas system, it is important to look behind the reported numbers. It is necessary to see the effects that the test and the testing system are having on the children and on what they are learning. It is essential to examine the effects of this system of testing on teachers. And it is critical to analyze the effects of this system of testing on children's lives.

We present here our strong assessment that the TAAS system of testing is reducing the quality and quantity of education offered to the children of Texas. Most damaging are the effects of the TAAS system of testing on poor and minority youths.

Our analysis draws on emerging research on high-stakes testing and on our individual investigations. These include a longitudinal analysis of instruction when test preparation materials become the curriculum, a multiyear study of Latino children's high school experiences, investigations of Latino elementary schools, and research in urban schools with predominantly Mexican American and African American children.[2] Our investigations have entailed the documentation of the effects of centralized testing in Texas beginning with the Perot reforms of the 1980s and on through the 1990s, when such tests were increasingly tied to high-stakes tests for children and school personnel.[3] Our investigations have included interactions over the past ten years with literally hundreds of public school teachers, representing all subjects and grades and a wide mix of urban and suburban districts, whom we have encountered through research projects and the teacher enhancement and school reform programs at the Rice University Center for Education. Our research required fieldwork in schools and classrooms and frequent interactions with students, teachers, and administrators, whose voices and experiences are vital to capture.

In essence, our investigations have permitted us to gather and triangulate data from a variety of sources over a multiyear period. From these investigations, we understand that there are a wide variety of responses to the TAAS. However, those we report are the most characteristic among the many schools, teachers, and students included in our research. The effects of the TAAS, which we describe here, represent strong, persistent trends emerging from the data. We are not describing isolated or aberrant cases. To the contrary, we have unavoidably encountered such cases in overabundance, and we have encountered them even in the course of pursuing other research topics.

Our analysis reveals that behind the rhetoric of rising test scores is a growing set of classroom practices in which test preparation activities are usurping a substantive curriculum. These practices are more widespread in those schools where administrators' pay is tied to test scores and where test scores have been historically low. These are the schools that are typically attended by children who are poor and African American or Latino, for many of whom English is not the dominant language. These are the schools that historically have had inadequate resources. In these schools, the pressure to raise test scores "by any means necessary" has frequently meant that a regular education has been supplanted by activities the sole purpose of which is to raise test scores on this particular test.

Because teachers' and administrators' job rewards under the TAAS system of testing are aligned to children's test scores, the TAAS system fosters an artificial curriculum. It is a curriculum aimed primarily at creating higher test scores, not a curriculum that will educate these children for productive futures. The testing system distances the content of the curriculum from the knowledge base of teachers and from the cultures and intellectual capacities of the children. It is creating an even wider gap between the curriculum offered to the predominantly white, middle- and upper-middle-class children in traditionally high-scoring schools and those in traditionally minority and poor schools.

In this chapter, we present what we are seeing as the direct, negative educational consequences of this system of testing and its harmful effects on the quality of education available to disadvantaged Latino and African American children. Under the TAAS system of testing, curriculum, instruction, school resources, and children are all adversely affected:

- The TAAS system of testing reduces the quality and quantity of curriculum.

- The TAAS system distorts educational expenditures, diverting scarce instructional dollars away from such high-quality curricular resources as laboratory supplies and books toward test preparation materials and activities of limited instructional value.

- The TAAS provokes instruction that is aimed at the lowest level of skills and information, and it crowds out other forms of learning, particularly for poor and minority students.

- TAAS-based teaching and test preparation violate what is known about how children learn.

- The TAAS is divorced from children's experiences and cultures.

- The TAAS imposes exit measures that are particularly inappropriate for students with limited English proficiency (LEP).

- The TAAS is widening the gap between the education of children in Texas's poorest (historically low-performing) schools and that available to more privileged children.

An analysis of the actual effects of the TAAS on children's educational experiences is especially important given the publicity that has surrounded both the TAAS scores and Texas children's performance on the National Assessment of Educational Progress (NAEP) exams. The latter exams present a mixed picture: there are some gains in the early grades, but Texas NAEP gains in the early grades do not seem to hold up in later grades. Also, the attention has been more on the *rate* of improvement on NAEP rather than actual improvement. Highly touted rates of improved scores (for example, that Texas was described as being in the top four "most improved states") mask the fact that even after such "gains," Texas students were still at or below average, registering lower than twenty-one of forty participating states. Hence, neither the TAAS, nor attempts to interpret Texas's NAEP rate gains as support for the TAAS, represent the actual status of education for youth in Texas.[4]

## THE TEXAS ACCOUNTABILITY SYSTEM AND MINORITY YOUTHS

The Texas Assessment of Academic Skills system of testing and test-driven curriculum was enacted by the Texas state legislature in the spring of 1990.[5] It is the most recent in a series of centralized, standardizing "reforms" in that state. It differs from earlier test systems in being increasingly tied to teacher and principal job security and pay.

The policy rhetoric surrounding the TAAS goes like this: by measuring student performance on a computer-scored standardized test, inferences can be drawn about the quality of teacher and principal performance, as well as the aggregate quality of the school. School ratings, periodically published in full-page spreads in the state's newspapers, now serve as barometers for the condition of education in the state.

Hence, important judgments about personnel and the quality of schooling now revolve around a single indicator. There clearly are serious problems when any single indicator is used to assess the quality of so complex an enterprise as educating children. This is why the use of a single indicator to assess learning or to make decisions about tracking, promotion, and graduation violates the ethics of the testing profession.[6]

However, in this chapter our focus is not on the technical problems that are typically raised for this and other tests (for example, probable impacts of particular questions, cutoff scores for passing, psychometric properties of the test), all of which are quite real. Rather, we want to focus on another consequence that is frequently overlooked: the direct, negative impact that this accountability system is having on the education of this state's most economically disadvantaged, minority children.

What we are seeing is not the "misuse" of the TAAS testing system, but the playing out of its inherent logic at the expense of our poorest, minority children. These are the children who comprise the preponderance of youths in large, urban school districts. For example, in the Houston Independent School District (HISD), 52.5 percent of all students are Latino and 34.1 percent are African American, while 10.6 percent are white. Moreover, 73 percent of the total receive free or reduced-price lunch.[7]

To assess fully the impact that this system of testing is having on the education of minority youths, it is essential to understand how this system is operationalized in classrooms. One of the misleading features of this testing system is the notion that publishing scores disaggregated by the race and ethnicity of the children alerts the public to inequities. In reality, these scores are misleading and diversionary: the scores loom so large that they overshadow discussion of other, more telling indicators of quality of education, among these the degree of segregation, the level of poverty, or the number of students graduating, taking the SATs, and going to college. Furthermore, the scores mask the inequities produced when schools raise test scores at the expense of substantive learning.

Drawing on our collective and extensive research, throughout this chapter we illuminate the ways in which this testing system harms the educational quality and educational opportunity of minority and economically disadvantaged youths. Our critique is organized around very specific and documented harmful effects of the TAAS system of testing on the quality of the curriculum, the quality of instruction, and on resource allocation for the education of minority youths.[8] Because of their dramatically increasing representation in our nation's largest school districts, a section below also addresses in some detail the even greater damaging effects of the TAAS test for youths with limited English proficiency in our schools.[9]

## THE EDUCATIONAL IMPACT OF THE TAAS

*In many urban schools, with students who are overwhelmingly poor and African American and Latino, the TAAS system of testing reduces the quality and quantity of subjects being tested by the TAAS.*

The pressure to raise TAAS scores leads teachers to spend class time, often several hours each week, drilling students on practice exam materials. This TAAS drill takes time from real teaching and learning: much of the drill time is spent learning how to fill in the bubbles for the test's answer sheets, how to weed out obviously wrong answers, and how to become accustomed to multiple-choice, computer-scored formats. In the name of "alignment" between course curricula and the test, TAAS drills are becoming the curriculum in our poorest schools.

The pressure to raise TAAS scores leads teachers to substitute commercial TAAS preparation materials for the substance of the curriculum. Principals, deans of instruction, and other building or central office administrators urge or even require teachers to set aside the course curriculum and use the TAAS preparation materials in their place.

Although the TAAS is supplanting a more substantial curriculum throughout the state, the problem emerges unevenly. It is more common in traditionally low-performing schools, the schools attended by low-income and nonwhite children. In contrast, middle-class children in white, middle-class schools are reading literature, learning a variety of forms of writing, and studying mathematics aimed at problem solving and conceptual understanding. In essence, these children continue to receive an education appropriate for their ages and grade levels, while poor and minority children are devoting class time to practice test materials, the purpose of which is to help children pass the TAAS. The TAAS system of testing thus widens the gap between the public education provided for poor and minority children and that of children in traditionally higher-scoring (that is, white and wealthier) schools.

Advocates of a state standardized system of testing frequently make the argument that "before TAAS, minority children were receiving nothing. Now at least, they are getting *something* (even if it is just exposure to the kinds of information that will be tested in the multiple-choice format)." We have seen no studies that have documented this claim. But we have seen a reduction in content, even in those schools historically underserved and with too few resources, when the TAAS becomes the focus. An experienced, white English teacher at Seguín High School (a pseudonym),[10] a predominantly Mexican HISD school,[11] underscores this point. She commented that she teaches "less" English each year: "Less as time goes on. Less as time goes on with the TAAS test thing. Because we have to devote so much time to the specific functions of the TAAS test, it's harder and harder [to teach English]."

Subjects tested by the TAAS (reading, writing, and mathematics) are reduced, in the test and in the test preparation materials, to isolated skills and fragments of fact. This artificial treatment of subjects into isolated components may enable children to recognize those components on a multiple-choice test. However, this treatment does not necessarily enable children to use these components in other contexts. For example, high school teachers report that although practice tests and classroom drills have raised the rate of passing for the reading section of the TAAS at their school, many of their students are unable to use those same skills for actual reading. These students are passing the TAAS reading section by being able to select among answers given. But they are not able to read assignments, to make meaning of literature, to complete reading assignments outside of class, or to connect reading assignments to other parts of the course such as discussion and writing.

Middle school teachers report that the TAAS emphasis on reading short passages, then selecting answers to questions based on those short passages, has made it very difficult for students to handle a sustained reading assignment. After children spend several years in classes where "reading" assignments were increasingly TAAS practice materials, their middle school teachers in more than one district reported that they were unable to read a novel even two years below grade level.

In writing, students are increasingly being asked to write repetitively in only the format of that year's TAAS writing objective. One African American parent, whose first son received an excellent fourth grade education in a Texas elementary school a few years ago, reported that when her second son entered fourth grade at the school in the fall of 1998, the entire fourth grade curriculum had disappeared. The teachers, facilities, and principal were all the same, but the fourth grade curriculum had essentially been replaced by daily writing of "the persuasive essay," according to the strict TAAS format for that essay.

The approved format for the TAAS essay, for all children in the state, is the "five paragraph essay." Within this essay format, long discredited by teachers of writing, each of five paragraphs contains exactly five sentences. Each paragraph begins with a "topic sentence," followed by three "supporting sentences" and a "concluding sentence," which essentially recaps the topic sentence. Paragraph one serves the essay in the same way the topic sentence serves each paragraph; the concluding paragraph essentially plays the role in the essay that each concluding sentence plays in its own paragraph.

Teachers of writing who work with their students on developing ideas, on finding their voices as writers, and on organizing papers in ways appropriate to both the ideas and the paper's intended audience find themselves in conflict with this prescriptive format. The format subordinates ideas to form, sets a single form out as "the essay," and produces, predictably, rote writing. Writing as it relates to thinking, to language development and fluency, to understanding one's audience, to enriching one's vocabulary, and to developing ideas has been replaced by TAAS writing to this format. "Writing" as TAAS preparation no longer bears any resemblance to what research shows to be writing as a developmental activity in children's language competency.

However, the essay is easy to score when testing large populations because what counts is the strict adherence to format rather than the development of ideas. Many teachers describe having to teach this format in terms of its intended audience: "Just think of yourself as writing for someone sitting in a cubicle in a bureaucracy, counting sentences and indentations." Others report teaching their students that there is "TAAS writing" and "real writing." Still others say that in their school teachers are required to have students do only TAAS writing, the five-paragraph essay, weekly or even daily *until* after the TAAS test (in other words, until late spring).

Students also complain about the persuasive essay. For example, an intellectually gifted, Mexican American senior male assigned to (that is, misplaced in) Seguín High School's "regular" track, feels that the school's priorities are misguided. In his view, the school should be preparing students for the SATs. On the subject of many of his peers' academic limitations, he provided the following commentary: "I've realized that the kids have good arguments here, but they have absolutely no argument skills. They probably have persuasive skills for the TAAS. Argument skills, none. The only argument they have is probably to curse. Say the F-word and that's it."

Reflecting on a conversation he had on the subject of the college application process with his friends, he further places the onus of students' limitations on the school itself:

> They [friends] were telling me that they are kind of fed up with that [the persuasive essay], because here are kids that are filling out scholarship applications and essays. They are writing essays, and they don't know how to write anything else but a persuasive essay for the TAAS. They prepare us for the TAAS, and we are not just test takers. I try to explain to people that we are not just persons who need to develop critical thinking skills on how to choose between five things. How to choose the correct answer out of five. That's nothing!

The required "TAAS objectives" or "TAAS prompts" that are to be drilled each day are often presented to teachers as five- to ten-minute exercises. However, teachers report that drilling to these prompts, often required by the administration if their students are poor or minority children (with a history of low scores), frequently usurps so much of the class period that little time is left for teaching and learning.

It is a myth that the TAAS sets the minimum standards and that teachers are encouraged to go beyond that. In many schools, it is the best-prepared teachers with the richest curricula who are required to scale back in order to teach to the sequence and format of the TAAS. In low-performing schools, even the most knowledgeable teachers are asked to set aside their lesson plans and materials to teach to the TAAS.

Whether children were being taught "nothing" before or whether they were being given a meaningful curriculum, the pressure to raise TAAS scores shows no evidence of opening children's access to great literature, to conceptual understanding in mathematics, to fluency in writing, or to other learning experiences that seriously address previous inadequacies in their education. Nor does the TAAS seem likely to do so. Under the current accountability system based on this test, financial rewards go to those schools where scores go up, not necessarily to those in need of serious upgrading of staff and materials. In addition, the statewide system of testing has not been accompanied by a parallel investment that could reduce inadequacies and inequities in low-performing schools. The result is that many very real problems persist, problems that are not addressed by more, and more centralized, measurement and testing, or problems that testing may exacerbate by its focus on a narrow set of measures rather than a comprehensive look at children's learning.

*The TAAS system of testing reduces the quality and quantity of course content in subjects not tested by the TAAS, because teachers are encouraged or required to substitute TAAS test preparation activities for the curriculum in those subjects.*

The study of science, social studies, art, and other subjects that are not tested by the TAAS is undermined by the TAAS system. For example, many science teachers in schools with poor and minority children are required by their principals to suspend the teaching of science for weeks, and in some cases for months, in order to devote science class time to drill and practice on the math sections of the TAAS. The first loss, of course, is the chance to learn science. The second is the chance to become highly knowledgeable in mathematics. Many science teachers have little background in mathematics; the "mathematics" they are "teaching" is drill and practice with commercial TAAS preparation materials.

The direct loss of both science and mathematics learning is clear. Less obvious, but equally important, is the way this TAAS practice widens the gap in science learning between children in middle-class, higher performing schools, who continue to study science, and poor and minority children, whose science classes are more frequently sacrificed for TAAS preparation.

Social studies is another core subject that is frequently suspended or interrupted for TAAS preparation. For instance, all history and social studies teachers in one Latino high school were told several months in advance of the TAAS to spend twenty minutes a day preparing students for the TAAS. According to one of these teachers, "Twenty minutes is just too much. By the time we get to teaching our history lesson, most of the time is gone. And then it's hard to recapture the rhythm of the previous day's lesson, which was also interrupted by the TAAS."

The content of elective subjects also often is set aside to make time for TAAS prep. Art teachers report that they are required to drill on the grammar sections of the TAAS. An ROTC instructor was assigning the five-paragraph essay each week, not to link writing to ROTC but to add another drill to the regimen, this time in a rote essay.

*The TAAS system distorts educational expenditures, diverting scarce instructional dollars away from such high-quality curricular resources as*

*laboratory supplies and books and toward test preparation materials
and activities of limited instructional value beyond the test.*

Under the TAAS, there is widespread pressure to spend instructional
dollars on test preparation materials and activities. These include expenditures on expensive materials for aligning the curriculum to the test,
for accountability systems, and for consultants. It also includes diverting
dollars from Texas's classrooms to out-of-state vendors of tests, test
preparation materials, consultants, and related materials.

The pressure to spend instructional dollars for test preparation is felt
most especially in schools with large populations of poor and minority
children, which have been historically underfunded. In these schools,
scarce instructional dollars are being diverted into materials and activities,
the only value of which is to increase TAAS scores, not to produce educated children who are well prepared for college or future work. For
example, to the extent that such schools had fewer sets of classroom nov-
els and other reading materials before, the pressure of the TAAS test does
not lead to such purchases. Rather, it tends to lead to the purchase of
costly, commercial test preparation materials. These provide practice in
answering multiple-choice, recall questions pertaining to brief passages
that are written explicitly for test preparation purposes.

This diversion of dollars further widens the gap between the quality
of education offered to poor and minority children and that provided to
wealthier children. Middle-class and wealthy districts either do not spend
money on these TAAS-related systems or they have the capacity to make
up the difference in local funding for schools; either way, wealthier districts continue spending money on high-quality instructional materials,
which advance their children's education and place them in the national
mainstream of what is considered to be a quality education.

Increasingly, expenditures for management and alignment systems are
displacing instructional expenditures, and expenditures for management
conferences and consulting on increasing compliance with the TAAS are
displacing programs of teacher learning and professional pedagogical
development. As the state curriculum becomes increasingly test driven, it
becomes difficult to disaggregate test preparation expenditures from
"curricular" expenditures. Administrators argue that materials aimed
at boosting test scores are in fact instructional expenses. Parents and
taxpayers, however, are often surprised to learn that what may appear to
be curricular and instructional items in budgets and expenditure lines
are not instructional materials in the traditional sense. Software, for
example, can be a means of providing students with up-to-date scientific
or historical information, with activities for manipulating geometric

figures, or for learning to conduct information searches. However, in schools dominated by the TAAS, software often focuses on test preparation drills, little different from drill-and-practice worksheets. The word "reading" may make the lay person think of books, magazines, and anthologies of literature, but in TAAS-controlled schools, reading may take the form of purchased practice tests of short reading passages.

The justification for these materials is often that they give students practice with the "basics," which they must master before "going on." However, among the schools we have visited, those where even low-achieving students are taught subject-matter content tend to have students who both learn more and score higher on the TAAS than those schools where TAAS preparation has displaced the curricular content.

In districts where schools' TAAS scores are tied to incentive pay for teachers or principals, and where TAAS-based performance contracts have replaced tenure, there is an even greater tendency for school personnel to shift dollars away from instruction and into the expensive TAAS preparation and alignment materials and consultants. Again, frequently these incentives are applied in schools or districts where the populations are poor or minority or both. And again, because such consultants and materials are focused narrowly on boosting test scores, they are unlikely to enhance children's capacity for thinking and learning in the many realms beyond the TAAS test.

The inversion of incentives needs to be examined systematically. If only those schools where scores increase receive additional funding (a form of merit reward), then the incentive to focus only on the TAAS will increase (to the detriment of more substantial learning). Likewise, if the neediest schools, which are least likely to have adequate resources, are trapped in that need until they can raise scores, they will see no compensating investments to bring their students opportunities to learn in line with those in more privileged schools. There is no plan to make a massive investment in the neediest schools. In fact, much of the public rhetoric is that low-performing schools do not deserve additional public investment. It is as if their poverty is tied in some puritanical sense to lack of virtue, with low scores as their scarlet letter of guilt.

*The TAAS system of testing emphasizes the lowest level of information and skills, crowds out other forms of learning, and disengages students in many urban schools—particularly those where children are poor and nonwhite.*

Teachers report that the pressure to drill for the TAAS has caused them to omit or severely decrease other forms of learning because of the lack of time or because their principals are urging them to devote time only to the types of activities that will be measured by the TAAS. Library research, independent projects, science experiments, oral histories, long-term writing assignments, writing assignments different from those on the test in a particular year, longer-term reading assignments that include related writing and speaking activities—all are being reduced, even though they are highly motivating for children. Such instructional activities, which engage children in higher-order problem solving and thinking, are deleted in those (poor, minority) schools where TAAS scores have been low.

The rigor of the academic learning is also sacrificed by courses like "TAAS math" and "TAAS English," which certain students are required to take to enable them to pass the exit exam. The curriculum in these classes is predictably fragmented and incoherent because teachers teach abstracted pieces of the curriculum in order to cover the various segments of the exam. Referred to as "local credit" courses, they do not count toward the twenty-four credits that are required for high school graduation. Since they are not "real" math and English courses, they are not taken very seriously by the students.

Placement in these courses also undermines learning as a result of wasteful and bureaucratic scheduling issues. If a student is enrolled in a fall TAAS course and takes and passes the exam in October, he or she will have to remain in the local credit course until the semester is over. An administrator from one of the larger, racially integrated HISD schools where such courses are offered told us that students start skipping class after they pass the TAAS test "since the course doesn't count toward high school credit anyway." According to this individual, TAAS courses are also wasteful if the students fail the fall exam because then they have to sign up a second time in another such course. This expands to a whole year the time that students are not in the regular curriculum. In addition to the TAAS courses, students must meet the normal math and English requirements for graduation. Additional requirements tend also to translate either into summer school attendance or graduating off schedule, if at all.

While white and middle-class children in this same HISD school overwhelmingly pass the TAAS test within the context of the normal curriculum, an entire segment of the school's population is being subjected to months, if not years, of TAAS preparation. By treating these students as if they are unteachable, the system itself engenders a cumulative deficit in students' knowledge, encouraging their resistance not to education, but to schooling.[12] Since the content of schooling is already deemed by many regular track youths (who are not honors students or college-bound) to be boring, unrewarding, and irrelevant to their lives, we are seeing the TAAS system of testing promote an even greater sense of alienation.

Preliminary research shows that those schools that score higher on the TAAS (usually wealthier, with fewer minority children) rarely teach directly to the TAAS. They teach children. They teach science, math, social studies, literature, writing, and the arts. They teach the subjects. A tortured logic governs the highly prescriptive administration of the TAAS in predominantly minority schools: if the scores increase, it is because the school taught more to the test; however, if the scores decrease, the school needs to teach more to the test.

Yet, teaching to the test, and thereby improving scores, does not indicate increased learning or improved capacity for complex problem solving. For example, one largely Hispanic, traditionally low-performing high school with virtually no library, a severe shortage of textbooks, and little laboratory equipment for its students spent $20,000 (almost its entire instructional budget) for a set of commercial test preparation materials. Even the school's best teachers were required to set aside their high-quality lessons and replace them with the test preparation activities. Scores on some sections of the TAAS did go up, but teachers report that students' actual capacity to read, to handle high school–level assignments, to engage in serious thought, and to be able to follow through on work actually declined.

This school, touted in the newspapers for increasing the TAAS passing rate on reading, is now searching for a way to counter what is seen by the faculty as a serious deficiency in the students' ability to read. It is clear that higher scores do not mean that children are learning to a higher level. Such scores may mean that nothing is being taught except TAAS preparation.

*The TAAS system of testing goes against what is known in research on children's learning.*

Research on children's learning shows that learning is not linear, that it must build on what children already know and understand, that it must engage children's active thinking, and that it must engage many senses.[13] In striking contrast, the TAAS reinforces one particular mode of learning. This cognitive impact of the test has not been seriously investigated. Classroom observations and teacher reports, however, raise critical questions about the sort of learning that is reinforced, the forms of learning that are subordinated to TAAS formats, and those that are increasingly structured out of test-dominated classrooms.

The TAAS mode of learning is to "master" brief, discreet, randomly selected pieces of information. The reading comprehension and grammatical sections of the writing TAAS, for example, cover isolated skills through the use of very brief written passages. These written passages are not intended to build a cumulative knowledge base; they are not meant to connect with children's understanding. The isolated skills are presented in fragments, carefully sequenced to match the fragmented and isolated skills in the Texas curriculum frameworks. Learning fragments, such as a fact or a skill out of context, is known to be counterproductive to understanding and to building cumulative skills that can be applied in an unfamiliar setting or to unfamiliar information in the future.

Two features of the TAAS and TAAS preparation materials are especially damaging to learning. First, under the TAAS system students are to choose among possible answers that are given to them; they rarely have to think on their own, puzzle out a problem, come up with a possible answer, or articulate an idea. This engenders passivity and a dependent learning style that fails to develop many essential cognitive skills. Second, the TAAS presents the child with choices, of which all but one are incorrect. To the extent that children, especially in poor and minority schools, are taught a curriculum and given test drills that are in the TAAS format, they are spending three-quarters of their learning time considering erroneous, "wrong" material. It is doubtful that there is any respectable learning theory that advocates children's continual exposure to incorrect material.

Again, the TAAS system places most at risk the children in schools (usually poor and minority) that heavily emphasize raising TAAS scores. These children not only fail to learn the same rich, complex material that children in middle-class schools learn, but they are simultaneously required to devote hours and hours each week to a de facto, worthless curriculum. By keeping children focused on these drills and these disembodied facts, the TAAS system of testing is denying them access to forms of knowledge and ways of knowing that can lead them beyond this minimal level into higher forms of learning. That is why one teacher said that yes, under the TAAS, certain students in her school who previously were not being taught much math (these were bilingual students, recently immigrated) are "getting more math now that we are testing everyone." But she also cautioned, "But of course, it's not real math—it's not what you would want for *your* children. It's just TAAS math." The opportunity costs of spending weeks, months, and even years on test drills that narrow learning modes and close off complex thought may be one of the costliest effects of the TAAS system of testing. It is a cost being borne by the least well served children in our schools.

*The generic curriculum inherent in the TAAS system of testing is divorced from children's experiences, language, and cultures.*

The TAAS system of testing is not respectful of, nor does it build on, children's personal experiences, the cultures of their families, nor the variations in learning style and interests that span any classroom. ("Subtractive schooling"[14] is a term that captures this problematic, ubiquitous feature of public schooling for U.S. minorities.) This use of a generic curriculum is frequently aggravated further by culturally and socially distant teachers who teach to the exam through traditional, teacher-centered lecture formats.

Important lessons about culture can be learned from the experiences of one Latina teacher, Ms. Moreno (a pseudonym), who teaches in one of the larger, virtually all-Mexican high schools. Through a rather energetic and lively style of teaching that includes "TAAS Pep Rallies" for her students, a majority of students in her classes every semester are able to pass the test.

When asked why they were able to learn from Ms. Moreno, students often referred to her use of *cariño* (or affection) in the classroom. They also said that she taught "the Mexican way," meaning that she used a lot of Spanish in the classroom and welcomed a high degree of interaction. An excerpt from an LEP student's written commentary about her heroic teacher appears below (in her exact words):

> One of the heroes I know is Ms. ____, she is a person that cares about people. I have her TAAS class and she is teachers in a way that everybody can understand her because, she talks in Spanish, and English. I think she is a strong person. Because she spent many hours teaching her students in the mornings and afternoons, she is always telling us that we can come to her room during our lunch period that she is going to be ready to teaches us. I come during my lunch period and she teaches me every problem I don't understand, and I feel very comfortable with her because she treats us like friends not like a student.[15]

Ms. Moreno was so committed to helping students pass the test that she, of her own initiative and without additional pay, held classes five days a week at seven o'clock in the morning to help students pass the TAAS. As one can see from her student's letter, her lunch hours were also dedicated to helping children. Through her commitment, cultural sensitivity, and her Mexican brand of caring, she singlehandedly enabled more children to pass the test than most of her colleagues combined.

She embodies the ethos that Gloria Ladson-Billings identifies as central to culturally relevant pedagogy for African American youth.[16] Motivated by a sense of shared fate and shared cultural assumptions, effective teachers of African American children see their role as one of "giving back to the community." Ms. Moreno is no different and just as effective.

Ms. Moreno attributes the lack of success of the majority of her colleagues to test anxiety and teachers' inability to teach to "this population." To prepare her students, she uses typical English-as-a-second-language (ESL) methodologies, even if her students are not in the ESL program (that is, they are English-speaking Mexican American). She laments her colleagues' penchant for teaching TAAS math through standard, teacher-centered lecture formats. She views manipulatives (geometric, patterned shapes) as particularly essential because they help students visualize relationships and therefore make sense of, and retain, information. While she is a firm believer that multisensory approaches work best for underprivileged youth, Ms. Moreno's capacity to help her students rise to her expectations also clearly is mediated by culturally relevant pedagogy.

The research literature makes clear that the learning of abstractions that have little connection to children's lives and cultures, or that present a monocultural, technical view of knowledge, yield little in long-term learning.[17] It is unfortunate and of great consequence that the problems of abstractions and the technical, fragmented sorts of facts and formulas associated with the TAAS combine with a historic inability of non-minority, middle-class teachers to promote widespread academic success with minority, low-income youths in segregated settings.[18] This Latina teacher's example strongly suggests how real academic achievement among underprivileged youths can be improved enormously through cultural awareness, sensitivity, and a commitment to social justice that no commercial test-preparation materials can possibly package. Attracting and supporting those teachers who are knowledgeable about their subjects, about children's learning, and also about children's cultures is a national need. It is one that will be difficult to fill when teachers are asked to bracket off their concern for children's whole development in order to process them through testing systems that undermine, rather than foster, these relationships.

*The TAAS exit test is particularly inappropriate for students with limited English proficiency.*

The TAAS system of testing has many negative effects on teaching, learning, and curriculum across the state. And, as we have discussed, many of the most harmful effects fall on those students whose education historically has lacked adequate resources and whose academic opportunities have been, by race and economic circumstance, severely limited.

Even given these general patterns, there is the need to focus more closely on the most rapidly growing student population in Texas: the children who, with their families, are recent immigrants. English is not the language of their family.

Harris County, Texas, helps to put this issue into perspective. The county has around three million people. The latest census data show that there are 875,000 Latinos in the county. While many of these are descendants of original Mexican families in this region, and others are second- or third- (or more) generation citizens, many others are recent arrivals. The schools call children of the latter group immediate immigrants—children who have arrived within the past three months. Several suburban counties in Texas show an increase of more than 80 percent in their Hispanic populations within the past five years.

The presence of these children, and their need for a quality education, is no longer an issue at the margins—either in Texas or in many other states. How they are taught, how they learn, and how their educational progress is evaluated are of central importance to these children, to their families, and to their communities. The failure of the TAAS system of testing to encompass a model of education that is appropriate for these children is telling not just because of problems the testing system is generating for these children. It is also important because it brings to light the ways in which the test, and the testing system, slight the relationship between children's learning and who they are.

The TAAS exit test results in a gap in student achievement that may be directly attributed to the test and not to these students' abilities. As newcomers at the high school level, students who are not fluent speakers of English are typically placed in the ESL curriculum (or "the ESL ghetto," as one scholar refers to it).[19] Angela Valenzuela refers to this placement practice as *cultural tracking*.[20] In the ESL track, students spend much of their day in courses that focus on English vocabulary and English reading without regard to their prior academic training. Their remaining subject matter courses are characteristically remedial and rarely, if ever, honors or college-prep classes. Rather than inferring that the immigrants' much needed—though often deficient—school-administered language support systems should be removed, however, it is necessary to focus attention on several consequences of cultural tracking. These relate directly to LEP students' test performance.

If lucky, LEP students are placed in ESL-subject-matter courses like ESL-math and ESL-biology, which approximate courses offered in the regular, mainstream, English-only track. Teachers offering these courses tend to be sensitive to issues that face language learners, particularly the sheer amount of time—between five and seven years—that it takes a young adult to gain native fluency in a second language. Consequently, teachers offer these subject matter courses to keep students from falling behind academically while they learn English. As one Seguín ESL teacher phrased it, "It's unfair to put their academics on hold while they (students) take time out to learn the language." Another motivation for teaching these courses is the ESL teachers' recognition of ample academic talent among their immigrant population. These teachers seek to capitalize on and nurture immigrant students' talents in and through ESL-subject-matter courses.

Theory would predict the prevalence of academic talent among many ESL youths, especially those schooled in their own country for many years prior to entering U.S. schools.[21] That is, the more students are schooled in their first language, the greater their conceptual grasp of academic subject matter (punctuation, how to summarize, arrive at conclusions, write papers, etc.). The greater their grasp of academic subject matter, the easier it is to transfer this knowledge to the second language.

Unfortunately, the more common situation in high schools—even those throughout the southwestern United States—is a scarcity of ESL-subject-matter courses, either because of a lack of resources to offer such courses or because of philosophical opposition, or both.[22] This results in ESL-remedial course placements, which in turn stall students' learning of the mainstream curriculum. This process masks the ways that the intellectual abilities and potential of so many talented immigrant students get compromised.

To appreciate and understand the magnitude of this waste in talent, one has to consider the characteristics of the immigrant population. Research shows that Mexican immigrants are a select group with average education levels that are higher than the national average for Mexico. They are risk takers who were able to delay gratification by accumulating capital to effectuate their passage across the border.[23] Studies, including Valenzuela's,[24] further show that immigrants and their children possess a progressive orientation toward schools and U.S. society generally. Moreover, since only 15 percent of the middle school–aged population attend secondary school in Mexico, to come across a critical mass of such students at the high school level is to encounter a truly "elite" crowd, which their ESL and Spanish language teachers readily recognize.

What must also be considered is that Mexico has a challenging national curriculum that is publicly subsidized and thus accessible to most children through the sixth year. By the fourth grade, students know the anatomy of the human body. By the sixth grade, students take the equivalent of U.S. ninth grade–level geometry.

Unfortunately, most school personnel are not sensitive to these kinds of possibilities—either because they cannot read a transcript from Mexico or because they simply assume that a good education is not possible there. As a result, youths get channeled systematically into the ESL ghetto. Even in instances when they are allowed to enjoy subject matter courses, immigrant youths are systematically denied the opportunity to achieve at an advanced academic level since none of these courses are offered at an honors' level. This structure helps explain why immigrant youths said in interviews that they used to know math or who further reported that they used to be smarter. In a word, many were "deskilled" as a result of having been schooled in the United States.[25]

Even if one considers that some amount of deskilling is occurring, the quantitative part of the Seguín High School study arrived at three significant and interrelated findings. First, within the regular, nonhonors track, immigrant youths outperform their United States–born counterparts. In multivariate analysis, these differences were consistently statistically significant, suggesting that immigrant youths have an edge, academically speaking. A second finding from survey data corroborated the ethnographic evidence that immigrant youths experience school significantly more positively than their United States–born peers. That is, they see teachers as more caring and accessible, and they rate the school climate in more positive terms as well. They are also much less likely to evade school rules and policies. These students' attitudes contrast markedly with those of their second- and third-generation counterparts, whose responses in turn are not significantly different from one another. Particularly striking is how generational status—and not gender or curriculum track placement—influences orientations toward schooling. These findings concur with research from numerous other large- and small-scale studies.[26] The third finding is that the level of schooling youths attain in Mexico or Latin America and their grades are significantly correlated. That is, for each year of schooling attained in Mexico or Latin America, achievement goes up, even after controlling for the quality of education they received (based on a subjective measure of school quality).

These three pieces of evidence together suggest that immigrant youths should be passing the TAAS test. And, since their chances of passing are in fact lower than their counterparts for whom English is the dominant language, it is logical to assume that their poor passing rates suggest more their difficulties with the English language, which is used on the test, than their potential to achieve academically at a high level. Their teachers frequently refer to this barrier as a chief explanation. In short, children of limited English proficiency are especially handicapped in their ability to exhibit their knowledge by the TAAS exit test.

*In conclusion, the TAAS is a ticket to nowhere.*

The TAAS is harmful to instruction by its rigid format, its artificial treatment of subject matter, its embodiment of discredited learning theories, its lack of attention to children's cultures and languages, and its emphasis on the accounting of prescribed learning. The test itself and the system of testing and test preparation have in poor and minority schools come to usurp instructional resources and supplant the opportunity for high-quality, meaningful learning.

This system of testing is therefore not the benign "reform" its political advocates claim. Nor is it the remedy for a malfunctioning bureaucratic system that is merely in need of stricter internal management and accountability. The TAAS system of testing exerts a direct, negative impact on the curriculum, creating new problems outlined here and exacerbating old ones related to historical inequities between rich/majority and poor/minority children. In addition, it masks the real problems of inequity that underlie the failure to educate children adequately. Because it shifts funds and scarce organizational and budgetary resources away from schools and into the coffers of the testing industry vendors, the futures of poor and minority children and the schools they attend are being compromised.

For the children, successful performance on the TAAS in no way ensures either a quality education or a promising future. An education aimed at TAAS scores unequivocally does reduce children's chances for a real education. The pressure to raise scores is greatest in our poorest, historically least well funded schools. To raise scores in those schools— absent a major investment in teacher knowledge, school facilities, and instructional materials—educators are diverting time, energy, and dollars away from the kind of instruction available in middle-class schools and into materials, the only purpose of which is to raise TAAS scores.

We conclude with an excerpt from fieldnotes, in which Valenzuela recorded an episode from Seguín High School that poignantly captures the human side of this misdirected and injurious policy:

> I attended Seguín's high school's graduation ceremony. In the middle of the ceremony after the class song was played, about eight

students stood up to chant the words scrawled on a large banner they held in their hands: "14 YEARS OF SCHOOL. MADE IT THIS FAR. WHY CAN'T WE WALK?" After the students chanted these phrases several times, three cops and six ushers approached the crowd to take away their banners. The audience booed the cops, including all or most of the graduates sitting in their seats. The hundreds of boos, which included parents', brought the ceremony to a halt. Some students were escorted out of the audience by the police while others left on their own. I could clearly see how this state-level policy of linking the TAAS test to high school graduation was sensed by everyone as unjust. It was only too fitting to see how this policy was "policed" in a final show of force to the would-be high school grads.[27]

Rather than youths failing schools, schools are failing our minority youths through the TAAS system of testing. In short, we fail to see how the state's interest is served by a policy that simultaneously diminishes young people's access to a substantive education and closes off their opportunity for graduation from high school, especially when this route represents their best hope for a socially productive life.

There is a critical need for additional, independent research that examines the effects of the TAAS system of testing on the curriculum in various school subjects, on children's capacities to learn and their sense of themselves as learners, on teachers' work, and on teachers' leaving (especially highly educated, highly qualified, and effective teachers) public schools where the TAAS is aligned with administrative bonuses and performance contracts. Virtually none of the effects on teaching, curriculum, and children that we summarize here are captured by analyses and reanalyses of individual or aggregate test score data.

In addition, there is a need for studies that do not rely merely on officially reported data on test scores and on tested students. There has been much analysis of the test score numbers, including analyses disaggregated by race. However, such studies have relied primarily on numbers provided by the state education agency and/or school districts. Furthermore, such studies are often carried out primarily by analysts employed by, or on contract to, the state or employed by organizations with continuing state contracts for such studies or for TAAS implementation, TAAS consulting, or training of teachers and administrators based on the TAAS.

There is also a need for public discourse surrounding the many ways in which to assess children's learning and evaluate their academic progress. Alternative assessments in most subject areas are not "alternative" except in the policy context. Through such professional organizations as the National Council of Teachers of English, the National Council of Teachers of Mathematics, the National Writing Project (and many regional writing projects), the Coalition of Essential Schools, and others, there is a broad and deep expertise on ways of understanding how and whether children are learning. Authentic means of documenting children's learning do not derive from management systems, nor are they intended to be tools of management. They are authentic to the extent that they are premised on a rich and complex view of curriculum subjects, on children's intellectual engagement with learning, and on an understanding of learning as developmental. They are authentic if they are able to encompass the relational part of teaching and learning. Ideally, they can encompass learning that honors the imagination and the open-ended possibilities that substantive learning supports. Authentic forms of assessment are ways of sharing information among children, their teachers, and their parents. They should be means by which adults can learn more about how to teach effectively not in a generic sense, but how better to teach "this child, these children."

There is at present an enormous gap in vocabulary and in ideology between those who teach and those who set policy. This gap must be addressed if the system is ever to be corrected; that is, if what is known about teaching and learning is ever going to shape large educational systems rather than be compromised by them. Ways of governing and managing schools, even big school systems, should not depend on forms of assessing children that undermine the very learning schools are intended to foster.

One step toward redressing this imbalance would be to examine the factors driving the present upside-down system of accountability. There is a need for independent research into the economic and political forces behind this system of testing and its promulgation across state legislatures and governors (and the business groups and test vendors advising them). The reliance within these testing and accountability systems on discredited theories of learning and on artificial representations of curricular content stems from the unexamined assumptions that permit the testing of children to be used for systems of management (and political) accountability. Research into ways in which these organizational, economic, and political forces are reshaping teaching and learning, and thereby restratifying children's opportunities to learn, would be far more productive than more studies on the validity of test questions or race-based trends in test scores. Helpful research studies would have to rely on field-based data across widely diverse student populations and school settings. Such studies would need to include the voices of educators and students in order to capture the complex dynamics that are rendered invisible by the current reliance on narrow sets of indicators. The effects on children from this system of testing need to be brought to light if we are to ensure that our public schools serve all children well.

CHAPTER EIGHT

# Should We End Social Promotion?
## Truth and Consequences*

## ROBERT M. HAUSER

Testing for readiness, achievement, or mastery plays a substantial—but not easily quantifiable—role in grade retention. It will play a greater role if the present movement toward test-based promotion policies continues. To shed light on this role, in this chapter I review the extent and consequences of grade retention in elementary and secondary school. Unfortunately, as this review will make clear, test-based promotion policies are likely to raise both the public and private costs of schooling without corresponding educational benefit.

In the first part of this chapter I review recent proposals for test-based grade promotion and retention. These proposals are based on politically attractive but scientifically unsupported claims about the benefits of retention, and minority students are more likely to be subject to them. Second, I outline what we know about rates, trends, and differentials in grade retention in the United States. Sound data are scarce, but current retention rates are much higher than is generally believed. At least 15 percent of pupils are retained between ages six to eight and ages fifteen to seventeen, and a substantial amount of retention occurs before or after

* An earlier version of this paper was given at the conference of the Harvard Civil Rights Project on Civil Rights and High Stakes Testing, Columbia University, December 1998. This draft is based largely on material in Chapter 6 of National Research Council, Committee on Appropriate Test Use, *High Stakes: Testing for Tracking, Promotion, and Graduation,* Jay Heubert and Robert Hauser, eds. (Washington, D.C.: National Academy Press, 1999). Samuel Messick, Marguerite Clarke, Jay P. Heubert, and Taissa S. Hauser contributed substantially to this chapter of the NRC report.

those ages. Retention rates are much higher for boys and members of minority groups than for girls and the white majority. And retention rates have grown substantially over the past two decades. Third, I review the scientific evidence about the effects of retention in grade. Several recent studies—purporting to show positive effects of grade retention—are in fact consistent with earlier findings that the academic benefits of retention typically are both temporary and costly. Even when previous academic performance and relevant social characteristics are controlled, past grade retention increases the likelihood of current school dropout. There is no evidence for claims that new policies will be coupled with effective remediation of learning deficits that would be worth their cost or would offset the well-established, long-term negative effects of retention.

## RECENT PROPOSALS FOR TEST-BASED GRADE PROMOTION AND RETENTION

Much of the current public discussion of high-stakes testing of individual students centers on calls for "an end to social promotion." In a memorandum to the secretary of education, President Bill Clinton wrote that

> [he had] repeatedly challenged States and school districts to end social promotions—to require students to meet rigorous academic standards at key transition points in their schooling career, and to end the practice of promoting students without regard to how much they have learned. . . . Students should not be promoted past the fourth grade if they cannot read independently and well, and should not enter high school without a solid foundation in math. They should get the help they need to meet the standards before moving on.[1]

In his 1999 State of the Union address, the president reiterated the proposal—to sustained applause—by calling for legislation to withhold federal education funds from school districts practicing social promotion. As recently as October 1999, President Clinton told a "summit" meeting of political and business leaders that "students who are held back because they fail to vault newly raised bars should be treated with tough love. . . . 'look dead in the eye some child who has been held back' and say, 'This doesn't mean there's something wrong with you, but we'll be hurting you worse if we tell you you're learning something when you're not.'"[2]

The Clinton administration's proposals for education reform strongly tied the ending of social promotion to early identification and remediation of learning problems. The president called for smaller classes, well-prepared teachers, specific grade-by-grade standards, challenging curricula, early identification of students who need help, after-school and summer school programs, and school accountability. He also called for "appropriate use of tests and other indicators of academic performance in determining whether students should be promoted."[3] The key questions are whether testing will be used appropriately in such decisions and whether early identification and remediation of learning problems will take place successfully.

Despite ample reason for doubt about their effectiveness and fairness, test-based requirements for promotion are not just being proposed; they are being implemented. According to a report by the American Federation of Teachers, forty-six states either have or are in the process of developing assessments aligned with their content standards. Seven of these states, up from four in 1996, require schools and districts to use the state standards and assessments in determining whether students should be promoted into certain grades.[4]

For some years, Iowa and California had taken strong positions against grade retention, based on research or on the reported success of alternative intervention programs.[5] But California's past policies have been repudiated by the current governor, Gray Davis, who has promoted a legislative package that will mandate test-based grade retention in elementary and secondary schools.

Governor George W. Bush of Texas has proposed that "3rd graders who do not pass the reading portion of the Texas Assessment of Academic Skills would be required to receive help before moving to regular classrooms in the 4th grade. The same would hold true for 5th graders who failed to pass reading and math exams and 8th graders who did not pass tests in reading, math, and writing. The state would provide funding for locally developed intervention programs."[6]

In 1998, New York City public schools chancellor Rudy Crew proposed that fourth and seventh graders be held back if they fail a new state reading test at their grade level, beginning in spring 2000. Crew's proposal initially combined testing of students with "a comprehensive evaluation of their course work and a review of their attendance records." A two-year delay in implementation of the tests would permit schools "to identify those students deemed most at risk and give them intensive remedial instruction."[7] However, late in the spring of 1999, under intense political pressure, Crew abandoned established policies and ordered thousands of third and sixth graders who had performed poorly on a new reading test to attend summer school and pass a new test at summer's end or be held back a year. The New York City public schools were promptly sued for violating their own rules.[8] The inappropriate reliance on performance on a single test came back to haunt the Crew administration when it turned out that the test was improperly normed, and thousands of students had been failed when they should have passed.[9]

In 1996–97 the Chicago public schools instituted a new program to end social promotion. Retention decisions are now based almost entirely on student performance on the Iowa Test of Basic Skills (ITBS) at the end of grades 3, 6, and 8. Students who fall below specific cutoff scores at each grade level are required to attend highly structured summer school programs and to take an alternative form of the test at summer's end.[10] At the end of the 1996–97 school year, 32 percent, 31 percent, and 21 percent of students failed the initial examination at grades 3, 6, and 8, respectively. Out of ninety-one thousand students tested overall, almost twenty-six thousand failed. After summer school, 15 percent, 13 percent, and 8 percent of students were retained at the three grade levels.[11]

The current enthusiasm for the use of achievement tests to end social promotion raises three concerns. First, much of the public discussion and some recently implemented or proposed testing programs appear to ignore existing standards for appropriate test use.[12] Second, there is persuasive research evidence that grade retention typically has no beneficial academic or social effects on students.[13] The past failures of grade retention policies need not be repeated. But they provide a cautionary lesson: making grade retention—or the threat of retention—an effective educational policy requires consistent and sustained effort. Third, public discussion of social promotion has made little reference to current retention practices—in which a very large share of American schoolchildren are already retained in grade. In part this is because of sporadic data collection and reporting, but even so, far more consistent statistical data are available about the practice of grade retention than, say, about academic tracking. It is possible to describe rates, trends, and differentials in grade retention using data from the U.S. Bureau of the Census, yet these data have not been used fully to inform the public debate.

## TRENDS AND DIFFERENTIALS IN GRADE RETENTION

In this section, I first consider the sources of evidence that are available for illuminating the trends and differentials in grade retention. Using these sources of evidence, I then report trends in the age of kindergarten entry, in retention in the primary and secondary grades, in overall retention after school entry, and in social differences in retention.

## Sources of Evidence

To support its analyses of high-stakes testing for promotion and retention, the National Research Council (NRC)'s Committee on Appropriate Test Use assembled and analyzed data on rates, trends, and differentials in grade retention.[14] Perhaps the most striking fact to surface from this effort to bring together existing data is that—despite the prominence of social promotion as an issue of educational policy—very little information about it is available. I doubt that governments currently make important policy decisions about any other social process with so little sound, basic, descriptive information.

No federal or independent agency monitors social promotion and grade retention. Occasional data on retention are available for some states and localities, but coverage is sparse, and little is known about the comparability of these data.[15] For example, the denominators of retention rates may be based on beginning-of-year or end-of-year enrollment figures. The numerators may include retention as of the end of an academic year or as of the end of the following summer session. Some states include special education students in the data; others exclude them. In the primary grades, retention is usually an all-or-nothing matter; in high school, retention may imply that a student has completed some requirements but has too few credits to be promoted.

Some states do not collect retention data at all or collect very limited data. For example, the NRC study found that thirteen states— Colorado, Connecticut, Illinois, Kansas, Montana, Nebraska, Nevada, New Hampshire, New Jersey, North Dakota, Pennsylvania, Utah, and Wyoming—collect no statewide data on grade retention. Twenty-two states, plus the District of Columbia, provide data on retention at some grade levels, but in some cases the data are very limited. For example, New York State collects such data only at the eighth-grade level.

Retention rates are highly variable across states. They are unusually high in the District of Columbia, where the student population is largely black. But the states with relatively low rates include some with relatively large minority populations as well, like South Carolina and Georgia. Retention rates tend to be relatively high in the early primary grades— though not in kindergarten—and in the early high school years.

The main federal source of information about education, the National Center for Education Statistics, provides essentially no statistics about grade retention or social promotion. For example, there are no data on this subject in current editions of its two major statistical compendiums, the *Digest of Education Statistics* and the *Condition of Education*.[16]

One egregious exception to the lack of federal information about grade retention and promotion is a recent Department of Education publication, *Taking Responsibility for Ending Social Promotion: A Guide for Educators and State and Local Leaders*.[17] While it also cites more reputable estimates of grade retention, the *Guide* features a "conservative" estimate from "1996 Current Population Statistics" that "only about 3 percent of students are two or more years over age for their grade (an indication that they have been retained at least once)."[18] This estimate is indefensibly low for three reasons. First, it covers only currently enrolled students, ignoring persons of normal school age who have fallen behind and dropped out. Second, by referring to K–12 students at all grade levels, it aggregates data for children in the primary grades, who have had few years at risk of retention, with data for children in higher grades, who have had many years at risk of retention. Third, by counting as "retained" only those students who are two or more years above the modal age for their grade, the *Guide* fails to include a large number of retained students. I cannot think of any rationale for this statistic, other than an effort to mislead the public about the true extent of grade retention.

The best current source of information on levels, trends, and differentials in grade retention is the *Current Population Survey* (CPS) of the U.S. Bureau of the Census. Using published data from the annual October School Enrollment Supplement of the CPS, it is possible to track the distribution of school enrollment by age and grade each year for groups defined by sex and race/ethnicity. These data have the advantage of comparable national coverage from year to year, but they say nothing directly about educational transitions or about the role of high-stakes testing in grade retention. We can infer the minimum rate of grade retention only by observing changes in the enrollment of children below the modal grade level for their age from one calendar year to the next. Suppose, for example, that 10 percent of six-year-old children were enrolled below first grade in October of 1994. If 15 percent of those children were enrolled below second grade in October of 1995, when they were seven years old, we would infer that at least 5 percent were held back in first grade between 1994 and 1995. Using this approach, the CPS data, and other data collected by the National Research Council's Committee on Appropriate Test Use, I review below trends in retention and social differentiation in retention.

## EXTENDED KINDERGARTEN ATTENDANCE

Historically, there was great variation in age at school entry in the United States. This variation had more to do with the labor demands of a farm economy and the availability of schooling to disadvantaged groups than with readiness for school. The variability declined as school enrollment completed its diffusion from middle childhood into younger and older ages.[19]

More recently, the age at entry into graded school gradually has crept upward since the early 1970s, reversing one of the major historic trends contributing to the growth of schooling in the United States. The Census Bureau's statistics on grade enrollment by age show that from the early 1970s to the late 1980s entry into first grade gradually came later in the development of many children. However, for the past decade there has been little change in age at school entry. Figure 8.1 shows percentages of six-year-old children who had not yet entered first grade as of October of the given year.[20] Among six-year-old boys, only 8 percent had not yet entered first grade in 1971,[21] but 22 percent were not yet in first grade in 1987, and 21 percent were not yet in first grade in

### FIGURE 8.1. PERCENTAGE OF SIX-YEAR-OLD CHILDREN WHO HAVE NOT ENTERED FIRST GRADE

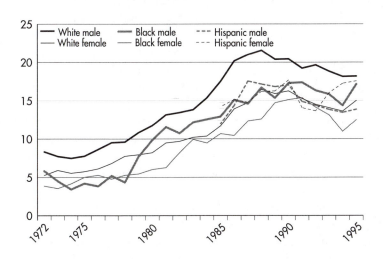

*Note:* Entries are three-year moving averages.
*Source:* U.S. Bureau of the Census, *Current Population Reports,* Series P-20.

1996. Among six-year-old girls, only 4 percent had not yet entered first grade in 1971, but 16 percent were not yet in first grade in 1987, and 17 percent were not yet in first grade in 1996. While boys are consistently more likely than girls to enter first grade after age six, there are only small differences between blacks and whites in age at entry into graded school, and these differences consistently favor black children. That is, six-year-old black children are slightly less likely than white children of the same age and sex to be enrolled below first grade or not enrolled in school. Also, six-year-old Hispanic boys are consistently more likely than white boys to have entered first grade. However, six-year-old Hispanic girls are less likely than white girls to have entered first grade.

It is not clear why age at school entry has risen. One contributing factor has been the influence of state laws on minimum age at school entry. Another—suggested by the initially slow school entry of white boys—is that some parents "red shirt" their children at an early age in order to give them an advantage in athletic competition later on. Early school retention is yet a third potential explanation of the trend.

Over the past two decades, attendance in kindergarten has been extended to two years for many children in American schools.[22] There is no single name for this phenomenon. As Lorrie A. Shepard reports in a 1991 paper, the names for such extended kindergarten classrooms include "junior-first," "prefirst," "transition," and "readiness room."[23] There are also no distinct categories for the first and second years of kindergarten in Census enrollment data. Fragmentary reports suggest that, in some places, kindergarten retention may have been as high as 50 percent in the late 1980s.[24] There are also reports of inappropriate use of cognitive tests in such decisions.[25] The degree to which early retention decisions originate with parents, such as when parents delay school entry to increase their children's chances for success in athletics, rather than with teachers or other school personnel is not known. Moreover, there are no regular national estimates of the prevalence of kindergarten retention, and none of the available state data indicate exceptionally high kindergarten retention rates. From occasional national surveys, Nancy L. Karweit suggests that "by first grade between 7 and 11 percent of children have been retained."[26]

Excepting the ubiquitous tendency for girls to enter (and complete) primary and secondary school at earlier ages than boys, there is little sign of social differentiation in age at school entry. Instead, as I demonstrate later in this chapter, socially differentiated patterns of grade retention begin to develop after entry into graded school, and they persist through secondary school.

## RETENTION IN THE PRIMARY AND SECONDARY GRADES

The term age-grade retardation refers to enrollment below the modal grade level for a child's age (and no broader meaning is either intended or implied). I have examined national rates of age-grade retardation by age, sex, and race/ethnicity for three-year age groups at ages six to seventeen from 1971 to 1996 and, also, parallel tabulations for young children by single years of age, 1971 to 1996. In each case, I have organized the data by birth cohort (year of birth), rather than by calendar year, so it is possible to see the evolution of age-grade retardation throughout the schooling of a birth cohort, as well as changes in age-grade retardation rates from year to year.[27]

The recent history of age-grade retardation is summarized in Figure 8.2 (page 160). It shows age-grade retardation at ages six to eight, nine to eleven, twelve to fourteen, and fifteen to seventeen among children who reached ages six to eight between 1962 and 1996. The horizontal axis shows the year in which an age group reached ages six to eight, so vertical comparisons among the trend lines at a given year show how age-grade retardation cumulated as a birth cohort grew older.

For example, consider children who were six to eight years old in 1987—the most recent cohort whose history can be traced all the way from ages six to eight up through ages fifteen to seventeen. At ages six to eight, 21 percent were enrolled below the modal grade for their age. By 1990, when this cohort reached ages nine to eleven, age-grade retardation grew to 28 percent, and it was 31 percent in 1993, when the cohort reached ages twelve to fourteen. By 1996, when the cohort reached ages fifteen to seventeen, the percentage who were either below the modal grade level or had left school was 36 percent. Almost all of the growth in retardation after ages twelve to fourteen, however, was due to dropout (4.8 percent), rather than grade retention among the enrolled.

One could read the rate of enrollment below the modal grade at ages six to eight as a baseline measure; that is, as if it did not necessarily indicate that grade retention had taken place. Relative to that baseline, increases in enrollment below the modal grade at older ages clearly show the net effects of retention in grade. This reading of the data would suggest that, in most birth cohorts, retention occurs mainly between ages to six to eight and nine to eleven or between ages twelve to fourteen and fifteen to seventeen.[28] This way of looking at the data surely understates the prevalence of grade retention, for much of it occurs within or below ages six to eight.

The series for ages fifteen to seventeen includes early school dropout, which is also shown as a separate series along the bottom of the figure.

FIGURE 8.2. PERCENTAGE OF CHILDREN ENROLLED BELOW MODAL
GRADE FOR AGE BY AGE GROUP AND YEAR IN WHICH
COHORT WAS SIX TO EIGHT YEARS OLD

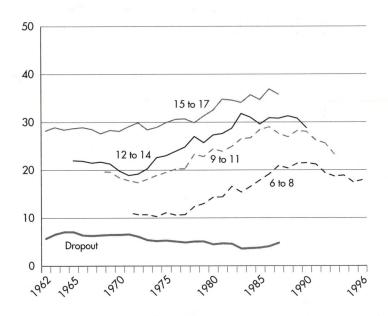

*Note:* Dropouts are included in the series at ages fifteen to seventeen.
*Source:* U.S. Bureau of the Census, *Historical Statistics,* Table A-3, persons six to seventeen.

Dropping out, rather than retention, evidently accounts for a substantial share of the increase in age-grade retardation between ages twelve to fourteen and ages fifteen to seventeen.

The trend in age-grade retardation at ages six to eight, nine to eleven, twelve to fourteen, and fifteen to seventeen can be read across Figure 8.2 from left to right. Age-grade retardation increased in every age group from cohorts of the early 1970s through those of the middle to late 1980s. Age-grade retardation increased at ages fifteen to seventeen after the mid-1970s, despite the slow decline in its early school dropout component throughout the period. That is, grade retention increased while the dropout rate decreased. Peak rates occurred earlier at older than at younger ages, suggesting that policy changes occurred in specific calendar years, rather than consistently throughout the life of successive birth cohorts. Among cohorts entering school after 1970, the percentage enrolled below the modal grade level was never less than 10 percent at ages six to eight, and it exceeded 20 percent for cohorts of the late 1980s. The trend lines suggest that age-grade retardation has declined slightly for cohorts entering school after the mid-1980s, but rates have not approached the much lower levels of the early 1970s.

Overall, a large share of each birth cohort now experiences grade retention during elementary school. Among children aged six to eight from 1982 to 1992, age-grade retardation reached 25 to 30 percent by ages nine to eleven.

## RETENTION AFTER SCHOOL ENTRY

Enrollment below first grade at age six is a convenient baseline against which to assess the effects of later grade retention. The comparisons of age-grade retardation at ages seven to nine with that at age six are shown in Figure 8.3 (page 162). There are two main patterns in the series. First, grade retention continues through the elementary years at each successive age. Retention cumulates rapidly after age six. For example, among children who were six years old in 1987, enrollment below the modal grade increased by almost five percentage points between ages six and seven and by five more percentage points between ages seven and nine. Second, there appears to have been a decline in retention between ages six and seven after the early 1980s. That is, comparing Figure 8.1 with Figure 8.3, we can infer a shift in elementary school grade retardation downward in age from the transition between ages six and seven to somewhere between ages four and six.

How much grade retention is there after ages six to eight? And does the recent growth in grade retardation by ages six to eight account for its observed growth at older ages? Figure 8.4 (page 163) shows changes in age-grade retardation between ages six to eight and each of the three older age groups.[29] Age-grade retardation grows substantially after ages six to eight as a result of retention in grade. For example, among children who reached ages six to eight between 1972 and 1985, almost 20 percent more were below the modal grade for their age by the time they were fifteen to seventeen years old. Among children who reached ages six to eight between the middle 1970s and the middle 1980s, grade retardation grew by about ten percentage points by ages nine to eleven, and it grew by close to five percentage points more by ages twelve to fourteen. Relative to ages six to eight, age-grade retardation at ages nine to eleven and twelve to fourteen increased for cohorts who were six to eight years

## FIGURE 8.3. CHANGE IN AGE-GRADE RETARDATION FROM AGE SIX TO AGES SEVEN TO NINE BY YEAR WHEN COHORT WAS SIX YEARS OLD

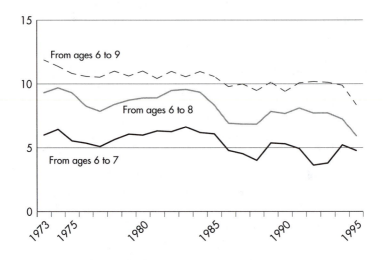

*Note:* Entries are three-year moving averages.
*Source:* U.S. Bureau of the Census, *Current Population Reports,* Series P-20.

old in the early 1970s; it was stable from the middle 1970s to the middle 1980s, and it has declined since then. However, the gap between retention at ages fifteen to seventeen and that at ages six to eight has been relatively stable—close to twenty percentage points—possibly excepting a very recent downward turn. Thus, the rise in age at entry into first grade—which is partly due to kindergarten retention—accounts for much of the overall increase in age-grade retardation among teenagers.

No national data are available to tell us the cumulative risk of grade retention across grades 1 to 12, but some states provide enough data to make such estimates.[30] For example, Texas has regularly reported the percentages of students who are retained at each grade level, and the rates are reported separately by race/ethnicity. Retention rates have been stable and high from 1990 onward, well before the new initiatives to "end social promotion." In other words, if all Texas students were subject to the failure rates of 1996–97, 17 percent would fail at least once between the first and eighth grades, and 32 percent

## FIGURE 8.4. CHANGE IN AGE-GRADE RETARDATION FROM AGES SIX TO EIGHT TO AGES NINE TO SEVENTEEN BY YEAR WHEN COHORT WAS SIX TO EIGHT YEARS OLD

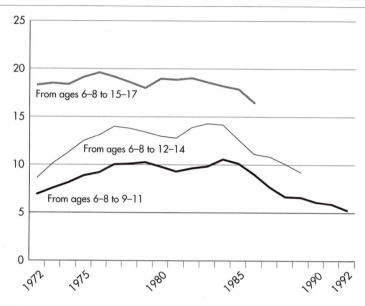

*Note:* Dropouts are included in the series at ages fifteen to seventeen. Entries are three-year moving averages.
*Source:* U.S. Bureau of the Census, *Historical Statistics,* Table A-3, Persons 6 to 17.

would fail at least once between ninth grade and high school completion.[31] Among African American students, the corresponding rates are 20 percent and 42 percent, and among Hispanic students they are 21 percent and 44 percent.[32]

In summary, grade retention is pervasive in American schools. It is important to think about the implications of "an end to social promotion" when ages at school entry are increasing and a large share of each new cohort of youths already experiences grade retention, particularly in light of the social differences in retention rates explored below.

## SOCIAL DIFFERENCES IN RETENTION

While there are similarities in the age pattern of grade retardation among major population groups—boys and girls and majority and minority groups—there are also substantial differences in rates of grade retardation among them, many of which develop well after school entry.

Figure 8.5 shows differences in grade-retardation between boys and girls
at ages six to eight and ages fifteen to seventeen. Overall, the sex differential gradually increases with age, from five percentage points at ages six
to eight to ten percentage points at ages fifteen to seventeen. That is,
boys are initially more likely than girls to be placed below the modal
grade for their age, and they fall further behind girls as they pass through
childhood and adolescence.

The differentiation of age-grade relationships by race and ethnicity is
even more striking. Figures 8.6 to 8.9 (pages 165–68) show trends in
the development of age-grade retardation by race/ethnicity in each of
the four age groups: six to eight years old, nine to eleven years old,
twelve to fourteen years old, and fifteen to seventeen years old. Unlike the
case of gender differentiation, at ages six to eight the rates of age-grade
retardation are very similar among whites, blacks, and Hispanics.
However, by ages nine to eleven the percentages enrolled below modal

FIGURE 8.5. PERCENTAGE ENROLLED BELOW MODAL GRADE AT
AGES SIX TO EIGHT AND AT AGES FIFTEEN TO SEVENTEEN BY
SEX AND YEAR COHORT REACHED AGES SIX TO EIGHT

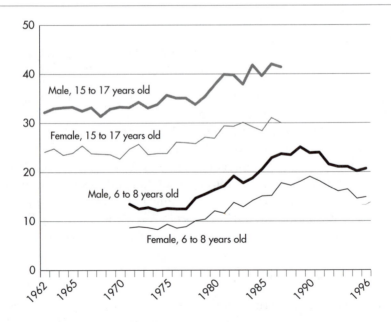

*Source:* U.S. Bureau of the Census, *Historical Statistics,* Table A-3, Persons 6 to 8
and 15 to 17.

grade levels are typically five to ten percentage points higher among blacks and Hispanics than among whites. The differentials continue to grow with age, and at ages fifteen to seventeen rates of grade retardation range from 40 to 50 percent among blacks and Hispanics, while they have gradually drifted up from 25 percent to 35 percent among whites. By ages fifteen to seventeen, there is also a differential between Hispanics and blacks, favoring the latter, that appears to follow from high rates of early school dropout among Hispanics. Figure 8.10 (page 169) shows the school dropout rates among fifteen- to seventeen-year-old whites, blacks, and Hispanics. There is almost no difference in the dropout rates between whites and blacks,[33] but Hispanics are much more likely to leave school at an early age. Thus, dropping out of high school early contributes very little to the observed difference in age-grade retardation between blacks and whites, which is mainly due to retention in grade. Dropping out early does, however, account in part for the difference in age-grade retardation between Hispanics and whites or blacks.

### FIGURE 8.6. PERCENTAGE ENROLLED BELOW MODAL GRADE AT AGES SIX TO EIGHT BY RACE/ETHNICITY AND YEAR

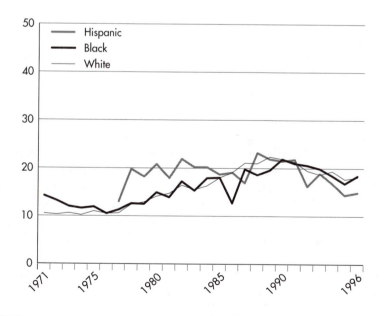

*Source:* U.S. Bureau of the Census, *Historical Statistics,* Table A-3, Persons 6 to 8.

FIGURE 8.7. PERCENTAGE ENROLLED BELOW MODAL GRADE AT
AGES NINE TO ELEVEN BY YEAR COHORT REACHED
AGES SIX TO EIGHT BY RACE/ETHNICITY

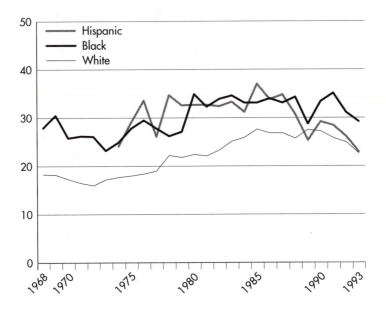

*Source:* U.S. Bureau of the Census, *Historical Statistics,* Table A-3, Persons 9 to 11.

In recent years, gender and race-ethnic differentials in age-grade retardation, even at young ages, are a consequence of school experience and not primarily of differentials in age at school entry. Social differentials in age-grade relationships are vague at school entry, but a hierarchy is clearly established by age nine, and it persists and grows through the end of secondary schooling. This growth can be explained only by grade retention. By age nine there are sharp social differentials in age-grade retardation, favoring whites and girls relative to blacks or Hispanics and boys. By ages fifteen to seventeen, close to 50 percent of black males have fallen behind in school—30 percentage points more than at ages six to eight—but age-grade retardation has never exceeded 30 percent among white girls of the same age range. If these rates and differentials in age-grade retardation are characteristic of a schooling regime in which social promotion is perceived to be the norm, it is cautionary to imagine what we might observe when that norm has been eliminated.

## FIGURE 8.8. PERCENTAGE ENROLLED BELOW MODAL GRADE AT AGES TWELVE TO FOURTEEN BY YEAR COHORT REACHED AGES SIX TO EIGHT BY RACE/ETHNICITY

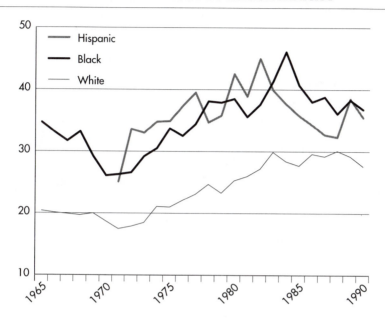

*Source:* U.S. Bureau of the Census, *Historical Statistics*, Table A-3, Persons 12 to 14.

## THE EFFECTS OF RETENTION

Determining whether the use of a promotion test produces better over-all educational outcomes requires weighing the intended benefits against unintended negative consequences for individual students and groups of students.[34] Most of the relevant research focuses on one outcome in particular—retention in grade. Although retention rates can change even when tests are not used in making promotion decisions, the use of scores from large-scale tests to make such decisions may be associated with increased retention rates.[35]

Increased retention is not a negative outcome if it benefits students. But are there positive consequences of being held back in school because of a test score? Does the student do better after repeating the grade, or would he have fared just as well or better if he had been promoted with his peers? Research data indicate that simply repeating a grade generally does not improve achievement;[36] moreover, it increases the dropout rate.[37]

FIGURE 8.9. PERCENTAGE ENROLLED BELOW MODAL GRADE OR
DROPPING OUT BY AGES FIFTEEN TO SEVENTEEN BY YEAR
COHORT REACHED AGES SIX TO EIGHT BY RACE/ETHNICITY

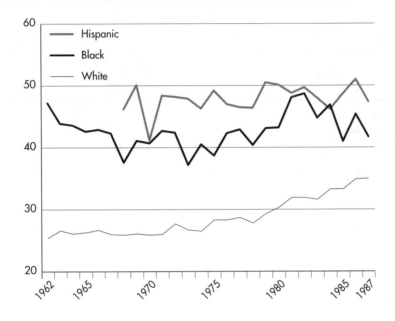

*Source:* U.S. Bureau of the Census, *Historical Statistics,* Table A-3, Persons 15 to 17.

## RETENTION AND ACADEMIC ACHIEVEMENT

Some of the clearest evidence regarding the effects of retention comes from C. Thomas Holmes' meta-analysis of sixty-three controlled studies of grade retention in elementary and junior high school through the mid-1980s.[38] When promoted and retained students were compared one to three years later, the retained students' average levels of academic achievement were at least 0.4 standard deviations below those of promoted students. In these comparisons, promoted and retained students were the same age, but the promoted students had completed one more grade than the retained students. Promoted and retained students were also compared after completing one or more grades—that is, when the retained students were a year older than the promoted students but had completed equal numbers of additional grades. Here, the findings were less consistent, but still negative. When the data were weighted by the

FIGURE 8.10. PERCENTAGE DROPPING OUT BY AGES FIFTEEN TO
SEVENTEEN BY YEAR COHORT REACHED AGES
SIX TO EIGHT BY RACE/ETHNICITY

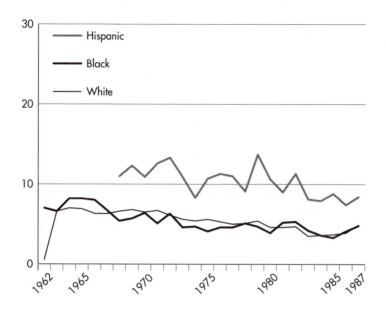

*Source:* U.S. Bureau of the Census, *Historical Statistics,* Table A-3, Persons 6 to 17.

number of estimated effects, there was an initially positive effect of retention on academic achievement after one more grade in school, but it faded away completely after three or more grades. When the data were weighted by the number of independent studies, rather than by the estimated number of effects on achievement, the average effects were negligible in every year after retention. Of the sixty-three studies reviewed by Holmes, fifty-four yielded overall negative effects of retention, and only nine yielded overall positive effects. Some studies had better statistical controls than others, but those with subjects matched on IQ, achievement test scores, sex, and/or socioeconomic status showed *larger* negative effects of retention than studies with weaker designs. Holmes concluded, "On average, retained children are worse off than their promoted counterparts on both personal adjustment and academic outcomes."[39]

Despite the seemingly conclusive findings of Holmes' review, there have been occasional new studies of the academic effects of retention. A study of Chicago children (undertaken in connection with an experiment in sustained educational intervention) found that "grade retention was significantly associated with lower reading and math achievement at age fourteen above and beyond a comprehensive set of explanatory variables."[40]

A more recent study of Baltimore schoolchildren by Karl L. Alexander, Doris R. Entwisle, and Susan L. Dauber concludes that grade retention does increase the chances of academic success.[41] That conclusion is explicit in the title of the book, *On the Success of Failure*. Alexander and his coauthors argued that earlier studies were methodologically weak. Along with legitimate criticisms, they dismissed many earlier studies precisely because they were old. (One wonders whether they would, for the same reason, dismiss the pioneering findings of natural scientists in the nineteenth century.) Their own investigation entailed an extensive longitudinal survey, following eight hundred children who entered first grade in 1982 for up to eight years, so long as they remained in the Baltimore public schools. They assessed academic achievement regularly, and they also looked at measures of self-concept, attitudes toward school, and achievement orientations. One important contribution of the book is a detailed account of the complex flows of students from one grade to the next—or to repeat a grade—and into and out of special education classifications. A vision of the schooling process as a linear progression through grade levels, possibly interrupted by retention, covers only a fraction of the experience of the Baltimore students.

Unfortunately, Alexander, Entwisle, and Dauber's analysis of the Baltimore data does not support their positive conclusions about the value of grade retention.[42] Most of the retention that they observed occurred at the first-grade level. Here, their stated conclusions about the effects of retention were plainly negative: "retainees fall farther and farther behind never-retained youngsters for as long as we can monitor their progress. . . . [A]ny lasting benefits of retention would be apparent within the time spans observed." However, for much smaller numbers of students who were retained at higher grade levels, the findings were in some cases neutral or positive. Nevertheless, the authors gradually shift their conclusions from negative to positive from earlier to later sections of the text. A close reading of their text, tables, and graphs makes it difficult to follow or to accept such conclusions.

Worse yet, there are serious methodological problems in Alexander, Entwisle, and Dauber's analysis, which were documented in an intensive review by Lorrie A. Shepard, Mary Lee Smith, and Scott F. Marion.[43] First, much of the analysis rests on comparisons of absolute test score gains of retained and promoted students. However, the test used in their study is vertically equated on the assumption that students learn more at lower than at higher grade levels. The standard deviations of the reading and math tests thus decline with grade level, and low-performing students typically have higher gain scores than high-performing students, even when they are falling further and further behind in relative terms. Second, Alexander and his coauthors failed to observe their own methodological rules for same-grade comparison when they looked at the nonacademic outcomes of retention. Shepard, Smith, and Marion conclude that the major empirical claims of Alexander, Entwisle, and Dauber could not be sustained.[44]

Nancy L. Karweit reports a larger-scale, but short-term, national study of the effects of retention, based on the Prospects database, an evaluation of the effects of Chapter 1 (federal support for education of economically disadvantaged students).[45] She was able to follow nearly ten thousand students in the grade 1 cohort of 1991 for their first three years of schooling. Thus, it was possible to compare the academic achievements of students who were retained in grade 1 with those of students who had not been retained, after both groups had completed grade 2. As is typically observed in retention studies, the retained students gained substantially in the year of retention, relative to their poor performance in the preceding year. However, by the end of the second grade, the retained students had fallen back relative to promoted students, though not as far behind as at the end of their first year in grade 1 (spring 1992). In these respects, the Prospects data are consistent with many previous studies of retention. Unfortunately, as Karweit notes, it is neither possible to sort out the effects of initial selection on poor test scores in spring 1992, nor to follow the cohort into higher grades. Retention fared better in comparisons between retained students and a small number of low-performing students in schools where there was no retention. However, Karweit observed that these retained and promoted students were poorly matched and cautioned readers that the comparisons should not be taken too seriously.

One other large-scale retention study, conducted by A. Gary Dworkin and his colleagues, was recently featured by the national newspaper *USA Today* as evidence that retention increases academic achievement.[46] In an analysis of longitudinal data supplied by the Texas Education Agency, Dworkin and his colleagues compared the academic achievements of elementary grade students who had failed the Texas

Assessment of Academic Skills (TAAS) and been retained with the much larger number of students who had failed the TAAS and had not been retained (only about 3 percent of TAAS failures were retained). Across several two- and three-year panels of observations, from grades 3 or 4 forward, students who had been retained frequently out-performed those who were promoted. The editorial writers of *USA Today*, like the authors of the study, were quick to attribute the test score gains of retained students to (assumed) remedial instruction that was withheld from the promoted students.

There are serious methodological problems in the Texas study and plausible alternative interpretations of the TAAS score gains. First, student coverage was poor: only about two-thirds of Texas students were initially covered at each grade level. Students who changed school districts were immediately lost, as were those who moved out of state. Consequently, retention rates were much lower among students included in the study by Dworkin than among all Texas students as reported by the Texas Education Agency.[47] Second, by limiting the study to students who had failed the TAAS, Dworkin and his colleagues followed only about 40 percent of covered students who were retained. Third, the retained students were so strongly selected for low test scores that one should expect to observe large increases in their scores in later years merely because of documented levels of year-to-year instability in test scores.[48] Fourth, the same-grade comparisons that one would normally prefer to examine in studies of retention are suspect in this case because of the systemic reforms carried out in Texas during the period of the study. Throughout the mid-1990s, the elementary school curriculum in Texas was revised to focus increasingly on preparation for the TAAS. For this reason—and because retained students completed each new grade one calendar year later than promoted students—it is not clear whether the superior test performance of retained students should be attributed to retention or to systemic, period-specific changes in school practices, such as "teaching to the test," that affected all students in specific grade levels. That is, one can attribute the observed improvements in test performance to retention in the Texas study only in the same way that one can attribute growth in educational attainment from one cohort to the next to being born in a later year; in each case, it pays to go through school more recently. There is no way to tie specific post-retention educational practices to the success of retained students, nor any basis for the belief that such practices, if they were successful, could be expanded to cover all students who might fail the TAAS.

It would perhaps be too much to say that grade retention cannot succeed, but surely there is no compelling evidence that it increases academic achievement on a large scale and in the long run. Correspondingly, there is no rationale for looking to grade retention as an educational panacea. To be sure, the available evidence is almost all based on typical educational practice, and one might believe that new practices would yield more favorable outcomes. However, if there are effective new practices, why not use valid assessments to identify students with learning difficulties and intervene before retention is the only alternative?

One of the frustrations of retention research is that—excepting three very early studies—there are no true field experiments. Many educational researchers dismiss this option because, they believe, it would be unethical. But if we truly do not know whether retention helps or hurts low-performing students, why would it be unethical to assign volunteers either to retention or promotion? Would this be any less ethical, say, than creating the variations in class size that have led to a new understanding of the value of very small class sizes in the primary grades? In my opinion, if there is truly continuing disagreement about the observational evidence on retention and academic achievement, then a large-scale field experiment is a logical choice. Surely, such an experiment would be preferable to massive interference in the lives of many of our most vulnerable children.

## RETENTION AND SCHOOL DROPOUT

The negative effects of grade retention on school dropout rates are even stronger and more consistent than its effects on academic achievement. For example, using data for several localities that included the 1979 to 1981 freshman classes from the Chicago public schools, James B. Grissom and Lorrie A. Shepard reported in 1989 that retention accelerated school dropout.[49] In a more recent analysis of data from Chicago—which predates the recent educational "reforms" in that city—Judy A. Temple, Arthur J. Reynolds, and Wendy T. Miedel found that retention between kindergarten and eighth grade increased dropout rates by twelve percentage points after controls for social background, program participation, school moves, and special education placement.[50] For two decades, the Chicago public schools have cycled through successive policies of loose and restrictive promotion, and it is not clear how long the present strict policies will hold.[51] But is there reason to doubt that the current regime of massive retention in Chicago will not also lead to increased dropout rates in future years?

Douglas K. Anderson produced an extensive, large-scale national study in 1994 of the effect of grade retention on high school dropout rates.[52] He analyzed data from the National Longitudinal Study of Youth for more than 5,500 students whose school attendance was followed annually from 1978–79 to 1985–86. With statistical controls for sex, race/ethnicity, social background, cognitive ability, adolescent deviance, early transitions to adult status, and several school-related measures, the study showed that students who were currently repeating a grade were 70 percent more likely to drop out of high school than students who were not currently repeating a grade.

Russell W. Rumberger and Katherine A. Larson analyzed high school dropout rates and rates for completion of the GED in longitudinal data from the National Educational Longitudinal Study (NELS) of 1988.[53] After controlling for social and family background, school characteristics, student engagement, and academic achievement in the eighth grade (based on test scores and grades), they found that being held back before eighth grade increased the relative odds of dropping out by twelfth grade by a factor of 2.56.[54] Furthermore, "Students who were held back before the eighth grade were more than four times as likely as students who were not held back to not complete high school or receive a GED by 1994."[55] Reliable negative evidence of that strength in a clinical trial would lead to its early termination.

## RACE, SOCIOECONOMIC STATUS, AND TEST-BASED PROMOTION

There are also strong relationships between race and socioeconomic status (SES) and the use of tests for promotion and retention. A national longitudinal study by Sean Reardon, using the NELS database, shows that certain students are far likelier than others to be subject to promotion tests in the eighth grade:

> Students in urban schools, in schools with high concentrations of low-income and minority students, and schools in southern and western states, are considerably more likely to have [high-stakes] test requirements in eighth grade. Among eighth graders, 35 percent of black students and 27 percent of Hispanic students are subject to [a high-stakes test in at least one subject] to advance to

ninth grade, compared to 15 percent of white students. Similarly, 25 percent of students in the lowest SES quartile, but only 14 percent of those in the top quartile, are subject to eighth grade [high-stakes test] requirements.[56]

Moreover, the study found that the presence of high-stakes eighth grade tests is associated with sharply higher dropout rates, especially for students at schools serving mainly students of low socioeconomic status. For such students, dropping out of school early—between the eighth and tenth grades—was 6 to 8 percent more likely than for students from schools that were similar excepting the high-stakes test requirement.[57]

What does it mean that minority students and low-SES students are more likely to be subject to high-stakes tests in eighth grade? Perhaps, as Reardon points out, such policies are "related to the prevalence of low-achieving students—the group proponents believe the tests are most likely to help."[58] Perhaps the adoption of high-stakes test policies for individuals serves the larger social purpose of ensuring that promotion from eighth to ninth grade reflects acquisition of certain knowledge and skills. Such tests may also motivate less able students and teachers to work harder or to focus their attention on the knowledge domains that test developers value most highly. But if, as the research suggests, retention in grade is not, on balance, beneficial for students,[59] it is cause for concern that low-SES children and minority students are disproportionately subject to any negative consequences.

Those who leave school without diplomas have diminished life chances. High dropout rates carry many social costs. It may thus be problematic if high-stakes tests lead individual students who would not otherwise have done so to drop out. There may also be legal implications if it appears that the public is prepared to adopt high-stakes test programs chiefly when their consequences will be felt disproportionately by minority students and students of low socioeconomic status.[60]

New York City appears to be following a similar cycle of strict and loose retention policies, in which the unsuccessful Promotional Gates program of the 1980s was at first "promising," then "withered," and was finally canceled by 1990, only to be revived in 1998 by a new central administration.[61] This cycle of policies, combining strict retention criteria with a weak commitment to remedial instruction, is likely to reconfirm past evidence that retention in grade is typically harmful to students.

Another important question is whether the use of a test in making promotion decisions exacerbates existing inequalities or creates new ones. For example, in their case study of a school district that instituted tests in order to raise standards, Mary Catherine Ellwein and Gene V. Glass found that test information was used selectively in making promotion and retention decisions, leading to what was perceived as negative consequences for certain groups of students.[62] Thus, although minorities accounted for 59 percent of the students who failed the 1985 kindergarten test, they made up 69 percent of the students who were retained and received transition services. A similar pattern was observed at grade 2.

In addition, there may be problems with using a test as the *sole* measure of the effectiveness of retention or other interventions (summer school, tutoring, and so on). This concern is related to the fact that the validity of test and retest scores depends in part on whether the scores reflect students' familiarity with actual test items or a particular test format. For example, there is evidence that improved scores on one test do not actually carry over when a new test of the same knowledge and skills is introduced.[63]

The current reform and test-based accountability systems of the Chicago public schools provide an example of high-stakes test use for individual students that raises serious questions about teaching to the test. Although Chicago is developing its own standards-based, course-specific assessment system, it currently remains committed to using the Iowa Test of Basic Skills as the yardstick for student and school accountability. Teachers are given detailed manuals on preparing their students for the tests.[64] Student test scores have increased substantially, both during the intensive summer remedial sessions—the Summer Bridge program—and between the 1996–97 and 1997–98 school years,[65] but the available data provide no means of distinguishing true increases in student learning from statistical artifacts or invalid comparisons. That is, the observed test-score gains might be produced by the combined effects of teaching to the test, repeated use of a similar test, and, in the case of the Summer Bridge program, the initial selection of students with low scores on the test.[66] Moreover, an evaluation of Chicago's policies conducted by the Consortium on Chicago School Research found that the students who had failed at the third, sixth, and eighth grade levels continued to do very poorly on the Iowa Test, even after summer school and retention. The evaluation also showed that students who failed the Iowa Test after Summer Bridge but were nevertheless promoted performed better than those who failed it but were retained.[67] Such results once again illustrate that grade retention typically has no lasting educational benefit.

## ALTERNATIVES TO RETENTION

The high rate of retention created by current evaluation practices, their disparate impact on minority youth, and the possibility of substantially increased, test-based retention raise a number of concerns. Among these are that the costs of grade repetition are large—both to those retained and those who must pay for repeated schooling. Another concern is that the presence of older students creates serious management problems for schools. Most important, the available evidence shows that retention has no lasting educational benefits. It typically leads to lower achievement than promotion and yields higher school dropout rates.

Thus, it is crucial to consider alternatives to simple test-based retention. For example, it is possible to imagine an educational system in which test-based promotion standards are combined with effective diagnosis and remediation of learning problems. Yet past experience suggests that American school systems may not have either the will or the means to enact such fair and effective practices. Such a system would include well-designed and carefully aligned curricular standards, performance standards, and assessments. Teachers would be well trained to meet high standards in their classrooms, and students would have ample notice of what they are expected to know and be able to do. Students with learning difficulties would be identified years in advance of high-stakes deadlines, and they and their parents and teachers would have ample opportunities to catch up before deadlines occur. Accountability for student performance would not rest solely or even primarily on individual students, but also, collectively, on educators and parents. There is no positive example of such a system in the United States, past or present, whose success is documented by credible research.

Some policymakers and practitioners favor an intermediate approach. They have rejected the simplistic alternatives of promoting or retaining students based on test scores. Instead, they favor testing early to identify students whose performance is weak, providing remedial education to help such students acquire the skills necessary to pass the test, and giving students multiple opportunities to retake different forms of the test in the hope that they will pass and avoid retention. Here, testing can play an important and positive role in early diagnosis and targeted remediation.

Intervention strategies appear to be particularly crucial from kindergarten through grade 2.[68] Some of the intensive strategies being used at this level include expanding preschool programs, giving children who are seriously behind their age-level peers opportunities to accelerate their instruction, and putting children in smaller classes with expert teachers.[69] Such strategies are being implemented in school districts across the country.[70] Data on their effectiveness are as yet unavailable.

These alternatives to social promotion and simple retention in grade should be tried and evaluated. At present only thirteen states require and fund such intervention programs to help low-performing students reach the state standards, and six additional states require intervention but provide no resources for carrying it out.[71] In my judgment, however, the effectiveness of such approaches will depend on the quality of the instruction that students receive after failing a promotion test, and it will be neither simple nor inexpensive to provide high-quality remedial instruction.

# CHAPTER NINE

# High-Stakes Testing and Civil Rights
## Standards of Appropriate Test Use
## and a Strategy for Enforcing Them*

## JAY P. HEUBERT

A s part of the national movement for standards-based reform in
public education, more and more states—about twenty at present—require students to pass large-scale, state tests as a condition of
receiving high school diplomas. Similarly, in response to concerns
about "social promotion," a growing number of states and school
districts now require students to pass standardized tests as a condition
of grade-to-grade promotion. Moreover, English-language learners
and students with disabilities are increasingly subject to these testing
requirements.[1]

* An earlier version of this article was presented at the Conference on the Civil
Rights Implications of High-Stakes Testing, held in New York City on December 6,
1998, under the sponsorship of the Civil Rights Project at Harvard University,
Columbia University Teachers College, and the Columbia University School of Law,
and published by *West's Education Law Reporter*, vol. 33, pp. 17–33, which holds
the copyright. This article also is based in part on a study by the National Research
Council, Jay P. Heubert and Robert M. Hauser, eds., *High Stakes: Testing for
Tracking, Promotion, and Graduation* (Washington, D.C.: National Academy
Press, 1999). The author is grateful to Robert Hauser, Samuel Messick, Marguerite
Clarke, Michael Feuer, Audrey Qualls, Lorraine McDonnell, and Jennifer
Hochschild for their contributions to pertinent parts of *High Stakes: Testing for
Tracking, Promotion, and Graduation*. The author is also grateful to Dr. Mark
Mendell of the National Institute for Occupational Safety and Health, who pro-
vided examples of federal and local regulations related to public health and welfare
that incorporate professional consensus standards.

By themselves, of course, tests do not produce improved teaching and learning, any more than a thermometer reduces fever. When good tests are used properly, however, the information they provide can contribute to improved teaching and learning. Combined with information from other sources, student test scores can alert educators, students, parents, and policymakers to educational problems and needs—of school districts, schools, teachers, and students—that warrant attention. They also can help identify promising educational practices that ought to be replicated. Conversely, "when test use is inappropriate, especially in making high-stakes decisions about individual students, it can undermine the quality of education and equality of opportunity."[2]

Unfortunately, as a 1999 study of high-stakes testing commissioned by Congress and conducted by the National Research Council (NRC) of the National Academy of Sciences found, some states and school districts use tests for tracking, promotion, and graduation in ways that are inappropriate.[3] For example, it is widely accepted that a test should be valid for the particular purpose for which it is being used. The NRC study—entitled *High Stakes: Testing for Tracking, Promotion, and Graduation* and referred to here as *High Stakes*—endorses this principle.[4] So do the *Standards for Educational and Psychological Testing*, issued jointly in December 1999 by the American Educational Research Association, the American Psychological Association, and the National Council on Measurement in Education and referred to here as the *Joint Standards*. Nonetheless, there is evidence that some tests used for tracking or promotion are not valid for these purposes.[5] Similarly, there is evidence in some states that students are not being taught the knowledge and skills that promotion and graduation tests measure. Such practices are inconsistent with the *Joint Standards*, which say that such tests should cover only the "content and skills that students have had an opportunity to learn,"[6] and with the standards for mastery tests articulated in *High Stakes*.[7]

For minority children, English-language learners, and students with disabilities, appropriate, nondiscriminatory test use is particularly important and the stakes associated with testing are particularly high. Such children tend to do less well on large-scale tests, even when such tests measure only basic skills. In the late 1970s, for example, when "minimum competency tests" gained popularity, 20 percent of black students, compared with 2 percent of white students, failed Florida's graduation tests and were denied high school diplomas.[8] Similarly, 1998 data from the Texas graduation tests show cumulative failure rates of 17.6 percent for black students and 17.4 percent for Hispanic students, compared with 6.7 percent for white students.[9] For students with disabilities, most of whom now participate in large-scale state assessments, recent data from fourteen states consistently show failure rates that are thirty-five to forty percentage points higher than those for nondisabled students.[10]

Moreover, states increasingly are raising the standards on their graduation tests to "world-class" levels, such as those embodied in the National Assessment of Educational Progress (NAEP). Based on 1996 NAEP data, 40 percent of all students would fail tests that reflect "world-class" standards, at least initially, and failure rates for minority students would be about 80 percent.[11] These predictions are consistent with recent data from Massachusetts and New York, where students have begun taking state tests that reflect "world-class" standards.[12] On such tests, failure rates for students with disabilities would be in the range of 75 to 80 percent.[13]

For these students, therefore, it is particularly important that tests be used to promote high-quality education for all children—the stated objective of standards-based reform in education—rather than to penalize students for not knowing what they have not been taught.[14] Unfortunately, as *High Stakes* recognizes, there is at present no satisfactory mechanism for ensuring that test makers and test users respect even widely accepted norms of proper test use.[15] The professional associations that produce the *Joint Standards* encourage compliance but lack monitoring and enforcement mechanisms. For courts and federal civil rights agencies, the reverse is true; they have complaint procedures and enforcement power, but lack specific, legally enforceable standards on the appropriate use of high-stakes tests. As a result, courts typically defer to state and local educators in testing cases, often respecting "local control" even when tests are used in ways that do not appear to meet professional standards.

The remainder of this chapter is divided into three sections. The first describes principles of appropriate test use articulated in *High Stakes* and in the newly promulgated *Joint Standards*, and considers their civil rights implications.[16] The second section explains why current methods of promoting appropriate test use are inadequate. The final section explores a promising strategy for promoting appropriate, nondiscriminatory use of high-stakes tests, under which the U.S. Department of Education would incorporate relevant norms of the testing profession into the legal standards that apply when high-stakes tests have a disproportionate adverse impact by race or national origin. Such an incorporation of professional norms into federal law is not without precedent. Indeed, in December 1999 the department's Office for Civil Rights (OCR) released a draft resource guide that, while not legally binding, aims to promote appropriate use of high-stakes tests.[17] The draft guidelines draw heavily on *High Stakes* and on the *Joint Standards*. It is, however, beyond the scope of this chapter to analyze this OCR draft.

## PRINCIPLES OF APPROPRIATE TEST USE AND THEIR IMPLICATIONS FOR CIVIL RIGHTS

In defining what constitutes appropriate use of tests for tracking, promotion, and graduation, *High Stakes* draws on the norms of the testing profession, reflected in the *Joint Standards*, and on empirical research assessing the effects of high-stakes testing policies and practices. *High Stakes* also adopts a three-part framework, drawn from an earlier NRC study, for determining whether a particular test use is appropriate.[18]

The three principal criteria are:

- *measurement validity:* whether a test is valid for a particular purpose and whether it accurately measures the test taker's knowledge in the content area being tested;

- *attribution of cause:* whether a student's performance on a test reflects knowledge and skill based on appropriate instruction or is attributable to poor instruction or to such factors as language barriers or disabilities unrelated to the skills being tested; and

- *effectiveness of treatment:* whether test scores lead to placements and other consequences that are educationally beneficial for students.[19]

For reasons discussed below, each criterion has important civil rights implications for the use of tests that carry high stakes.

### MEASUREMENT VALIDITY

Under this criterion, there must be evidence that a test is valid for the particular purpose for which it is being used, that the constructs it measures are relevant in making the decision in question, that the test actually measures those constructs, and that the test is reliable and accurate. It is beyond the scope of this chapter to explore these in detail,[20] but these standards have important civil rights implications and warrant at least brief discussion here.

First, there are important differences between *placement* tests, such as tests used for tracking, and *mastery* tests, such as tests used in awarding or withholding high school diplomas. A test used to make promotion decisions could be viewed as either,[21] though most current promotion tests measure mastery.[22]

A placement test is used for predictive purposes: to determine which *future* setting or educational treatment would be most beneficial for particular students. Thus, for example, a test used to assign students to different tracks should provide information about which available level of instruction would most benefit each student. This, in turn, requires a close fit between what the placement test measures and the curriculum in each of the possible tracks in the particular grade and school. Tests intended to measure mastery, such as graduation exams and most promotion tests, should provide a close fit between what the test measures and what students have already been taught in the schools of the state or district that administers the test.[23]

There is evidence, however, that these standards are not always met when tests are used in decisions about tracking, promotion, and graduation.[24] Such validity problems are a civil rights issue for minority students and English-language learners, who are disproportionately placed in low-track classes, retained in grade, and denied high school diplomas on the basis of test scores.

The discrepancy between what graduation tests measure and what students have been taught is likely to be greatest when test standards are high and instruction is weak. As *High Stakes* notes, "to the extent that all students are expected to meet world-class standards, there is a need to provide world-class curriculum and instruction to all students. However, in most of the nation, much needs to be done before a world-class curriculum and world-class instruction will be in place."[25] Moreover, when policymakers use high-stakes tests to spur or "lead" changes in curriculum and instruction, there is inevitably—by design— a gap between what the tests measure and what students have been taught. *High Stakes* therefore recommends that "tests should be used for high-stakes decisions about individual mastery only after implementing changes in teaching and curriculum that ensure that students have been taught the knowledge and skills on which they will be tested."[26] As noted above, the *Joint Standards* take a similar position on the need for a close fit between what mastery tests for promotion and graduation measure and what students have been taught.

Minority students are often overrepresented among those who do not receive high-quality curriculum and instruction, including, for example, being assigned to low-track classes.[27] There are also many students with disabilities whose Individualized Education Plans (IEPs) do not ensure that they receive the instruction they need to pass large-scale promotion and graduation tests. This discrepancy exists in part because such students traditionally have not been included in large-scale assessment programs.[28] Similarly, English-language learners often have not had the opportunity to acquire the levels of English proficiency they need to pass such tests. As a result, these students are among those likeliest to benefit from policies that ensure that students actually have been taught the facts and skills on which they will be tested before the tests are used for high-stakes decisions.

Second, the choice of constructs plays an important role where high-stakes tests are concerned. "If a high-school graduation test emphasizes reading and writing rather than science or mathematics, then graduation rates for males and females, as well as for English-language learners, will be quite different. . . . Any finite number of subjects covered by the test are likely to yield different graduation rates for different groups because they underrepresent the broad construct of school learning."[29] Moreover, such problems are likely to be even greater with new generations of performance assessments, if only because these typically measure fewer constructs than traditional standardized tests do.[30]

There are ways of reducing these and other problems due to the inherent imprecision of test scores,[31] which can be considerable. These include giving tests in a variety of subjects,[32] giving students multiple opportunities to demonstrate mastery before being retained in grade or denied a diploma,[33] and using a test only with groups for which the test constructs are reasonably well measured.[34]

It is also important to weigh information other than test scores in making decisions about student tracking, promotion, and graduation. *High Stakes* emphasizes that educators should always buttress test score information with "other relevant information about the student's knowledge and skills, such as grades, teacher recommendations, and extenuating circumstances" when making high-stakes decisions about individual students.[35] This is consistent with current standards of the testing profession, which state that "in elementary or secondary education, a decision or characterization that will have a major impact on a test taker should not automatically be made on the basis of a single test score. Other relevant information . . . should be taken into account if it will enhance the overall validity of the decision."[36] Current practice is not always consistent with this principle, however, particularly in states and school districts that automatically deny high school diplomas or promotion to students who fail a test, regardless of their performance on other measures of achievement.[37] This, too, is a civil rights issue, both because minority students and English-language learners tend to do less well on such tests and because such students are likelier than white students to be subject to high-stakes promotion or graduation tests in the first place.[38]

## PROPER ATTRIBUTION OF CAUSE

Use of a test is appropriate only if educators and others draw proper inferences from a student's test scores; what requires validation is not the test itself but rather the inferences derived from the test scores and the actions that follow.[39] In order to make the correct inferences, educators need to question some common assumptions. For example, ordinarily people assume both that a student has received proper instruction and that the student's test performance reflects his or her actual knowledge and skill. This is not always the case, however, and the assumption is less often warranted where minority students, English-language learners, and students with certain disabilities are concerned.

A student's poor performance may be attributable to poor instruction. We know, for example, that students in low-track classes, disproportionate numbers of whom are students of color and/or English-language learners, typically receive "far less than a world-class curriculum."[40] This is so even though federal law requires that low-achieving, disadvantaged students receive "accelerated," "enriched," and "high-quality" curricula; "effective instructional strategies"; and "highly qualified instructional staff."[41] Reflecting these realities, the testing profession's *Joint Standards* provide that "when test results substantially contribute to making decisions about student promotion or graduation, there should be evidence that the test adequately covers only the . . . content and skills that the curriculum has afforded students an opportunity to learn."[42] Thus, standards of appropriate test use require test users to teach students the knowledge and skills that promotion and graduation tests measure before students are subject to test-based retention in grade or diploma denials.

Poor performance may also stem from factors unrelated to the knowledge and skills being tested—such as poor health on the day of the test, construct-irrelevant disabilities, or language barriers—that prevent a student from demonstrating what he or she actually knows. For example, if a blind student takes a test without accommodation—using the standard paper-and-pencil version, complete with bubble sheet—it is impossible to tell how much of the student's poor performance is due to the disability and how much is attributable to lack of subject matter knowledge.

Similarly, if an English-language learner scores poorly on a high-stakes mathematics test in English—and mathematics tests increasingly rely on word problems—it is impossible to know what portion of the poor performance is due to limited English proficiency and what portion is attributable to limited knowledge of mathematics. The *Joint Standards* recognize this basic threat to test validity. Standard 7.7 states that "where the level of linguistic or reading ability is not part of the construct of interest, the linguistic or reading demands of the test should be kept to the minimum necessary for the valid assessment of the intended construct."[43]

More generally, there is a duty to investigate competing explanations of poor performance. "It is imperative to account for various plausible rival interpretations of low test performance [such as] anxiety, inattention, low motivation, fatigue, limited English proficiency, or certain sensory handicaps other than low ability."[44] "Influences associated with variables such as socioeconomic status, ethnicity, gender, cultural background, or age may also be relevant."[45]

Last but not least, when test performance differs across groups, there is an obligation to collect, report, and analyze relevant data on such differences. *High Stakes* recommends that policymakers "monitor both the intended and unintended consequences of high-stakes assessments on all students and on significant subgroups of students, including minority students, English-language learners, and students with disabilities."[46] The *Joint Standards* provide that "when the use of a test results in outcomes that affect the life chances or educational opportunities of examinees, evidence of mean test score differences should, where feasible, be examined . . . to determine that such differences are not attributable to . . . construct-irrelevant variance."[47]

In sum, test makers and test users are under an obligation to report, examine, and discount plausible rival interpretations of low scores, particularly for minority students, English-language learners, students with disabilities, and students who may have received poor instruction. Implementation of these standards would benefit many students in these groups.

### EFFECTIVENESS OF TREATMENT

Under this criterion, a test use is appropriate only if test scores lead to placements and other consequences that are educationally beneficial for the students who are subject to the treatment or placement; it is inappropriate to use tests to place students in settings that are demonstrably ineffective educationally. According to the *Joint Standards*, "the validity of test scores for placement or promotion decisions rests, in part, upon evidence about whether students, in fact, benefit from the differential instruction." This principle is consistent with established standards of the profession, which consider consequential validity, that is, the effectiveness of resulting treatments, to be an important aspect of appropriate test use.[48]

Thus, for example, a 1982 study of special education placements concluded that "decisions about a student's track placement should be based on predictions about what track will produce the most beneficial expected educational outcome for the student [being placed]."[49] Even if a test has strong predictive validity, there is a need for further evidence that children will learn more effectively in one setting than another.[50]

Based on a careful review of empirical research, *High Stakes* concludes that certain placements and treatments are typically ineffective, whether based on test scores or other information. One such treatment is simple retention in grade, where students are obliged to repeat, without effective educational interventions, the very grades they have just failed:

> Grade retention policies typically have positive intentions but negative consequences. The intended positive consequences are that students will be more motivated to learn and will consequently acquire the knowledge and skills they need at each grade level. The negative consequences, as grade retention is currently practiced, are that retained students persist in low achievement levels and are likely to drop out of school. Low-performing students who have been retained in kindergarten or primary grades lose ground both academically and socially relative to similar students who have been promoted. In secondary school, grade retention leads to reduced achievement and much higher rates of school dropout. At present, the negative consequences of grade retention policies typically outweigh the intended positive effects. Simple retention in grade is an ineffective intervention.[51]

*High Stakes* reaches a similar conclusion about placement of students in typical low-track classes: "As tracking is currently practiced, low-track classes are typically characterized by an exclusive focus on basic skills, low expectations, and the least-qualified teachers. Students assigned to low-track classes are worse off than they would be in other placements. This form of tracking should be eliminated. Neither test scores nor other information should be used to place students in such classes."[52]

The weight of the research evidence on the negative consequences of simple retention in grade and placement in typical low-track classes suggests an emerging consensus among scholars on these points. The use of test scores or other information for such purposes is therefore inappropriate: "Neither a test score nor any other kind of information can justify a bad decision."[53] These findings have obvious civil rights implications because minority students, English-language learners, and students with certain disabilities are highly overrepresented among those retained in grade and placed in low-track classes.

In sum, *High Stakes* offers general criteria of appropriate test use—measurement validity, proper attribution of cause, and effectiveness of treatment—that apply broadly to existing and new tests used for student tracking, promotion, and graduation and that have important implications for students of color, English-language learners, and students with disabilities.

## WHY STANDARDS OF APPROPRIATE TEST USE ARE NOT ENFORCED

If the standards of appropriate test use described above were enforced consistently, many existing high-stakes testing programs would look quite different, and there would be closer scrutiny of tracking, promotion, and graduation tests that produce disproportionate adverse impact. Improper test use is due, in part, to the fact that standards of appropriate test use are unenforced and, at present, unenforceable. Congress recognized as much when it asked the NRC to identify not only norms of appropriate, nondiscriminatory test use but also "methods, practices, and safeguards" to help ensure that test developers and test users actually abide by such norms.

The problem is that both of the existing mechanisms for promoting appropriate test use—professional discipline and legal enforcement—have been ineffective.[54] The remainder of this section focuses on why this is so. It turns out that the two existing methods have complementary shortcomings: the profession has detailed norms of appropriate test use but no mechanisms for enforcing them, while the legal system has well-established enforcement mechanisms but poorly defined standards of appropriate test use.

### PROFESSIONAL DISCIPLINE

Most of the professional standards that govern educational testing have their source in the *Joint Standards*[55] and the *Code of Fair Testing Practices in Education*.[56] These standards have been developed by organizations whose members comprise most of the testing profession itself. Recent versions of the *Joint Standards*, moreover, reflect an awareness of, and concern about, the negative effects that high-stakes tests can have on minority students, English-language learners, and students with disabilities. They contain sections focusing in some detail on fairness in testing, testing individuals of different linguistic backgrounds, testing students with disabilities, and "opportunity to learn" issues. They also contain clear statements regarding the obligations of test developers and test users to minimize the negative consequences of improper test use. For example, Standard 13.1 provides that:

> Where educational testing programs are mandated by school, district, state, or other authorities, the ways in which test results are intended to be used should be clearly described. It is the responsibility of those who mandate the use of tests to monitor their impact and to identify and minimize potential negative consequences. Consequences resulting from the uses of the test, both intended and unintended, should also be examined by the test user.[57]

Where professional discipline is concerned, therefore, the problem is not a lack of standards but rather a lack of enforcement mechanisms. In theory, the organizations that promulgate the *Joint Standards* could monitor test use—or at least respond to complaints—and impose sanctions on individuals or organizations that violate norms of appropriate test use. In practice, however, compliance with the *Joint Standards* is voluntary for members of the American Educational Research Association and the National Council on Measurement in Education, most of whom are academics and researchers. These organizations encourage compliance via "ethical guidelines," but they conduct no monitoring of test practice and possess no procedures for investigating complaints or imposing sanctions.[58] The American Psychological Association does have standing policies for monitoring and enforcing its ethical principles, but violations appear to result, at most, in expulsion from the organization.[59]

As a result, compliance depends on the good faith and good judgment of test developers and test users. As the Office of Technology Assessment puts it, "the test-taker's fate rests on the assumption that good testing practice has been upheld by both the test developer when it constructed the test and the test user (such as the school) when it selected, interpreted, and made a decision on the basis of the test."[60] If this assumption were valid, of course, there would be no improper test use.

In reality, test developers are under financial pressure to accommodate the wishes of their customers, who often can take their business elsewhere. It is therefore unusual, though not unheard of, for test developers to challenge publicly test uses that they consider inappropriate.[61] Test users, in turn, are often under strong political pressure to adopt and use tests in ways that may not be consistent with professional standards for test use. For example, in discussing Chicago's decision to rely so heavily on standardized test scores in making promotion decisions, the school district's chief accountability officer said, "we decided to be credible to the public. . . . Our problem comes with explaining it to educators, why we don't use other indicators."[62]

Furthermore, many of those who use tests and test results, including educators, do not know about the *Joint Standards* and are "untrained in appropriate test use."[63] As a result, there is real debate over whether the *Joint Standards* have actually led to improved test use.[64] It is clear, in any event, that the organizations that promulgate the *Joint Standards* do not enforce them in any meaningful way.

## LEGAL CHALLENGES

The second existing mechanism for enforcing norms of appropriate test use is legal enforcement. Federal law often has been used, in fact, to challenge educational tests that have disproportionate adverse impact by race or national origin. Some of these claims rest on constitutional grounds.[65] As discussed below, others are based on civil rights statutes and regulations.

Unlike the professional organizations described above, courts and administrative agencies have no shortage of enforcement mechanisms. Under federal law, students and parents have the legal right to initiate lawsuits if they believe that high-stakes tests discriminate against them on the basis of race or national origin. Certain federal civil rights statutes— including Title VI of the Civil Rights Act of 1964,[66] which prohibits recipients of federal funds from discriminating on the basis of race or national origin—also allow parents and students to file complaints with an administrative agency, the U.S. Department of Education's Office for Civil Rights. The courts and OCR both have procedures for reviewing complaints, determining whether illegal behavior has occurred, and imposing sanctions on wrongdoers.

What federal civil rights law lacks is not enforcement mechanisms but specific standards defining the appropriate use of educational tests. Under Title VI regulations,[67] for example, when a test has "disproportionate, adverse impact" by race or national origin, a recipient of federal funds must show that use of the test is "educationally necessary."[68] But neither Title VI nor its current regulations provide standards that would help define the circumstances under which it is educationally necessary to use a high-stakes test that has disproportionate, adverse impact by race or national origin or under which specific educational treatments or placements are "adverse."

Without such standards, and in the absence of definitive decisions by the U.S. Supreme Court, lower courts have responded inconsistently in cases involving high-stakes educational tests. Various courts have defined "educationally necessary" more or less stringently. Some courts require school officials to show that the test use is "demonstrably necessary to meeting an important educational goal."[69] Others require "a substantial legitimate justification" for the challenged policy or practice,[70] or require proof of a "manifest relationship" between a test requirement and an educational objective.[71] With regard to whether particular educational placements are adverse, some courts have found that low-track placements are educationally beneficial or "remedial," while other courts have found such placements to be educationally harmful "dead ends."[72] No reported decision considers whether simple retention in grade is beneficial or adverse. Courts also have varied in the weight they accord to test-use standards, relying more frequently on test developers' user manuals or on the judgments of state and local educators than on the *Joint Standards* themselves.[73] Finally, some court decisions in testing cases pay little attention to empirical research on how the use of high-stakes tests can affect students' educational opportunities or life chances.[74]

In sum, the existing approaches for promoting appropriate test use have complementary strengths and limitations: professional standards lack enforcement, and federal civil rights enforcement mechanisms lack standards.

## A HYBRID ALTERNATIVE

There is an important need to ensure that high-stakes tests are used appropriately, especially as such test use expands, standards rise, and the number of students likely to fail increases significantly. Congress recognized as much when it commissioned *High Stakes*. But if current mechanisms are inadequate, how are standards of appropriate test use to be enforced? There are a number of possible approaches, which are by no means mutually exclusive.[75]

One promising approach would be to link federal civil rights enforcement with explicit standards of appropriate test use and existing research on the efficacy of different educational placements and treatments. Such a linkage could be achieved if OCR were to adopt standards under Title VI for the use of tests in student tracking, promotion, and graduation. A high-stakes test having disproportionate impact by race or national origin would be considered educationally necessary under Title VI only if the test user (with assistance from the test developer) could show that the test is being used in a manner consistent with applicable standards of appropriate test use such as those discussed above. These standards, together with research findings on which a substantial consensus among scholars has been reached, would also be applied—by courts in judicial proceedings and by OCR in administrative actions—in determining whether educational placements and treatments are beneficial or adverse for the students affected and whether there exist equally feasible alternative assessment methods that have a less disproportionate impact.

A basic question is whether OCR should formulate its own standards of appropriate test use or instead incorporate relevant standards from the *Joint Standards* and scholarly literature such as the *High Stakes* report. Both approaches have precedents. In other contexts, the U.S. Department of Education has adopted detailed regulations as part of OCR's civil rights enforcement activities. Two examples are the regulations adopted under Title IX, a sex discrimination statute,[76] and Section 504, a statute forbidding recipients of federal funds from discriminating on the basis of disability.[77] Moreover, the federal government has already adopted detailed test-use standards, though in the context of employment rather than education.[78]

Precedents also exist for the incorporation of existing professional standards into federal law and regulation. For example, when Congress enacted the Occupational Safety and Health Act of 1970, it expressly required the secretary of labor to promulgate as a federal occupational safety and health standard "any national consensus standard" that national professional organizations had already agreed upon.[79] State and local governments also rely on the standards of various professional organizations in adopting legally binding building codes.[80]

Either approach—formulation of new OCR standards or adoption of relevant existing professional standards—would serve important educational objectives. First, consistent standards of appropriate test use would be enforceable in all states and school districts.[81] Second, publicity about these standards and relevant educational research would help educate policymakers, educators, parents, and students about proper and improper test use, particularly where high-stakes tests have a disproportionate adverse impact. Third, while the enforcement of uniform test-use standards would not eliminate all ambiguities and questions of judgment, it would plainly reduce uncertainty, particularly if the standards are clear and the research indicates substantial consensus among scholars. It would also reduce the need for judges to develop their own standards or for OCR to review complaints on an ad hoc basis.

Several considerations suggest that it would be preferable for the federal government to incorporate relevant existing professional standards for appropriate test use rather than to develop and enforce its own. First, new standards would inevitably differ from, and conflict with, those that already exist. Such differences would spark disputes that would take time and energy to resolve when the need is for timely implementation of appropriate standards that reflect broad consensus.

Second, any decision to adopt enforceable standards for test use under Title VI would produce controversy. Precisely because high-stakes testing is so popular among political leaders, educational policymakers, and the public,[82] any federal effort to regulate it would surely raise objections, including all the usual concerns about intrusive civil rights enforcement, judicial involvement in education, and the role of the federal government in education. In a political climate that favors devolution and a reduced federal role, these concerns could create significant barriers. Rules drafted by the government, however, would probably arouse more resistance than would a decision by the government to adopt relevant standards developed over decades through a process of professional consensus.

In commissioning the study that became *High Stakes*, Congress recognized both the increasingly important role that educational tests play in determining the life chances of young people and the need for new "methods, practices and safeguards" to ensure appropriate, non-discriminatory use of tests for tracking, promotion, and graduation. Decades of experience with the *Joint Standards* have shown that unenforceable standards will not ensure appropriate test use. Similarly, judicial and administrative enforcement of Title VI has not, to date, prevented improper use of high-stakes tests that have disproportionate, adverse impact by race or national origin.

Thus, whether the Department of Education formulates its own standards or incorporates relevant standards that already exist, it is important that such standards be legally enforceable in administrative or judicial proceedings. This, in turn, means that Title VI standards for test use should be promulgated as regulations rather than as guidelines or in some other form.[83] Such an approach, combining enforceable norms of test use with existing law-enforcement mechanisms, would help ensure the integrity of high-stakes testing programs and protect millions of students, especially minority students and English-language learners, against the serious consequences of inappropriate test use.

# $\mathcal{N}otes$

NOTES TO CHAPTER 1

1. National Research Council, Committee on Appropriate Test Use, *High Stakes: Testing for Tracking, Promotion, and Graduation,* Jay P. Heubert and Robert M. Hauser, eds. (Washington, D.C.: National Academy Press, 1999); Sean Reardon, "Eighth-grade Minimum Competency Testing and Early High School Dropout Patterns," paper presented at the annual meeting of the American Educational Research Association, New York, April 1996.
2. Ronald Reagan, "Education," in Fred L. Israel, ed., *Ronald Reagan's Weekly Radio Addresses to the Nation,* vol. 1 (Wilmington, Del.: Scholarly Resources, Inc., 1983), pp. 97–98.
3. National Commission on Excellence in Education, *A Nation at Risk* (Washington, D.C.: U.S. Government Printing Office, 1983).
4. Susan Walton, "States' Reform Efforts Increase as Focus of Issues Shifts," *Education Week,* December 7, 1983, p. 5.
5. In Arkansas, Hillary Clinton headed the Education Standards Committee, which proposed a set of reforms. The committee did not recommend mandatory teacher competency testing, but the idea had more than 75 percent public support in the surveys that Dick Morris was running for Governor Clinton. The resulting legislation, including the bitterly controversial mandatory teacher test, was enacted in a special session of the Arkansas state legislature and led to Governor Bill Clinton's claim to being an "education governor." See David Maraniss, *First in His Class: The Biography of Bill Clinton* (New York: Touchstone Books, 1995), pp. 410–15.
6. Eileen White, "Poll Finds Public Endorsement of School Reforms," *Education Week,* August 31, 1983, pp. 1–10.
7. Chris Pipho, "Tracking the Reforms, Part 12," *Education Week,* May 12, 1986, p. 20.
8. David Hoffman, "George Bush Promises to Keep," *Washington Post,* January 20, 1989, p. A25; *America 2000: An Education Strategy* (Washington, D.C.: U.S. Department of Education, 1991).

9. Bill Clinton and Al Gore, *Putting People First: How We Can All Change America* (New York: Times Books, 1992), pp. 84–85.

10. Howard Kurtz, "Bush and Gore Launch Dueling TV Ads on Education," *Washington Post,* March 18, 2000, p. A5; Peter Schrag, "Education and the Election," *The Nation,* March 6, 2000, http://www.thenation.org.

11. Lynn Olson, "Few States Are Now in Line with Bush Testing Plan," *Education Week,* January 31, 2001, available at http://www.edweek.org.

12. Alan B. Krueger, "Reassessing the View that American Schools are Broken," *Federal Reserve Board of New York Economic Policy Review,* March 1998, p. 31.

13. David C. Berliner and Bruce J. Biddle, *The Manufactured Crisis: Myths, Fraud, and the Attack on America's Public Schools* (Reading, Mass.: Addison-Wesley, 1995), pp. 34–35. (Italics in the original.)

14. Ibid., p. 44.

15. See Christopher Jencks and Meredith Phillips, "America's Next Achievement Test: Closing the Black-White Test Score Gap," *The American Prospect* 40 (September–October 1998): 44–53.

16. David J. Hoff, "Gap Widens between Black and White Students on NAEP," *Education Week,* September 6, 2000, http://www.edweek.org/ew/ewstory.cfm?slug=01naep.h20.

17. Differences in average scores across countries often appear to put the United States in a relatively weak position compared to other nations. However, such averages mask an enormous array of issues and are not an adequate basis for making inferences about national academic performance. For example, different nations have different proportions of their youths in secondary education and test them at different ages. Thus, the U.S. performance looks poorer relative to some other countries that educate smaller proportions of the population and in which secondary school lasts to a later age.

18. John A. Hartigan and Alexandra K. Wigdor, eds., *Fairness in Employment Testing: Validity Generalization, Minority Issues, and the General Aptitude Test Battery* (Washington, D.C.: National Academy of Sciences, 1989).

19. Richard Murnane et al., *The Role of Cognitive Skills in Explaining Inequality in the Earnings of American Workers: Evidence from 1985 and 1991* (Stanford, Calif.: National Center for Postsecondary Improvement, Stanford University, 1988); Richard Murnane, John Willett, and Frank Levy, "The Growing Importance of Cognitive Skills in Wage Determination," *Review of Economics and Statistics* 77 (May 1995): 251–66.

20. Joseph Altonji and Charles Pierret, "Employer Learning and Statistical Discrimination," *Quarterly Journal of Economics* 116, no. 1 (2001): 1–37.

21. The poverty level for a single person in 1993 was $7,463 (*Statistical Abstract of the United States,* U.S. Bureau of the Census, Washington, D.C., 1995, p. 481). Bishop does not provide baseline incomes. We estimate that, given a base of approximately $6,900 for non-MCE graduates, a $694 increase (more than a 10 percent increase) for MCE graduates results in an average estimated income of $7,794. Thus, graduates of MCEs hovered just over the official poverty line, and those of non-MCEs hovered just below it. In real terms,

both remain poor. Neither kind of graduate could readily sustain an independent existence.

22. Robert J. Sternberg, *Successful Intelligence* (New York: Plume, 1996); Robert J. Sternberg and Richard K. Wagner, "Controversies: The g-ocentric View of Intelligence and Job Performance Is Wrong," *Current Directions in Psychological Science* 2, no. 1 (1993): 1–5; *What Work Requires of Schools* (Washington, D.C.: U.S. Department of Labor, Secretary's Commission on Achieving Necessary Skills, 1991, 1992).

23. Signithia Fordham and John Ogbu, "Black Students' School Success: Coping with the 'Burden of "Acting White,"'" *The Urban Review* 18, no. 3 (1986): 176–206; John Ogbu, *Minority Education and Caste: The American System in Cross-Cultural Perspective* (New York: Academic Press, 1978).

24. See, for example, Richard Herrnstein and Charles Murray, *The Bell Curve* (New York: Free Press, 1994).

25. But see Philip J. Cook and Jens Ludwig, "The Burden of 'Acting White': Do Black Adolescents Disparage Academic Achievement?" in Christopher Jencks and Meredith Phillips, eds., *The Black-White Test Score Gap* (Washington, D.C.: Brookings Institution Press, 1998), pp. 375–400.

26. Claude Steele, "A Threat in the Air: How Stereotypes Shape the Intellectual Identities and Performance of Women and African Americans," *American Psychologist* 52, no. 6 (1997): 613–29; Claude Steele and Joshua Aronson, "Stereotype Threat and the Intellectual Performance of African Americans," *Journal of Personality and Social Psychology* 69, no. 5 (1995): 797–811.

27. See, for example, Milbrey W. McLaughlin and Lorrie A. Shepard, *Improving Education through Standards-based Reform: A Report by the National Academy of Education Panel on Standards-based Education Reform* (Stanford, Calif.: The National Academy of Education, 1995).

28. See, for example, Francis X. Clines, "Cheating Report Renews Debate over Use of Tests to Evaluate Schools," *New York Times,* June 12, 2000, p. A16.

29. Richard Elmore and Robert Rothman, eds., *Testing, Teaching, and Learning: A Guide for States and School Districts* (Washington, D.C.: National Academy Press, 1999).

30. For example, in Houston a dramatic rise in the TAAS was not matched by increases in the Stanford 9; on this nationally normed test students performed poorly. Melanie Markley, "HISD Doesn't Shine on National Test," *Houston Chronicle,* March 23, 1998.

31. David Grissmer et al., "Improving Student Achievement: What NAEP Test Scores Tell Us," RAND Corporation, Santa Monica, Calif., 2000.

32. Ibid., p. 59.

33. Walt Haney, "The Myth of the Texas Miracle in Education," *Education Policy Analysis Archives* 8, no. 41 (August 2000): Part 7; Stephen P. Klein et al., "What Do Test Scores in Texas Tell Us?" RAND Corporation, Santa Monica, Calif., 2000.

34. Fordham and Ogbu, "Black Students' School Success"; Ogbu, *Minority Education and Caste.*

35. For example, Linda Darling-Hammond, *Doing What Matters Most: Investing in Quality Teaching* (New York: National Commission on Teaching and

America's Future, 1998); Mark Fetler, "Where Have All the Teachers Gone?" *Education Policy Analysis Archives* 5, no. 2 (January 1997), available at http://olam.ed.asu.edu/epaa.

36. In the fall of 2000, 95 percent of high school seniors passed New York State's required English Regents Exam because the passing score was lowered from 65 to 55. At the 65 score, only 75 percent of the state's seniors would pass and only 53 percent of New York City seniors would pass. Kate Zernike, "Most Seniors Pass Regents Exam with a Lower Cutoff Score," *New York Times,* November 10, 2000, available at http://www.nytimes.com.

37. Walt Haney, *Supplementary Report on Texas Assessment of Academic Skills Exit Test (TAAS-X)* (Chestnut Hill, Mass.: Boston College, 1999); Haney, "The Myth of the Texas Miracle in Education." Martin Carnoy of Stanford University takes issue with Haney's findings. Carnoy and his colleauges associate the rise minority students' retention rates not with the TAAS, but with reforms implemented in Texas in the mid-1980s. Martin Carnoy, Susanna Loeb, and Tiffany L. Smith, "Do Higher State Test Scores in Texas Make for Better School Outcomes?" paper presented at the annual meeting of the American Educational Research Association, New Orleans, April 2000. Haney recently also has stated that the trend toward increased retention and dropout among Texas's minority students first began in the early 1980s. Walt Haney, "Revisiting the Myth of the Texas Miracle in Education: Lessons about Dropout Research and Dropout Prevention," paper presented at "Dropouts in America," conference at the Harvard Graduate School of Education, Cambridge, Mass., January 13, 2001.

38. Haney, *Supplementary Report on Texas Assessment of Academic Skills Exit Test.*

39. Jencks and Phillips, *The Black-White Test Score Gap.*

40. Hoff, "Gap Widens between Black and White Students on NAEP."

41. C. Thomas Holmes, "Grade Level Retention Effects: A Meta-analysis of Research Studies," in Lorrie A. Shepard and Mary Lee Smith, eds., *Flunking Grades: Research and Policies on Retention* (London: Falmer Press, 1989).

42. Karl L. Alexander, Doris R. Entwisle, and Susan L. Dauber, *On the Success of Failure: A Reassessment of the Effects of Retention in the Primary Grades* (Cambridge: Cambridge University Press, 1994).

43. Alfonso Caramazza, Michael McCloskey, and B. Green, "Naive Beliefs in 'Sophisticated' Subjects: Misconceptions about Trajectories of Objects," *Cognition* 9, no. 2 (1981): 117–23; Howard Gardner, *The Unschooled Mind* (New York: Basic Books, 1992); Jean Lave, "The Culture of Acquisition and the Practice of Understanding," in James W. Stigler, Richard A. Shweder, and Gilbert Herdt, eds., *Cultural Psychology: Essays in Comparative Human Development* (Cambridge: Cambridge University Press, 1990).

44. Elmore and Rothman, *Testing, Teaching, and Learning.*

45. American Educational Research Association, American Psychological Association, and National Council on Measurement in Education, *Standards for Educational and Psychological Testing* (Washington, D.C.: American Psychological Association, 1999); National Research Council, *High Stakes.*

46. Paul Black and Dylan Wiliam, "Inside the Black Box: Raising Standards through Classroom Assessment," *Phi Delta Kappan* 80, no. 2 (October 1998): 139–48.

47. Jacques Steinberg, "Student Failure Causes States to Retool Testing Programs," *New York Times,* December 22, 2000, p. A19; Kevin Bushweller, "Delay High-States Graduation Exam, Alaska Board Says," *Education Week,* January 10, 2001, p. 25; Darcia Harvis Bowman, "Arizona Posed to Revisit Graduation Exam," *Education Week,* November 29, 2000, p. 16; Scott S. Greenberger and Sandy Coleman, "State Proposes Changes to MCAS," *Boston Globe,* January 5, 2001; Jessica L. Sandheim, "Calif. Board Votes to Pare Down New Graduation Test," *Education Week,* November 13, 2000, p. 27.

## NOTES TO CHAPTER 2

1. Leon Kamin, *The Science and Politics of IQ* (Potomac, Md.: Lawrence Erlbaum Associates, 1974).

2. Nicholas Lemann, "The Structure of Success in America," *The Atlantic Monthly,* August 1995, available at http://www.theatlantic.com/issues/95sep/ets/grtsort1.htm; Nicholas Lemann, "The Great Sorting," *The Atlantic Monthly,* September 1995, available at http://www.theatlantic.com/issues/95sep/ets/grtsort2.htm.

3. Alexandra K. Wigdor and Wendell R. Garner, eds., *Ability Testing: Uses, Consequences, and Controversies* (Washington, D.C.: National Academy Press, 1982), pp. 119–51.

4. Patricia Broadfoot, *Education, Assessment and Society* (Buckingham, England: Open University Press, 1996); Allan Hansen, *Testing Testing: The Social Consequences of the Examined Life* (Berkeley: University of California Press, 1994).

5. Kamin, *The Science and Politics of IQ.*

6. Alabama, Florida, Georgia, Hawaii, Indiana, Louisiana, Maryland, Massachusetts, Michigan, Minnesota, Mississippi, Nevada, New Jersey, New Mexico, New York, North Carolina, Ohio, South Carolina, Tennessee, Texas, Virginia, and West Virginia.

7. Alaska, Illinois, Maine, Oregon, and Pennsylvania.

8. Michigan, New York, and Tennessee.

9. New York, Ohio, and Tennessee.

10. Bruce L. Wilson and Gretchen B. Rossman, *Mandating Academic Excellence* (New York: Teachers College Press, 1993); William A. Firestone, Margaret E. Goertz, and Gary Natriello, *From Cashbox to Classroom* (New York: Teachers College Press, 1997).

11. Kennon M. Sheldon and Bruce J. Biddle, "Standards, Accountability, and School Reform: Perils and Pitfalls," *Teachers College Record* 100, no. 1 (1998): 164–80.

12. National Research Council, Committee on Appropriate Test Use, *High Stakes: Testing for Tracking, Promotion, and Graduation,* Jay P. Heubert and Robert M. Hauser, eds. (Washington, D.C.: National Academy Press, 1999).

13. Decision of Judge Edward C. Prado, *GI Forum et al.* v. *Texas Education Agency et al.,* Civil Action no. SA-97-CA-1728-EP, January 7, 2000, p. 2.

14. Linda Darling-Hammond and Beverly Falk, "Policy for Authentic Assessment," in A. Lin Goodwin, ed., *Assessment for Equity and Inclusion: Embracing All Our Children* (New York and London: Routledge, 1997).

15. *The Strategy for Raising Standards* (Albany: New York State Education Department, 1995).

16. New York State Education Department, "Q&A—New Assessment System: Message from the Deputy Commissioner," *School Executive's Bulletin,* June/July 1996.

17. New York State Education Department, "Questions and Answers: Raising Standards, Building Local Capacity, and Reporting Results," *School Executive's Bulletin,* May 1996.

18. *Regents Examinations, Regents Competency Tests, and Proficiency Examinations—School Administrators Manual* (Albany: New York State Education Department, 1996).

19. *Statistical Profiles of Public School Districts* (Albany: New York State Education Department, 1997).

20. Here we are treating limited English proficiency as an exogenous factor reflecting student background, rather than as an endogenous factor reflecting school effectiveness.

21. *Minnesota Graduation Standards Planning Guide for Parents of Children with Disabilities,* Minnesota Department of Children, Families, and Learning, 1998, available at http://children.state.mn.us/grad/special%20ed.htm.

22. *Basic Standards Testing: Establishing a District Process for Including Limited English Proficient (LEP) Students,* Minnesota Department of Children, Families, and Learning, 1998, available at http://cfl.state.mn.us/GRAD/inclus.htm.

23. Roy Wilkins Center for Human Relations and Social Justice, *Analysis of the 1996 Minnesota Basic Standards Test Data,* Hubert H. Humphrey Institute of Public Affairs, University of Minnesota, Minneapolis, 1997.

24. Claude Steele, "A Threat in the Air: How Stereotypes Shape Intellectual Identity and Performance," *American Psychologist* 52, no. 6 (June 1997): 613–29.

NOTES TO CHAPTER 3

1. National Center on Education and the Economy, *America's Choice: High Skills or Low Wages* (Rochester, N.Y.: National Center on Education and the Economy, 1990); National Commission on Excellence in Education, *A Nation at Risk* (Washington, D.C.: U.S. Government Printing Office, 1983).

2. *The National Education Goals Report: Building a Nation of Learners* (Washington, D.C.: National Education Goals Panel, 1992), p. xi.

3. National Research Council, Committee on Appropriate Test Use, *High Stakes: Testing for Tracking, Promotion, and Grade Retention,* Jay P. Heubert and Robert M. Hauser, eds. (Washington, D.C.: National Academy Press, 1998).

4. John H. Bishop and Ferran Mane report in this volume that graduation from a high school requiring minimum competency tests is a significant predictor of wages and earnings. They use the term significant to refer to statistical significance, which means that repeated sampling of a population would be unlikely to obtain by chance the difference in wages and earnings associated with minimum competency testing. However, with very large samples, even a small relationship can be statistically significant without being socially significant. My argument is that these relationships tend to be small—so small that they are not useful for allocating workers to positions or generating predictions about individual worker productivity. Their predictive validities are so low that any strict use will result in massive injustices and misallocations of workers. In fact, in Table 4.7 of their appendix it appears that most of the estimates are not even statistically significant. For example, of eighteen estimates by socioeconomic status of the earnings associated with graduation from a high school that required a minimum competency test, only three of the coefficients were statistically significant.

5. The following analysis draws heavily upon my own recent work, but I add to this evidence the findings of several other studies. See Henry Levin, "Educational Performance Standards and the Economy," *Educational Researcher* 27, no. 4 (May 1998): 4–10.

6. Edwin Ghiselli, *The Validity of Occupational Aptitude Tests* (New York: John Wiley and Sons, 1966).

7. John A. Hartigan and Alexandra K. Wigdor, eds., *Fairness in Employment Testing: Validity Generalization, Minority Issues, and the General Aptitude Test Battery* (Washington, D.C.: National Academy of Sciences, 1989).

8. John Bishop, "Incentives for Learning: Why American High School Students Compare Poorly to Their Counterparts Overseas," in Commission on Workforce Quality and Labor Market Efficiency, U.S. Department of Labor, ed., *Investing in People: A Strategy to Address America's Workforce Crisis,* Background Papers, vol. 1 (Washington, D.C.: U.S. Government Printing Office, 1989), pp. 1–84.

9. Francisco Rivera-Batiz, "Quantitative Skills and Economic Success in the Labor Market," *IUME Briefs* (New York: Institute for Urban and Minority Education, Teachers College, Columbia University, 1994).

10. Richard Murnane et al., *The Role of Cognitive Skills in Explaining Inequality in the Earnings of American Workers: Evidence from 1985 and 1991* (Stanford, Calif.: National Center for Postsecondary Improvement, Stanford University, 1998).

11. See, for example, ibid.; Richard Murnane, John Willett, and Frank Levy, "The Growing Importance of Cognitive Skills in Wage Determination," *Review of Economics and Statistics* 77 (May 1995): 251–66; Rivera-Batiz, "Quantitative Skills and Economic Success in the Labor Market."

12. Murnane et al., *The Role of Cognitive Skills in Explaining Inequality in the Earnings of American Workers;* Murnane, Willett, and Levy, "The Growing Importance of Cognitive Skills in Wage Determination."

13. James S. Coleman and Thomas Hoffer, *Public and Private High Schools* (New York: Basic Books, 1987).

14. Ibid.; Murnane, Willett, and Levy, "The Growing Importance of Cognitive Skills in Wage Determination."

15. Steven W. Raudenbush and Rafa M. Kasim, "Cognitive Skill and Economic Inequality: Findings from the National Adult Literacy Survey," *Harvard Educational Review* 68, no. 1 (Spring 1998): 33–79.

16. Irwin S. Kirsch et al., *Adult Literacy in America: A First Look at the Results of the National Adult Literacy Survey* (Washington, D.C.: National Center for Education Statistics, U.S. Department of Education, 1993).

17. Raudenbush and Kasim, "Cognitive Skill and Economic Inequality," p. 48.

18. The interpretation of the relation between literacy and earnings from the NALS data by Bishop and Mane in this volume overstates the degree to which test scores "predict" earnings in this data set because earnings also "predict" test scores through the occupational placements reinforcing literacy skills that are associated with different earnings levels.

19. Carmi Schooler, "Psychological Effects of Complex Environments during the Life Span," in Carmi Schooler and K. Warner Schaie, eds., *Cognitive Functioning and Social Structure over the Life Course* (Norwood, N.J.: Ablex, 1987), pp. 24–49.

20. Organisation for Economic Co-operation and Development (OECD) and Statistics Canada, *Literacy, Economy, and Society* (Paris: OECD, 1995), pp. 87–114.

21. Murnane et al., *The Role of Cognitive Skills in Explaining Inequality in the Earnings of American Workers.*

22. Derek A. Neal and Willam R. Johnson, "The Role of Premarket Factors in Black-White Wage Differences," *Journal of Political Economy* 104, no. 5 (1996): 869–95.

23. David Grissmer, Ann Flanagan, and Stephanie Williamson, "Does Money Matter for Minority and Disadvantaged Students? Assessing the New Empirical Evidence," in William J. Fowler, Jr., ed., *Developments in School Finance, 1997,* NCES 98-212 (Washington, D.C.: National Center for Education Statistics, U.S. Department of Education, 1998), pp. 13–30.

24. See, for example, Raudenbush and Kasim, "Cognitive Skill and Economic Inequality."

25. Neal and Johnson, "The Role of Premarket Factors in Black-White Wage Differences."

26. William R. Johnson and Derek Neal, "Basic Skills and the Black-White Earnings Gap," in Christopher Jencks and Meredith Phillips, eds., *The Black-White Test Score Gap* (Washington, D.C.: Brookings Institution, 1998), pp. 480–97.

27. Samuel Bowles and Herb Gintis, *Productive Skills, Labor Discipline, and the Returns to Schooling* (Amherst, Mass.: Department of Economics, University of Massachusetts, 1996).

28. Samuel Bowles and Herb Gintis, *Schooling in Capitalist America* (New York: Basic Books, 1976).

29. Robert Sternberg, *Successful Intelligence: How Practical and Creative Intelligence Determine Success in Life* (New York: Plume, 1997).

30. Raudenbush and Kasim, "Cognitive Skill and Economic Inequality."

31. Gordon Berlin and Andrew Sum, *Toward a More Perfect Union: Basic Skills, Poor Families and Our Economic Future,* Occasional Paper 3 (New York: Ford Foundation Project on Social Welfare and the American Future, 1988).

32. Earl Hunt, *Will We Be Smart Enough?* (New York, Russell Sage Foundation, 1995).

33. Hartigan and Wigdor, *Fairness in Employment Testing,* pp. 149–71.

34. John E. Hunter and Frank L. Schmidt, "Fitting People to Jobs: The Impact of Personnel Selection on National Productivity," in Marvin D. Dunnette and Edwin A. Fleishman, eds., *Human Capability Assessment* (Hillsdale, N.J.: Lawrence Erlbaum Associates, 1982), Chapter 7.

35. Hartigan and Wigdor, *Fairness in Employment Testing,* pp. 235–48; Henry M. Levin, "Ability Testing for Job Selection: Are the Economic Claims Justified?" in Bernard Gifford, ed., *Test Policy and the Politics of Opportunity Allocation: The Workplace and the Law* (Boston: Kluwer Academic Publishers, 1989), pp. 211–32.

36. Jeremy D. Finn and Charles M. Achilles, "Answers and Questions about Class Size: A Statewide Experiment," *American Educational Research Journal* 27, no. 3 (1990): 557–77.

37. *What Work Requires of Schools* (Washington, D.C.: U.S. Department of Labor, Secretary's Commission on Achieving Necessary Skills, 1991, 1992).

38. *New Standards Student Performance Standards,* vols. 1–3 (Washington, D.C.: New Standards, 1997).

39. Russell Rumberger and Henry M. Levin, "Schooling for the Modern Workplace," in Commission on Workforce Quality and Labor Market Efficiency, U.S. Department of Labor, ed., *Investing in People,* vol. 1, pp. 85–143.

40. Lauren Resnick and John Wirt, eds., *Linking School and Work: Roles for Standards and Assessment* (San Francisco: Jossey-Bass, 1996).

41. Robert L. Linn, "Work Readiness Assessment: Questions of Validity," in Resnick and Wirt, *Linking School and Work,* p. 246.

42. Jong-Il Kim and Lawrence J. Lau, "The Sources of Economic Growth in the East Asian Newly Industrialized Countries," *Canadian Journal of Economics* 29, no. 2 (1996): S448-454.

43. For example, see references in Henry Levin and Carolyn Kelley, "Can Education Do It Alone?" *Economics of Education Review* 13, no. 2 (June 1994): 97–108; David Levine, *Reinventing the Workplace: How Business and Employees Can Both Win* (Washington, D.C.: Brookings Institution, 1996).

44. Sandra E. Black and Lisa M. Lynch, "How to Compete: The Impact of Workplace Practices and Information Technology on Productivity," *NBER Working Paper* No. 6120 (Cambridge, Mass.: National Bureau of Economic

Research, 1997); Claire Brown, Michael Reich, and David Stern, "Becoming a High-Performance Work Organization: The Role of Security, Employee Involvement, and Training," *The International Journal of Human Resource Management* 4, no. 2 (1993): 247–75; Levin and Kelley, "Can Education Do It Alone?"; Levine, *Reinventing the Workplace.*

45. The opposite is also true. That is, 42 percent of those with scores one standard deviation above the mean would be expected to have job productivity levels below the mean, and about one-third of those two standard deviations above the mean (the top 3 percent of the test population) would be expected to have job productivity levels below the mean.

46. *What Work Requires of Schools*; Sternberg, *Successful Intelligence.*

47. Wendy Hopfenberg et al., *The Accelerated Schools Resource Guide* (San Francisco: Jossey-Bass, 1993).

48. Mark Kelman, "Concepts of Discrimination in 'General Ability' Job Testing," *Harvard Law Review* 104, no. 6 (1991): 1158–1247.

NOTES TO CHAPTER 4

1. Caroline Hendrie, "Urban League Effort Targets Young Achievers," *Education Week,* July 14, 1999.

2. James A. Kulik and Chen-Lin Kulik, "Effects of Accelerated Instruction on Students," *Review of Educational Research* 54, no. 3 (Fall 1984): 409–25; David Monk, "Subject Area Preparation of Secondary Mathematics and Science Teachers and Student Achievement," *Economics of Education Review* 13, no. 2 (1994): 125–45; John Bishop, "The Impact of Curriculum-Based External Examinations on School Priorities and Student Learning," *International Journal of Education Research* 23, no. 8 (1996): 3–124.

3. Pam Belluck, "Reason Is Sought for Lag by Blacks in School Effort," *New York Times,* July 4, 1999, pp. 1, 15.

4. M. Ward, "A Day in the Life," *New York Teacher* (January 1994).

5. Interview with counselor at a wealthy suburban school, August 1997.

6. Arthur G. Powell, Eleanor Farrar, and David Cohen, *The Shopping Mall High School: Winners and Losers in the Educational Marketplace* (Boston: Houghton Mifflin, 1985), p. 9.

7. Surveys of college admission officers suggest they are increasing the weight that they attach to taking rigorous courses in high school and doing well in these courses. Grades in high school have always been the number one consideration. Standardized test scores have now become the second most important consideration, displacing class rank. Class rank is becoming less important because an increasing number of high schools are refusing to calculate class rank. National Association of College Admission Counselors, 1993, as reported in the *Ithaca Journal,* October 23, 1993.

8. Jean Johnson and Steve Farkas, *Getting By: What American Teenagers Think about Their Schools* (New York: Public Agenda, 1997), pp. 1–54.

9. The analyses by Lillard and by Lillard and DeCicca of longitudinal data from the National Education Longitudinal Study in 1988 (NELS: 88) found that different specifications produced different estimates of their impact on dropout rates. Models that controlled for state fixed effects and examined the effect of introducing a state MCE tended to find no effect. Dean Lillard, "The Effects of State Mandates and Markets on Time to Completion and High School Dropout Decisions," College of Human Ecology, Cornell University, Ithaca, N.Y., 1997, pp. 1–32; Dean Lillard and Phillip DeCicca, "The Effects of State Graduation Requirements on High School Dropout Decisions," College of Human Ecology, Cornell University, Ithaca, N.Y., 1997, pp. 1–27; Dean Lillard and Phillip DeCicca, "State Education Policy and Dropout Behavior: An Empirical Investigation," College of Human Ecology, Cornell University, Ithaca, N.Y., 1997, pp. 1–23.

10. Richard P. Phelps, Thomas M. Smith, and Nabeel Alsalam, *Education in States and Nations* (Washington, D.C.: U.S. Department of Education, National Center for Education Statistics, 1996), pp. 73, 149.

11. The population of seventeen-year-olds was used as the base rather than eighteen-year-olds because the number of eighteen-year-olds may be inflated by in-migration of college students and military personnel.

12. Since information from the two different sources is not completely consistent, separate regressions were run using indicators of state graduation requirements taken from each source.

13. The control variables characterizing the demographic background of the state's high school–age youth were as follows: a parents' education index, equal to the average of the percentage of parents with a high school diploma and the percentage of parents with a university degree; incidence of poverty for children under eighteen; the percentage of the population that is foreign born; the percentage of public school students who are African American; and the percentage of public school students who are Hispanic.

14. A dummy variable for New York State was used to test whether the voluntary Regents exams have any impact on dropout rates.

15. The results of the regression analysis are presented in Table 4.5. Four of the six coefficients on the state MCE variable are negative, but none comes even close to statistical significance at the 10 percent level. The only significant coefficient on the MCE variable is positive.

16. For graduation rates, the variable for Carnegie unit requirements is negative and similar in magnitude to the enrollment rate regressions, but far from statistical significance.

17. Barbara Lerner, "Good News about American Education," *Commentary* 91, no. 3 (1990): 19–25.

18. Causal effects will be smaller because early literacy levels influence completed schooling, because additional schooling raises literacy, and because working in white-collar and professional and managerial jobs raises literacy and increases the probability of returning to school for further education.

19. J. C. Hauser and Thomas M. Daymont, "Schooling, Ability and Earnings: Cross-sectional Evidence 8–14 Years after High School," *Sociology of Education*

50 (July 1977): 182–206; Paul Taubman and Terence Wales, "Education as an Investment and a Screening Device," in F. Thomas Juster, ed., *Education, Income and Human Behavior* (New York: McGraw-Hill, 1975); Henry Farber and Robert Gibbons, "Learning and Wage Dynamics," *Quarterly Journal of Economics* 111, no. 3 (1996), pp. 1007–47.

20. M. H. Brenner, "The Use of High School Data to Predict Work Performance," *The Journal of Applied Psychology* 52, no. 1 (1968): 29–30; *General Aptitude Test Battery Manual* (Washington, D.C.: U.S. Department of Labor, 1970); John Hartigan and Alexandra K. Wigdor, *Fairness in Employment Testing* (Washington, D.C.: National Academy Press, 1989); John Bishop, "The Productivity Consequences of What Is Learned in High School," *Journal of Curriculum Studies* 22, no. 2 (1990): 101–26.

21. Richard Murnane, John Willett, and Frank Levy, "The Growing Importance of Cognitive Skills in Wage Determination," *Review of Economics and Statistics* 77, no. 2 (May 1995): 251–66.

22. Joseph Altonji and Charles Pierret, "Employer Learning and Statistical Discrimination," *Quarterly Journal of Economics* 116, no. 1 (2001): 1–37.

23. Science, civics, and writing are included in the MCE assessments of New York, New Jersey, Ohio, Massachusetts, and many other states.

24. Bishop, "The Productivity Consequences of What Is Learned in High School."

25. "America's Toughest Assignments: Solving the Education Crisis," CBS Special, September 6, 1990.

26. The regression models predicting college attendance and wages included controls for reading and math test scores in grade 12; grade point average; courses taken in high school, whether courses were remedial or honors; extracurricular activities; paid employment during senior year; TV and homework hours; religion; reading for pleasure; attitudes; a disabilities indicator; family demographics; marital and parental status at the end of grade 12; dummies for region and for rural, suburban, or urban residence; and six variables describing the quality of the school. The variables describing the quality of the school were a dummy variable for Catholic schools and for other private schools, average teacher salary, proportion of teachers with a master's degree or higher, average daily pupil attendance rate, and principal reports of school problems. When wage rates or earnings is the dependent variable, months attending college full-time and months attending college part-time (both current and past) are included as control variables. Otherwise the models predicting wages and the models predicting college attendance were the same. The results of the analysis for graduates categorized by gender and by reading and mathematics test scores are presented in Table 4.6. Results for graduates categorized by socioeconomic status and ethnicity are presented in Table 4.7.

27. Over the course of the 1980s, jobs became more cognitively complex and employers started demanding higher-level cognitive skills. An increase in the payoff in relation to years of schooling resulted. The rise in the wage premium for graduating from an MCE high school during the 1980s documented here is probably part of the same phenomenon.

28. The MCE coefficient for the low test score group is not significantly less than zero, but it is significantly smaller than the coefficient in the middle test score group. This may reflect the fact that around 1990, many education reformers, such as the late Albert Shanker, began urging employers to reward achievement in high school. Employers in jurisdictions with MCEs were apparently more responsive to these urgings. The reward for reading and math achievement in high school apparently has risen more in communities with MCE graduation requirements than in communities without such requirements.

29. Sherman N. Tinkelman, "Regents Examinations in New York State after 100 Years," State University of New York, State Department of Education, Albany, N.Y., 1966, p. 12.

30. Ibid.

31. The stakes for teachers and school administrators were higher because information on numbers of students taking and passing each exam were published in local newspapers and on the Internet. While students' stakes were low compared to European and Asian curriculum-based examination systems, they appear to have been sufficient to improve the achievement of New York students substantially. When the socioeconomic characteristics of students are controlled, New York students outperform comparable students in other states by about one grade level equivalent. See John Bishop, Joan Y. Moriarty, and Ferran Mane, "Diplomas for Learning, Not Seat Time: The Impacts of New York Regents Examinations," *Economics of Education Review* 19, no. 4 (2000): 333–49.

32. Charisse Jones, "New York City to Stiffen Rules for Graduating," *New York Times,* May 2, 1994, p. A1.

33. For example, in the new Regents English exam, four essays written under timed conditions, responding to source material or literature, account for more than half of the points in the exam. The following is an example of a writing prompt: "Write a critical essay in which you discuss two pieces of literature you have read from the perspective of the statement that is provided to you in the 'critical lens.' In your essay, provide a valid interpretation of the statement as you have interpreted it, and support your opinion using specific references to appropriate literary elements from the two works. (Critical lens: 'The test of a courageous person is the ability to bear defeat without losing heart.')" The following is another sample prompt: "Write an article for the community health newsletter. Using relevant information from text and graphs, discuss the factors that influence teenage smoking and the implications of those factors for reducing teenage smoking." See http://www.nysed.gov/rscs/test123.html for examples of the new Regents exams, scoring rubrics, and a complete description of the testing program.

34. The method of drawing the sample and conducting the interviews is described in David Monk and Samid Hussein, "Resource Allocation Implications of Increased High School Graduation Expectations," in Jim Wycoff, ed., *Educational Finance to Support High Learning Standards* (Albany, N.Y.: New York State Board of Regents, 1997). The site visitors wrote a short report about

each district. In eight of the school districts, interviews were recorded. About sixty hours of tape were generated.

35. From taped interviews conducted as part of the All Regents Study, a study directed by Bill Miles, district superintendent of the Otsego Northern Catskills, Board of Cooperative Extension Services.

36. Ibid.

37. Ibid.

38. Ibid.

39. Ibid.

40. Ibid.

41. Ibid.

42. Ibid.

43. This recommendation was intended to induce school districts to consider ending social promotion at transitions between elementary and middle school and between middle and high school. It leaves the decision in the hands of local school boards, teachers, and administrators. State mandates on grade promotion specifying competencies that must be achieved are not feasible or desirable. The committee felt that the best way of responding to the needs of struggling students was to provide extra instruction during the school year and during the summer. The threat of retention in grade is, currently, often used to induce students to attend summer school or after-school programs. Since students naturally want to move up to the next grade with their friends, the possibility of being retained (particularly at transitions between buildings) is a powerful incentive to study. Yet, it should be employed only as a last resort. Grade retention rates are quite high in grade 9 in New York State. It might make more sense to make graduation from middle school more contingent on student achievement in order to induce middle school students to work harder and their teachers to set higher standards.

44. Safety Net Study Group, "Providing Fairness and Maintaining High Standards for All Students," report to the commissioner of education, New York State Education Department, Albany, N.Y., June 1998, pp. 1–28.

45. Interview conducted by John Bishop of "Bob," a teacher in Calgary, Alberta, Canada, May 1996.

46. New York State Board of Regents, *State Aid to Public Schools in New York State,* draft recommendations, November 1998, http://stateaid.nysed.gov/regents99.html.

47. Bishop, "The Impact of Curriculum-Based External Examinations on School Priorities and Student Learning."

48. Ibid.

49. Altonji and Pierret, "Employer Learning and Statistical Discrimination."

## NOTES TO CHAPTER 5

1. This is a grim scenario that continues to be taken for granted and hawked by many observers, commentators, commissions, academics, and policymakers. There are, however, opposing arguments based on substantial evidence that

our educational problems have been vastly overgeneralized and are neither universal nor nation-threatening. Nonetheless, good news about the public schools is either ignored or gets short shrift. See David C. Berliner, "Mythology and the American System of Education," *Phi Delta Kappan* 75, no. 8 (1993): 632–40; Gerald W. Bracey, "The Second Bracey Report on the Condition of Public Education," *Phi Delta Kappan* 74, no. 2 (1992): 104–17; Gerald W. Bracey, "The Third Bracey Report on the Condition of Public Education," *Phi Delta Kappan* 75, no. 2 (1993): 104–17; George F. Madaus, "Do We Have a Crisis in Education? The Fashioning and Amending of Public Knowledge and Discourse about Public Schools," address at the annual meeting of the American Educational Research Association, San Francisco, April 17, 1995; Daniel Tanner, "A Nation 'Truly' at Risk," *Phi Delta Kappan* 75, no. 4 (1993): 288–97. For a full discussion of why the proclamation of generalized bad news eclipses the good, see George F. Madaus, "Do We Have a Crisis in Education?"

2. *From Gatekeeper to Gateway: Transforming Testing in America* (Chestnut Hill, Mass.: National Commission on Testing and Public Policy, 1990).

3. For a more complete listing of the purported benefits of high-stakes "authentic" assessments, see George F. Madaus, "A National Testing System: Manna from Above: An Historical/Technological Perspective," *Educational Assessment* 1, no. 1 (1993): 9–26.

4. Jay R. Campbell, Kristin E. Voelkl, and Patricia L. Donahue, *NAEP 1996 Trends in Academic Progress* (Washington, D.C.: National Center for Education Statistics, 1997), p. 67.

5. Ibid.

6. The average for white thirteen-year-olds on the NAEP scale was 281 scale score points; for black seventeen-year-olds it was 286.

7. Gail T. McLure, Anji Sun, and Michael J. Valiga, *Trends in Advanced Mathematics and Science Course-Taking and Achievement among ACT-Tested High School Students: 1987–1996* (Iowa City, Iowa: American College Testing Program, 1997).

8. Robert Linn and Lloyd Bond, *Studies of the Extent of Adverse Impact of Certification Rates on Federally Protected Groups and the Extent to which Assessment Exercises Are Free of Bias and Unfairness: A Report Submitted to the National Board for Professional Teaching Standards* (Detroit: National Board for Professional Teaching Standards, 1994); Christopher Jencks and Meredith Phillips, *The Black-White Test Score Gap* (Washington, D.C.: Brookings Institution Press, 1998).

9. Susan Sturm and Lani Guinier, "The Future of Affirmative Action: Reclaiming the Innovative Ideal," *California Law Review* 84, no. 4 (1996), pp. 953–1035. The fact that test results can detect that something is wrong was first recognized in the early 1960s. At that time, intervention programs such as Head Start and Title I were initially justified on the grounds that an achievement gap existed between disadvantaged and other children. This gap was defined in terms of standardized-test performance levels. See A. J. Biemiller, "Aid to Elementary and Secondary Education," in U.S. House General Subcommittee on Education,

Committee on Education and Labor, *Hearings on H.R. 2361 and H.R. 2362,* 89th Cong., 1st sess., January 29, 1966, vol. I. Anthony Celebrezze, then secretary of health, education, and welfare, testified before a congressional hearing committee arguing for the passage of the Elementary and Secondary Education Act of 1965 and cited standardized test results to justify enactment. He pointed out, "You will find that by the end of the third year [grade] this student [in central Harlem in New York City] is approximately 1.2 grades behind the national average and 1.1 grades behind the New York City average. By the time he gets to the sixth grade, he is 2.1 grades below the national average and two grades below the New York average. And by the time he gets to the eighth grade, he is 2 1/2 grades below the national average and approximately 2 grades below the New York average. . . . The students continue to get further and further behind in terms of standardized test norms." (Anthony Celebrezze, in House Committee on Education and Labor, *Hearings on Education Act of 1965, H.R. 2361 and H.R. 2362,* 89th Cong., 1965, p. 89).

10. For example, in grade 12 only 2 percent of students are classified at the advanced level. Nonetheless, about 50 percent of all seniors take either the SAT-I or ACT each year. About 16 percent of that 50 percent score higher than one standard deviation above the mean; this constitutes about 8 percent of all seniors. This figure is four times as high as the 1994 NAEP "advanced" category percentage. In other words, large numbers of seniors scoring in the top 16 percent of students on the ACT or SAT-I math sections would not reach the NAEP "advanced" attainment level. It is questionable whether this makes intuitive sense; that is, are the NAEP math achievement levels defensible, particularly given that the SAT-I and ACT are important in the students' lives while the NAEP is a "drop from the sky" event without any personal consequences?

11. Daniel Koretz and Sheila I. Barron, *The Validity of Gains on the Kentucky Instructional Results Information System (KIRIS)* (Santa Monica, Calif.: RAND, 1998).

12. W. Hamilton, *Discussions in Philosophy and Literature, Education, and University Reform,* 2d ed. (London: Longman, 1853), p. 769, cited in George Madaus and Thomas Kellaghan, "Curriculum Evaluation and Assessment," in Philip W. Jackson, ed., *Handbook of Research on Curriculum* (New York: MacMillan, 1992), p. 121.

13. Edmond G. A. Holmes, *What Is and What Might Be?* (London: Constable, 1911), p. 128.

14. For a development of these principles see George F. Madaus, "The Influence of Testing on the Curriculum," in Daniel Tanner, ed., *Critical Issues in Curriculum* (Chicago: University of Chicago Press, 1988), pp. 8–121.

15. Donald T. Campbell, "On the Conflicts between Biological and Social Evolution and between Psychology and Moral Tradition," *American Psychologist* 30, no. 12 (1975): 1103–26. The Heisenberg uncertainty principle states that you cannot measure an electron's position without distorting its velocity and vice versa.

16. The validity of this assertion was confirmed in the late 1980s by a West Virginia physician, John Cannell. Surprised and curious about the above-average scores

obtained by some local students on nationally normed achievement tests, Cannell collected standardized test results from states and school districts across the country. He found that most states and districts were reporting above-average scores. When subsequent study of what came to be called the "Lake Wobegon" effect was undertaken, one of the explanations advanced for the almost universally above-average results was that schools routinely taught directly to the test, and even to specifically known test questions. John Cannell, *National Normed Elementary Achievement Testing in America's Public Schools: How All Fifty States Are above the National Average* (Albuquerque: Friends for Education, 1987); John J. Cannell, *The "Lake Wobegon" Report: How Public Educators Cheat on Standardized Achievement Tests* (Albuquerque: Friends for Education, 1989).

17. Thus, back in the 1930s, writing about the New York State Regents examination, F. T. Spaulding noted that teachers felt they had to abandon locally developed curriculum guides in favor of the curriculum defined by the Regents examinations. F. T. Spaulding, *High School and Life: The Regent's Inquiry into the Character and Cost of Public Education* (New York: McGraw-Hill, 1938). A recent study in Israel concluded that the introduction of three different high-stakes tests by the Ministry of Education narrowed the process of education, "making it merely instrumental and unmeaningful." Elana Shohamy, *The Power of Tests: The Impact of Language Tests on Teaching and Learning,* occasional papers (Washington, D.C.: National Foreign Language Center, Johns Hopkins University, 1993), p. 17.

18. A clear example of this surfaced during the minimum competency test hearings, sponsored by the National Institutes of Education. A principal from New York explained how high-stakes, multiple-choice tests had affected reading instruction in her school. The tests dictated not only the content focus of instruction, but also the form that instruction took. The principal told how her students practiced "reading" by reading dozens of little paragraphs and answering related multiple-choice questions. Further, when a section on synonyms and antonyms was dropped from the test, the practice materials on synonyms and antonyms were dropped from the teacher's arsenal of instructional techniques. National Institute of Education, Minimum Competency Testing Clarification Hearings, hearings held June 8, 9, 10, 1981, Washington, D.C., ERIC document nos. 215000, ED215001, and ED215002.

19. George F. Madaus and Vincent Greaney, "The Irish Experience in Competency Testing: Implications for American Education," *American Journal of Education* 93, no. 2 (1985): 268–94; Madaus, "The Influence of Testing on the Curriculum."

20. See also Laura S. Hamilton, E. Michael Nussbaum, and Richard E. Snow, "Interview Procedures for Validating Science Assessments," *Applied Measurement in Education* 10, no. 2 (1997): 181–200.

21. The study consisted of a closed-end questionnaire to which 2,229 teachers responded (45 percent response rate), and six case studies in urban districts with large minority enrollments. For technical details and a full report of the findings see George Madaus et al., *The Influence of Testing on Teaching Math and*

*Science in Grades 4–12* (Chestnut Hill, Mass.: Center for the Study of Testing, Evaluation, and Educational Policy, Boston College, 1992), Appendix D.

22. In the eighteenth and nineteenth centuries in Britain, pioneers of examinations believed that self-interest was the main motive for study, and since study involved drudgery, it was necessary to link important rewards or sanctions to learning (George Madaus and Thomas Kellaghan, *Student Examination Systems in the European Community: Lessons for the United States*, contractor report submitted to the Office of Technology Assessment, U.S. Congress, 1991; George Madaus and Thomas Kellaghan, "National Testing: Lessons for America from Europe," *Educational Leadership* 49, no. 3 (1991): 87–93). Adam Smith in the eighteenth century expressed the need for extrinsic rewards linked to examinations when he wrote:

> The public can encourage the acquisition of those most essential parts of education, by giving small premiums, and little badges of distinction, to the children of the common people who excel in them.
>
> The public can impose upon almost the whole body of the people the necessity of acquiring those most essential parts of education, by obliging every man to undergo an examination or probation in them before he can obtain the freedom in any corporation, or be allowed to set up any trade either in a village or town corporate (Adam Smith, "An Inquiry into the Nature and Causes of the Wealth of Nations" [Chicago: *Encyclopedia Britannica*, 1990], p. 384).

23. Thomas Kellaghan, George Madaus, and Anastasia E. Raczek, "The Use of External Examinations to Improve Student Motivation," American Educational Research Assocation, Washington, D.C., 1996.

24. For further discussion, see Florence R. Webb, Martin V. Covington, and James W. Guthrie, "Carrots and Sticks: Can School Policy Influence Student Motivation?" in Tommy M. Tomlinson, ed., *Motivating Students to Learn: Overcoming Barriers to High Achievement* (Berkeley, Calif.: McCutchan Publishing Corporation, 1993), pp. 99–124.

25. These positions are mirrored by advocates of testing who emphasize an instrumental, qualification-gathering aspect of education and a view of instruction as being driven by measurement (measurement-driven instruction), now often described as outcome-based education (see Nigel Brooke and John Oxenham, "The Influence of Certification and Selection on Teaching and Learning," in John Oxenham, ed., *Education Versus Qualifications? A Study of Relationships between Education, Selection for Employment and the Productivity of Labour* [London: Allen & Unwin, 1984], pp. 147–75; Ronald Philip Dore, *The Diploma Disease: Education, Qualification, and Development* [London: Allen & Unwin, 1976]). The positions contain three ingredients: a clear concept of educational goals or standards, a test that measures the goals, and high stakes associated with test results to act as a driving force (James Popham, "Measurements as an Instructional Catalyst," *New Directions for Testing and*

*Measurement,* no. 17 [1983]: 19–30; James Popham, "The Merits of Measurement-Driven Instruction," *Phi Delta Kappan* 68, no. 9 [1987]: 680–82; James Popham et al., "Measurement-Driven Instruction: It's on the Road," *Phi Delta Kappan* 66, no. 9 [1985]: 628–35).

26. Kellaghan, Madaus, and Raczek, "The Use of External Examinations to Improve Student Motivation."

27. See Carol Dweck and E. L. Leggett, "A Social-Cognitive Approach to Motivation and Personality," *Psychological Review* 95, no. 2 (1988): 256–73.

28. Kellaghan, Madaus, and Raczek, "The Use of External Examinations to Improve Student Motivation."

29. *An Examination System for the Nation* (Pittsburgh, Pa., and Rochester, N.Y.: Learning Research and Development Center and the National Center on Education and the Economy, 1990).

30. Wilfred Sheed, *Transatlantic Blues* (New York: Dutton, 1982), p. 117.

31. Kellaghan, Madaus, and Raczek, "The Use of External Examinations to Improve Student Motivation."

32. Edward L. Deci, Robert J. Vallerand, and Luc G. Pelletier, "Motivation and Education: The Self-Determination Perspective," *Educational Psychologist* 26, nos. 3/4 (1991): 325–46.

33. Edward L. Deci, *Intrinsic Motivation and Self-Determination in Human Behavior* (New York: Plenum Publishers, 1985); Edward L. Deci et al., "Effects of Performance Standards on Teaching Styles: Behavior of Controlling Teachers," *Journal of Educational Psychology* 74, no. 6 (1982): 852–59.

34. John U. Ogbu, "Immigrant and Involuntary Minorities in Comparative Perspective," in Margaret A. Gibson and John U. Ogbu, eds., *Minority Status and Schooling: A Comparative Study of Immigrant and Involuntary Minorities* (New York: Garland, 1991); Claude Steele, "A Threat in the Air: How Stereotypes Shape Intellectual Identity and Performance," *American Psychologist* 52, no. 6 (1997): 613–29.

35. Kellaghan, Madaus, and Raczek, "The Use of External Examinations to Improve Student Motivation."

36. Ibid.

37. The authentic assessment movement emerged in the late 1980s. See Ruth Mitchell, *Testing for Learning: How New Approaches to Evaluation Can Improve American Schools* (New York: Free Press, 1992); Grant Wiggins, "A True Test: Toward More Authentic and Equitable Assessment," *Phi Delta Kappan* 70, no. 9 (1989): 703–13. Underlying the movement is the belief that student learning and progress are best assessed by tasks that require active engagement, such as producing extended responses or a tangible product, investigating complex problems, generating material for portfolios, performing exhibitions, or carrying out experiments.

38. Data on how the use of performance assessment might impact different groups over an extended time frame do not exist in the United Kingdom or elsewhere.

39. Sally Thomas, George F. Madaus, and Anastasia E. Raczek collected *both* teacher assessments and standard task assessments for 17,718 students in 590 schools in

one large local education authority across nine attainment targets. In English, these topics were reading, writing, spelling, and handwriting. In mathematics, the topics were number operations, probabilities, and collecting, recording, processing, and handling data. In science, the topics were types and uses of materials, and earth and atmosphere. The standard tasks are examples of what advocates of the authentic assessment movement in this country call for. The teacher assessments are just that—teacher judgments about student attainment on the same areas of the national curriculum measured by the standard tasks. For further details of the study see Sally Thomas, George Madaus, and Anastasia E. Raczek, "Comparing Teacher Assessments and Standard Task Results in England: The Relationship between Pupil Characteristics and Attainment," *Assessment in Education: Principles, Policy & Practice 5*, no. 2 (1998): 213–46.

40. For a discussion of validity issues surrounding the use of readiness tests for entrance or retention, see Lorrie A. Shepard and Mary Lee Smith, "Academic and Emotional Effects of Kindergarten Retention in One School District," in Lorrie A. Shepard and Mary Lee Smith, eds., *Flunking Grades: Research and Policies on Retention* (London: Falmer Press, 1989), pp. 79–107.

41. Amelia E. Kreitzer, George Madaus, and Walt Haney, "Competency Testing and Dropouts," in Lois Weis, Eleanor Farrar, and Hugh G. Petrie, eds., *Dropouts from School: Issues, Dilemmas, and Solutions* (Albany: State University of New York Press, 1989), pp. 129–52.

42. Kreitzer, Madaus, and Haney calculated what is sometimes called attrition rate. Attrition rates are calculated by subtracting the graduation rate from 100 percent. The graduation rates were calculated by the Department of Education (DOE) by dividing the number of public school graduates by the ninth-grade enrollment four years earlier. The rates were adjusted by DOE for migration and students who are unclassified by grade. For details, see ibid.

43. Ibid.

44. Data from the 1988 and 1990 National Education Longitudinal Surveys on students who were required to pass one or more MCTs in eighth grade in 1988 were examined in order to find out if such students were more likely to have dropped out of school by tenth grade than students who did not have to meet such a requirement. Sean F. Reardon, "Eighth Grade Minimum Competency Testing and Early High School Dropout Patterns," paper presented at the Annual Meeting of the American Educational Research Association, New York, April 8, 1996.

45. Ibid., p. 5.

46. Mark Fassold identified a student as a TAAS dropout if (1) the student failed an exam, after which he or she missed the remaining exams before his or her class's scheduled graduation; and conjunctively, (2) the student did not drop out for one of eighteen specified reasons on a "dropout-exit-reason code" used by the state, and he or she did not defer from taking the test. Some of the specified reasons included job, military, pregnancy, poor attendance, and age. Mark A. Fassold, *Adverse Racial Impact of the Texas Assessment of Academic Skills* (San Antonio, Tex.: Mexican American Legal Defense and Education Fund, 1996).

47. Socioeconomic status was defined solely by participation in the school lunch program.

48. Linda Darling-Hammond and Beverly Falk, "Using Standards and Assessments to Support Student Learning," *Phi Delta Kappan* 79, no. 3 (1997): 190–99; Shepard and Smith, "Academic and Emotional Effects of Kindergarten Retention in One School District."

49. Texas Education Agency, *Comprehensive Biennial Report on Texas Public Schools: A Report to the 75th Texas Legislature* (Austin: Texas Education Agency, 1996).

50. Gary G. Wehlage and Robert A. Rutter, "Dropping Out: How Much Do Schools Contribute to the Problem?" *Teachers College Record* 87, no. 3 (1986): 374–92.

51. Madaus and Greaney, "The Irish Experience in Competency Testing: Implications for American Education."

52. See Ina V. S. Mullis et al., *Mathematics and Science Achievement in the Final Year of Secondary School: IEA's Third International Mathematics and Science Study* (Chestnut Hill, Mass.: Center for the Study of Testing, Evaluation, and Educational Policy, Boston College, 1998), Table B5, Appendix B.

53. See ibid., Appendix A.

54. *From Gatekeeper to Gateway,* p. 2.

55. Ibid., p. 31, emphasis in original.

56. Ibid., p. 13, emphasis added. One of the seventeen commissioners endorsing this recommendation was Bill Clinton, then governor of Arkansas.

57. Derek Bell, "A Commission on Race? Wow," *New York Times,* June 14, 1997, p. A23.

58. Barry J. Zimmerman, Albert Bandura, and Manuel Martinez-Pons, "Self-Motivation for Academic Attainment: The Role of Self-efficacy Beliefs and Personal Goal Setting," *American Educational Research Journal* 29, no. 3 (1992): 663–76.

## NOTES TO CHAPTER 6

1. Monty Neill, *Testing Our Children: A Report Card on State Assessment Systems* (Cambridge, Mass.: FairTest, 1997); Monty Neill, "Transforming Student Assessment," *Phi Delta Kappan* 79, no. 1 (1997): 34–40, 58; Edward Roeber, Linda A. Bond, and Selena Connealy, *Annual Survey of State Student Assessment Programs* (Washington, D.C.: Council of Chief State School Officers, 1997).

2. David Grissmer and Ann Flanagan, *Exploring Rapid Achievement Gains in North Carolina and Texas* (Washington, D.C.: National Education Goals Panel, 1998); "Quality Counts '98," *Education Week,* January 8, 1998.

3. Grissmer and Flanagan, *Exploring Rapid Achievement Gains in North Carolina and Texas.*

4. Daniel Koretz, "Arriving in Lake Wobegon: Are Standardized Tests Exaggerating Achievement and Distorting Instruction?" *American Educator*

(Summer 1988): 8–15, 46–52; George Madaus, "The Influence of Testing on the Curriculum," in Laura N. Tanner, ed., *Critical Issues in the Curriculum, 87th Yearbook of the National Society for the Study of Education, Part I* (Chicago: University of Chicago Press, 1988), pp. 83–121; Lorrie Shepard, "Inflated Test Score Gains: Is the Problem Old Norms or Teaching the Test?" *Educational Measurement: Issues and Practice* 9, no. 3 (1990): 15–22.

5. Meredith Markley, "HISD Doesn't Shine on National Test," *Houston Chronicle,* March 23, 1998, available at http://www.houstonchronicle.com.

6. Meredith Lawton, "Panel Finds No Tests Comparable to Ones Clinton Espouses," *Education Week,* June 17, 1998, p. 38.

7. George F. Madaus et al., *The Influence of Testing on Teaching Math and Science in Grades 4–12* (Chestnut Hill, Mass.: Center for the Study of Testing, Evaluation, and Educational Policy, Boston College, 1992); Thomas A. Romberg et al., "Curriculum and Test Alignment," in Thomas A. Romberg, ed., *Mathematics Assessment and Evaluation* (Albany: State University of New York Press, 1992), pp. 61–74.

8. "Quality Counts '98"; Improving America's Schools Act of 1994, Public Law 103-382, Title I, 108 Stat. 3523–3527.

9. Grissmer and Flanagan, *Exploring Rapid Achievement Gains in North Carolina and Texas.*

10. David Hoff, "Board Won't Revise State NAEP Scores," *Education Week,* May 19, 1999, pp. 1, 13; Improving America's Schools Act of 1994.

11. Clyde M. Reese et al., *NAEP 1996 Mathematics Report Card for the Nation and the States* (Washington, D.C.: National Center for Education Statistics, Office of Educational Research and Improvement, U.S. Department of Education, 1997).

12. Jay R. Campbell et al., *NAEP 1994 Reading Report Card for the Nation and the States* (Washington, D.C.: National Center for Education Statistics, Office of Educational Research and Improvement, U.S. Department of Education, 1996).

13. Patricia L. Donahue et al., *NAEP 1999 Reading Report Card for the Nation and the States* (Washington, D.C.: National Center for Education Statistics, Office of Educational Research and Improvement, U.S. Department of Education, 1999).

14. Linda Bond, Edward Roeber, and David Braskamp, *Trends in State Student Assessment Programs,* Fall 1996 (Washington, D.C.: Council of Chief State School Officers, 1996); Edward Roeber, Linda Bond, and Arie van der Ploeg, *State Student Assessment Programs Database, 1993–1994* (Washington, D.C.: Council of Chief State School Officers, 1994); "State Competency Testing Mandates," *Education Week,* June 8, 1992.

15. Bond, Roeber, and Braskamp, *Trends in State Student Assessment Programs;* Roeber, Bond, and van der Ploeg, *State Student Assessment Programs Database.*

16. Noe Medina and Monty Neill, *Fallout from the Testing Explosion: How 100 Million Standardized Exams Undermine Equity and Excellence in America's*

*Public Schools,* 3d ed., rev. (Cambridge, Mass.: FairTest, 1990); Neill, *Testing Our Children.*

17. Neill, *Testing Our Children.*
18. Madaus, "The Influence of Testing on the Curriculum."
19. Madaus, *The Influence of Testing on Teaching Math and Science in Grades 4–12.*
20. Bond, Roeber, and Brasskamp, *Trends in State Student Assessment Programs;* Roeber, Bond, and van der Ploeg, *State Student Assessment Programs Database.*
21. Reese et al., *NAEP 1996 Mathematics Report Card for the Nation and the States.*
22. Bond, Roeber, and Braskamp, *Trends in State Student Assessment Programs;* Roeber, Bond, and van der Ploeg, *State Student Assessment Programs Database.*
23. This means that there is no more than a 5 percent chance that these relationships could have occurred by chance due to sampling.
24. Although both increased the percentage at "basic" and reduced the percentage at "below-basic," they did not do so to a level of statistical significance.
25. Reese et al., *NAEP 1996 Mathematics Report Card for the Nation and the States.*
26. Glen E. Robinson and David P. Brandon, *NAEP Test Scores: Should They Be Used to Compare and Rank State Educational Quality* (Arlington, Va.: Educational Research Service, 1994).
27. Reese et al., *NAEP 1996 Mathematics Report Card for the Nation and the States;* Campbell et al., *NAEP 1994 Reading Report Card for the Nation and the States.*
28. Ibid.
29. Neill, *Testing Our Children.*
30. Ibid.
31. Ibid.
32. Grissmer and Flanagan, *Exploring Rapid Achievement Gains in North Carolina and Texas.*
33. Lynn Olson, "A Question of Value," *Education Week,* May 13, 1998, pp. 27, 30–31; William L. Sanders, "Value-Added Assessment," *The School Administrator* (December 1998): 24–27.
34. Monty Neill, *High Stakes Tests Do Not Improve Student Learning* (Cambridge, Mass.: FairTest, 1998).
35. Grissmer and Flanagan, *Exploring Rapid Achievement Gains in North Carolina and Texas.*
36. Albert H. Kauffman, "Plaintiffs' Post-Trial Brief," *GI Forum et al.* v. *Texas Education Agency et al.,* Civil Action no. SA-97-CA-1278EP, U.S. District Court for the Western District of Texas, San Antonio Division, 1999.
37. Donahue et al., *NAEP 1999 Reading Report Card for the Nation and the States.*
38. Grissmer and Flanagan, *Exploring Rapid Achievement Gains in North Carolina and Texas.* For further discussion of Texas, see Gary Orfield, "Strengthening Title I: Designing a Policy Based on Evidence," available at

http://www.educationnews.org/strengtheningtitlei.htm (draft chapter from a forthcoming book on Title I, edited by Orfield); and McNeil and Valenzuela, this volume.

39. Paul E. Barton and Richard S. Coley, *Growth in School: Achievement Gains from the Fourth to the Eighth Grade, Policy Information Report* (Princeton, N.J.: Educational Testing Service, 1998); Grissmer and Flanagan, *Exploring Rapid Achievement Gains in North Carolina and Texas.*

40. Barton and Coley, *Growth in School,* p. 10.

41. Ibid., p. 17

42. Kauffman, "Plaintiffs' Post-Trial Brief."

43. Walt Haney, *Supplementary Report on Texas Assessment of Academic Skills Exit Test (TAAS-X),* prepared for plaintiffs and submitted to the court in *GI Forum et al.* v. *Texas Education Agency et al.* (plaintiffs are represented by the Mexican American Legal Defense and Educational Fund, San Antonio, Tex.); Kauffman, "Plaintiffs' Post-Trial Brief." Haney has conducted a further investigation of Texas, with similar overall findings. See Walt Haney, "The Myth of the Texas Miracle in Education," *Education Policy Analysis Archives* 8, no. 4 (2000), available at http://epaa.asu.edu/epaa/v8n41; Walt Haney, "Revisiting the Myth of the Texas Miracle in Education: Lessons about Dropout Research and Dropout Prevention," paper presented at "Dropouts in America," conference at the Harvard Graduate School of Education, Cambridge, Mass., January 13, 2001.

44. Ibid.

45. Ibid.

46. Madaus, "The Influence of Testing on the Curriculum"; Medina and Neill, *Fallout from the Testing Explosion;* Neill, *High Stakes Tests Do Not Improve Student Learning.*

47. Neill, *Testing Our Children;* Monty Neill, "State Exams Flunk Test of Quality," *The State Education Standard,* Spring 2000, pp. 31–35, available at http://www.fairtest.org; Norman Frederiksen, "The Real Test Bias: Influences of Testing on Teaching and Learning," *American Psychologist* 39, no. 3 (1984): 193–202; Lauren B. Resnick and Daniel P. Resnick, "Assessing the Thinking Curriculum: New Tools for Educational Reform," in Bernard R. Gifford and Mary C. O'Connor, eds., *Future Assessments: Changing Views of Aptitude, Achievement, and Instruction* (Boston: Kluwer Academic Publishers, 1989); Mary C. Shafer and Sherian Foster, "The Changing Face of Assessment," *Principled Practice in Mathematics and Science Education* (Madison: Wisconsin Center for Educational Research, Fall 1997), pp. 1–7; Grant P. Wiggins, "A True Test: Toward More Authentic and Equitable Assessment," *Phi Delta Kappan* 70, no. 9 (May 1989): 703–13; Grant P. Wiggins, *Assessing Student Performance: Exploring the Purpose and Limits of Testing* (San Francisco: Jossey-Bass, 1993); Dennie P. Wolf et al., "To Use Their Minds Well: Investigating New Forms of Student Assessment," in Gerald Grant, ed., *Review of Research in Education,* vol. 17 (Washington, D.C.: American Educational Research Association, 1991), pp. 31–74.

48. Neill, "Transforming Student Assessment," pp. 34–40, 58; Lorrie A. Shepard, "The Role of Assessment in a Learning Culture," *Educational Researcher* 29, no. 7 (October 2000): 4–14.

49. Neill, personal discussion. Linda McNeil has documented in great detail the damage to high-quality programs for low-income students done by a focus on high-stakes tests. Linda McNeil, *Contradictions of School Reform* (New York: Routledge, 2000).

50. Neill, personal notes of "Summit," May 10, 1999.

51. Neill, "Transforming Student Assessment."

52. Paul Black and Dylan Wiliam, "Inside the Black Box: Raising Standards Through Classroom Assessment," *Phi Delta Kappan* 80, no. 2 (1998): 139–48.

53. Ibid., p. 141.

54. Ibid.

55. Ibid.

56. Resnick and Resnick, "Assessing the Thinking Curriculum."

57. Black and Wiliam, "Inside the Black Box," p. 144 (emphasis in original).

58. Ibid.

59. Mano Singham, "The Canary in the Mine: The Achievement Gap Between Black and White Students," *Phi Delta Kappan* 80, no. 1 (1998): 8–15; see also Monty Neill, "Some Pre-requisites for the Establishment of Equitable, Inclusive, Multicultural Assessment Systems," in Michael T. Nettles and Arie L. Nettles, eds., *Equity and Excellence in Educational Testing and Assessment* (Norwell, Mass.: Kluwer Academic Publishers, 1995).

60. Black and Wiliam, "Inside the Black Box."

61. Ibid.

62. For a discussion and critique of Kentucky's exams, see Betty Lou Whitford and Ken Jones, "Kentucky Lesson: High Stakes School Accountability Undermines a Performance-Based Curriculum Vision," in Betty Lou Whitford and Ken Jones, eds., *Accountability, Assessment and Teacher Commitment: Lessons from Kentucky's Reform Efforts* (Albany: State University of New York Press, 2000), pp. 9–26.

63. Monty Neill, personal communications, February and May 1999; New York Performance Standards Consortium, miscellaneous materials in the process of development, Urban Academy, New York, 1999.

64. Neill, *Testing Our Children.*

65. "Findings," *Teacher Magazine,* September 1994.

66. *January 1999 Progress Report: Outcomes Study: New York Networks for School Renewal* (New York: New York University Institute for Education and Social Policy, 1999).

67. *Educational Standards and Assessment Act* (Albany: Legislative Bill Drafting Commission, 11298-01-9, 1999).

68. Mary Barr, *California Learning Record* (El Cajon, Calif.: Center for Language in Learning, 1994).

69. FairTest, "U.S. Agency Adopts Learning Record," *FairTest Examiner* (Spring 1999).

70. Myra Barrs et al., *The Primary Language Record: Handbook for Teachers* (London: Centre for Language in Primary Education, 1988).

71. Winfield Cooper and Mary Barr, *The Primary Language Record and The California Learning Record in Use* (El Cajon, Calif.: Center for Language in Learning, 1995).

72. Phyllis J. Hallam, *1998 Inter-site Moderation Follow-up Study* (El Cajon, Calif.: Center for Language in Learning, 1998); see also The Learning Record at http://www.learningrecord.org.

73. FairTest, "U.S. Agency Adopts Learning Record"; Barr, *California Learning Record*.

74. James Ridgeway, "From Barrier to Lever: Revising Roles for Assessment in Mathematics Education," NISE Brief, vol. 2, no. 3, University of Wisconsin, Madison, January 1998.

75. Neill, "State Exams Flunk Test of Quality," pp. 31–35. See also National Forum on Assessment, *Principles and Indicators for Student Assessment Systems* (Cambridge, Mass.: FairTest, 1995).

## NOTES TO CHAPTER 7

1. That this use of the test violates the professional ethics of the testing profession and goes against standards for test use is discussed in a comprehensive report by the National Research Council, Committee on Appropriate Test Use, *High Stakes: Testing for Tracking, Promotion, and Graduation*, Jay P. Heubert and Robert M. Hauser, eds. (Washington, D.C.: National Academy Press, 1999).

2. Linda M. McNeil, *Contradictions of Control: School Structure and School Knowledge* (New York: Routledge, 1988); Linda M. McNeil, *Contradictions of Reform: The Educational Costs of Standardized Testing* (New York: Routledge, 2000); Angela Valenzuela, "Mexican American Youth and the Politics of Caring," in Elizabeth Long, ed., *From Sociology to Cultural Studies*, Sociology of Culture Annual Series, vol. 2 (London: Blackwell, 1997); Angela Valenzuela, "Subtractive Schooling: U.S.-Mexican Youth and the Politics of Caring," *Reflexiones 1998: New Directions in Mexican American Studies* (Austin: University of Texas, Center for Mexican American Studies, 1998); Angela Valenzuela, *Subtractive Schooling: U.S.-Mexican Youth and the Politics of Caring* (Albany: State University of New York Press, 1999).

3. Linda M. McNeil, "The Politics of Texas School Reform," *Politics of Education Association Yearbook* (1987): 199–216.

4. *NAEP 1996 Mathematics: Cross-State Data Compendium for the Grade 4 and Grade 8 Assessment* (National Center for Education Statistics 98-481); *NAEP 1998: Reading Report for the Nation and the States*; NAEP 1999 State Facts (http://www.negp.gov). For national trends, also see U.S. Department of Education, National Center for Education Statistics, *The Condition of Education 1999*, Washington, D.C. To the extent that there are real increases in

NAEP scores, we may be observing a testing effect. Kris Sloan suggests that since the NAEP is not a high-stakes test, its use in states like Texas, where high-stakes examinations are used, may translate into higher scores since Texas students are not only more likely to take it more seriously, but in addition are "test savvy." (Correspondence between Kris Sloan and Angela Valenzuela, April 2000.)

5. *Texas Student Assessment Program Technical Digest for the Academic Year 1996–97* (Austin: Texas Education Agency, 1998).

6. National Research Council, *High Stakes.*

7. *District and School Profiles, 1993–94* (Houston: Houston Independent School District). See also *District and School Profiles, 1997–98* (Houston: Houston Independent School District), 1998.

8. Because the TAAS test has changed over the years, longitudinal analyses are impossible due to an incomparability of data. Currently, the key testing benchmarks established by the State Board of Education and the Texas Education Agency are at the fourth-, eighth-, and tenth-grade levels. See *Texas Student Assessment Program Technical Digest for the Academic Year 1996–97.*

9. In the Houston Independent School District alone, fifty-eight thousand students (or 27.6 percent) were classified as LEP youth. (*District and School Profiles, 1997–98*).

10. As researchers, we could not use the actual names of those studied or their schools because of the intense pressure attached to the official view of these tests within the state government, school districts, and the media.

11. Besides being a segregated school, Seguín (pseudonym) mirrors other national trends. The dropout rate is at least 50 percent, while the state and national dropout rates for Latinos are both around 40 percent. See Rafael Valdivieso, *Must They Wait Another Generation? Hispanics and Secondary School Reform* (Washington, D.C.: Hispanic Policy Development Project, 1986); Ricardo Romo and Nestor Rodriguez, *Houston Evaluation of Community Priorities* (Austin, Tex.: Tomas Rivera Center, 1994). Between 1,200 and 1,500 students enter the ninth grade each year, and only 400 to 500 students graduate in any given year. In March of 1993, 19 percent of the senior class had passed all three portions of the TAAS test. A year later, slightly more (21 percent) had passed all three portions, resulting in a ranking that still made Seguín one school above the worst high school in the entire district. In 1993–94, 540 seniors were enrolled, and only 350 graduated. About 100 students actually showed up for graduation. Low expectations are virtually built into this school: were students to progress normally from one grade to the next, there would be no space to house them. As things stand, Seguín's 3,000-plus student body is crammed into a physical facility capable of housing no more than 2,600 students. Due to the school's high failure and dropout rates, more than half of the school population is always comprised of freshmen. Although their TAAS test scores have increased in more recent years, this reflects reduced numbers of students reaching the tenth grade test; graduation rates have remained low.

12. Valenzuela, *Subtractive Schooling*.

13. Howard Gardner, *The Unschooled Mind: How Children Think and How Schools Should Teach* (New York: Basic Books, 1991); Susan Ohanian, *One Size Fits Few: The Folly of Educational Standards* (Portsmouth, N.H.: Heinemann, 1999); Peter Sacks, *Standardized Minds: The High Price of America's Testing Culture and What We Can Do to Change It* (Cambridge, Mass.: Perseus Books, 1999).

14. Valenzuela, "Mexican American Youth and the Politics of Caring"; Valenzuela, "Subtractive Schooling"; Valenzuela, *Subtractive Schooling*.

15. Written assignment for an English class by a senior female student at Seguín, dated September 14, 1994.

16. Gloria Ladson-Billings, *The Dreamkeepers: Successful Teachers of African American Children* (San Francisco: Jossey-Bass Publishers, 1994).

17. Ibid.; Valenzuela, *Subtractive Schooling*.

18. Robert A. DeVillar, "The Rhetoric and Practice of Cultural Diversity in U.S. Schools: Socialization, Resocialization, and Quality Schooling," in Robert A. DeVillar, Christian J. Faltis, and James P. Cummins, eds., *Cultural Diversity in Schools: From Rhetoric to Practice* (Albany, N.Y.: State University of New York Press, 1994).

19. Guadalupe Valdés, "The World Outside and Inside Schools: Language and Immigrant Children," *Educational Researcher* 27, no. 6 (1998): 4–18.

20. Valenzuela, *Subtractive Schooling*.

21. James Cummins, *Bilingualism and Special Education: Issues in Assessment and Pedagogy* (Clevedon, England: Multilingual Matters 6, 1984); Tove Skutnabb-Kangas and James Cummins, *Minority Education: From Shame to Struggle* (Clevedon, England: Multilingual Matters 40, 1988).

22. Laurie Olsen, *Made in America: Immigrant Students in our Public Schools* (New York: New Press, 1997); Valdés, "The World Outside and Inside Schools."

23. For reviews, see Raymond Buriel, "Academic Performance of Foreign- and Native-born Mexican Americans: A Comparison of First-, Second-, and Third-Generation Students and Parents," report to the Inter-University Program for Latino Research, Social Science Research Council, 1987; Raymond Buriel, "Immigration and Education of Mexican Americans," in Aida Hurtado and Eugene Garcia, eds., *The Educational Achievement of Latinos: Barriers and Successes,* University of California Latino Eligibility Study (Santa Cruz: University of California, Santa Cruz, 1994).

24. Valenzuela, *Subtractive Schooling*.

25. A caveat is in order here. Though Valenzuela observed a critical mass of highly adept immigrant/LEP youths in her study, not all immigrant youths come with advanced academic skills (for example, see Olsen, *Made in America*). While the issue of cultural tracking persists for such students, other additional issues also would have to be taken into account. For instance, many of these youths will perform poorly because of incorrect assignment to courses, a lack of availability of support services, unfamiliarity with testing,

limited or no test-taking skills, cultural biases within the test, and test-taking anxiety. When students come to the United States with limited prior educational experiences, they are indeed among the most vulnerable to academic failure.

26. Maria Eugenia Matute-Bianchi, "Situational Ethnicity and Patterns of School Performance among Immigrant and Nonimmigrant Mexican-descent Students," in Margaret A. Gibson and John U. Ogbu, eds., *Minority Status and Schooling: A Comparative Study of Immigrant and Involuntary Minorities* (New York: Garland Publishing, 1991); Kao Grace and Marta Tienda, "Optimism and Achievement: The Educational Performance of Immigrant Youth," *Social Science Quarterly* 76, no. 1 (1995): 1–19.

27. Angela Valenzuela, field notes, June 5, 1996.

## Notes to Chapter 8

1. William Jefferson Clinton, "Helping Schools End Social Promotion," Memorandum for the Secretary of Education, press release (Washington, D.C.: The White House, 1998), pp. 1–2.

2. Jacques Steinberg, "Clinton Urges Tough Love for Students Who Are Failing," *New York Times,* October 1, 1999.

3. Clinton, "Helping Schools End Social Promotion," p. 3.

4. *Making Standards Matter 1997: An Annual Fifty-State Report on Efforts to Raise Academic Standards* (Washington, D.C.: American Federation of Teachers, 1997). The states are Arkansas, Florida, Louisiana, New Mexico, North Carolina, South Carolina, and West Virginia. A report from the Council of Chief State School Officers lists five states with required testing for promotion: Louisiana, North Carolina, New York, South Carolina, and Virginia. (Survey of State Student Assessment Programs, [Washington, D.C.: Council of Chief State School Officers, 1998]).

5. Catherine George, *Beyond Retention: A Study of Retention Rates, Practices, and Successful Alternatives in California, Summary Report* (Sacramento: California Department of Education, 1993); Iowa Department of Education, Early Childhood Network, The Primary Program, Position Statements, "Retention, Tracking, and Extra Year Programs," http://www.state.ia.us, July 13, 1998.

6. Robert C. Johnston, "Texas Governor Has Social Promotion in His Sights," *Education Week,* February 11, 1998.

7. Jacques Steinberg, "Chancellor Vows to Fail Students Lacking in Skills," *New York Times,* April 21, 1998.

8. Randal Archibold, "Suit Threatened over School Promotion Rules," *New York Times,* August 17, 1999.

9. Anemona Hartocollis, "Miscalculation on Scores Shows a Weakness of Tests," *New York Times,* September 17, 1999; Randal Archibold, "8600 in Summer School by Error, Board Says," *New York Times,* September 16, 1999.

10. The *1997–1998 Guidelines for Promotion in the Chicago Public Schools* also list minimum report card requirements and a minimum attendance requirement, but "students who score at or above grade level on both the Reading and Mathematics sections of the ITBS are excepted from the latter requirement" (Chicago: Chicago School Reform Board of Trustees, Bureau of Student Assessment, 1997). This use of the ITBS appears to be in conflict with the publisher's recommendations about "inappropriate purposes" of testing: "If a retention decision is to be made, classroom assessment data gathered by the teacher over a period of months is likely to be a highly relevant and accurate basis for making such a decision. A test score can make a valuable contribution to the array of evidence that should be considered. However, a test score from an achievement battery should not be used alone in making such a significant decision" (H. D. Hoover et al., *Interpretive Guide for School Administrators: Iowa Test of Basic Skills, Levels 5–14* [Iowa City, Iowa: Riverside Publishing Company, 1994]. However, the test publisher (but not the developers) have endorsed this use of the ITBS by the Chicago public schools.

11. Between 2 and 3 percent of students failed the initial exam at each grade level but were ultimately waived into the next grade (*The Summer Bridge: Helping Chicago's Public School Students Bridge the Gap* [Chicago: Chicago Public Schools, 1998]).

12. National Research Council, Committee on Appropriate Test Use, *High Stakes: Testing for Tracking, Promotion, and Graduation,* Jay P. Heubert and Robert M. Hauser, eds. (Washington, D.C.: National Academy Press, 1999), Chapter 6.

13. The failure of past programs is recognized in President Clinton's initiative to end social promotion: "Ending social promotions by simply holding more students back is the wrong choice. Students who are required to repeat a year are more likely to eventually drop out, and rarely catch up academically with their peers. The right way is to ensure that more students are prepared to meet challenging academic standards in the first place" (Clinton, "Helping Schools End Social Promotion").

14. National Research Council, *High Stakes,* Table 6-1.

15. Lorrie A. Shepard and Mary Lee Smith, "Academic and Emotional Effects of Kindergarten Retention in One School District," in Lorrie A. Shepard and Mary Lee Smith, eds., *Flunking Grades: Research and Policies on Retention* (London: Falmer Press, 1989), pp. 79–107.

16. National Center for Education Statistics, U.S. Department of Education, Office of Education Research and Improvement, *Digest of Education Statistics, 1998,* NCES 1999-032 (Washington, D.C.: U.S. Government Printing Office, 1999); National Center for Education Statistics, U.S. Department of Education, Office of Education Research and Improvement, *Condition of Education, 1999,* NCES 1999-022 (Washington, D.C.: U.S. Government Printing Office, 1999).

17. *Taking Responsibility for Ending Social Promotion: A Guide for Educators and State and Local Leaders* (Washington, D.C.: U.S. Department of Education, 1999).

18. Ibid., p. 6. There is no such publication as "Current Population Statistics." Apparently, the reference is to *Current Population Reports,* Series P- 20, No. 500, which reports school enrollment by age in October 1996. However, I cannot reproduce exactly the estimates reported in *Taking Responsibility for Ending Social Promotion,* and the Department of Education has not responded to my request for their source.

19. Beverly Duncan, "Trends in Output and Distribution of Schooling," in Eleanor B. Sheldon and Wilbert E. Moore, eds., *Indicators of Social Change* (New York: Russell Sage Foundation, 1968); National Research Council, *A Common Destiny: Blacks and American Society,* Gerald D. Jaynes and Robin M. Williams, Jr., eds. (Washington, D.C.: National Academy Press, 1989).

20. *Current Population Reports,* "School Enrollment: Social and Economic Characteristics of Students" (Washington, D.C.: U.S. Bureau of the Census, various years). Unpublished data for 1996 were generously provided by Census Bureau staff. Percentages shown in Figure 8.1 are three-year moving averages and do not agree exactly with the annual estimates reported in the text.

21. The percentages include those enrolled below grade 1 and a small share of six-year-olds who were not enrolled in school. The data are virtually unchanged if nonenrolled children are eliminated from the analysis: neither the trends nor the differences by race/ethnicity and sex are affected.

22. Another relevant factor is change in state or local requirements about the exact age a child must reach before entering kindergarten or first grade.

23. Lorrie A. Shepard, "Negative Policies for Dealing with Diversity: When Does Assessment and Diagnosis Turn into Sorting and Segregation?" in Elfrieda H. Hiebert, ed., *Literacy for a Diverse Society: Perspectives, Practices, and Policies* (New York: Teachers College Press, 1991), pp. 279–98.

24. Lorrie A. Shepard, "A Review of Research on Kindergarten Retention," in Shepard and Smith, *Flunking Grades,* pp. 64-78; Shepard, "Negative Policies for Dealing with Diversity."

25. Shepard, "Negative Policies for Dealing with Diversity," p. 287; Lorrie A. Shepard, Sharon Lynn Kagan, and Emily Wurtz, eds., *Principles and Recommendations for Early Childhood Assessments,* prepared for the National Educational Goals Panel by the Goal 1 Early Childhood Assessments Resource Group (Washington, D.C.: U.S. Government Printing Office, 1998).

26. Nancy L. Karweit, *Grade Retention: Prevalence, Timing, and Effects,* CRESPAR Report no. 33 (Baltimore: Johns Hopkins University Center for Social Organization of Schools, March 1999).

27. These data have been assembled from *Historical Statistics,* Table A-3, "Persons 6 to 17 Years Old Enrolled below Modal Grade, 1971 to 1995," which is available from the U.S. Bureau of the Census at http://www.census.gov/population/ socdemo/school/report95/taba-3.txt, and from selected publications in the P-20 series of *Current Population Reports,* "School Enrollment: Social and Economic Characteristics of Students," from the U.S. Bureau of the Census (nos. 241, 260, 272, 286, 303, 319, 333, 346, 360, 400, 408, 413, 426, 439, 443, 452, 460, 469, 474, 479, 487, and 492).

Unpublished data for 1996, as well as corrections in the *Historical Statistics,* Table A-3, were kindly provided by Census Bureau staff.

28. We ignore the logical possibility that age-retardation at younger ages could be counterbalanced by double promotion at older ages.

29. Again, early school dropout (at ages fifteen to seventeen) is counted as age-grade retardation.

30. National Research Council, *High Stakes,* Table 6-1.

31. *Comprehensive Biennial Report on Texas Schools: A Report to the 76th Texas Legislature* (Austin: Texas Education Agency, December 1998).

32. To estimate these rates, I multiplied the complements of the reported failure rates across grade levels to estimate the probability of never being failed. The complement of that estimate is the probability of having failed at least once.

33. Dropping out by ages fifteen to seventeen does not indicate ultimate rates of failure to complete high school because large numbers of youth complete regular schooling through age nineteen or, alternatively, pass the GED exam through their late twenties. Robert M. Hauser, "Indicators of High School Completion and Dropout," in Robert M. Hauser, Brett V. Brown, and William R. Prosser, eds., *Indicators of Children's Well-Being* (New York: Russell Sage Foundation, 1997).

34. American Educational Research Association, American Psychological Association, and National Council on Measurement in Education, *Standards for Educational and Psychological Testing* (Washington, D.C.: American Psychological Association, 1985); Joint Committee on Testing Practices, *Code of Fair Testing Practices in Education* (Washington, D.C.: National Council on Measurement in Education, 1988); Samuel Messick, "Validity," in Robert L. Linn, ed., *Educational Measurement,* 3d ed. (Washington, D.C.: American Council on Education, 1989); National Research Council, *High Stakes.*

35. Caroline Hendrie, "Do or Die," *Education Week,* August 6, 1997.

36. C. Thomas Holmes, "Grade Level Retention Effects: A Meta-Analysis of Research Studies," in Shepard and Smith, *Flunking Grades,* pp. 16–33; Ernest R. House, "Policy Implications of Retention Research," in Shepard and Smith, *Flunking Grades,* pp. 202–13.

37. R. Gampert and P. Opperman, "Longitudinal Study of the 1982–83 Promotional Gates Students," paper presented at the Annual Meeting of the American Educational Research Association, New Orleans, April 1988; James B. Grissom and Lorrie A. Shepard, "Repeating and Dropping Out of School," in Shepard and Smith, *Flunking Grades,* pp. 34–63; Lynn Olson, "Education Officials Reconsider Policies on Grade Retention," *Education Week,* May 16, 1990; Douglas K. Anderson, "Paths through Secondary Education: Race/Ethnic and Gender Differences," Ph.D. thesis, University of Wisconsin-Madison, 1994; Linda Darling-Hammond and Beverly Falk, "Using Standards and Assessments to Support Student Learning: Alternatives to Grade Retention," in *Report to the Chancellor's Committee on Grade Transition Standards* (New York: National Center for Restructuring Education, Schools and Teaching, Teachers College, Columbia University, 1995); Stuart Luppescu et al., *School Reform, Retention*

*Policy, and Student Achievement Gains* (Chicago: Consortium on Chicago School Research, 1995); Sean Reardon, "Eighth-Grade Minimum Competency Testing and Early High School Dropout Patterns," paper presented at the annual meeting of the American Educational Research Association, New York, April 1996.

38. Holmes, "Grade Level Retention Effects."
39. Ibid., p. 27.
40. Ann R. McCoy and Arthur J. Reynolds, "Grade Retention and School Performance: An Extended Investigation," discussion paper 1167-98 (Madison: Institute for Research on Poverty, University of Wisconsin-Madison, 1998); also, see Arthur Reynolds, "Grade Retention and School Adjustment: An Explanatory Analysis," *Educational Evaluation and Policy Analysis* 14, no. 2 (1992): 101–21.
41. Karl L. Alexander, Doris R. Entwisle, and Susan L. Dauber, *On the Success of Failure* (Cambridge, England: Cambridge University Press, 1994).
42. Throughout the following discussion, I have focused on same-grade comparisons of promoted and retained students, where the scores of promoted students are lagged one calendar year behind those of retained students. That is, the retained students have taken one more year to complete each grade. These comparisons are usually more favorable to retained students than same-age comparisons, in which they are one grade level behind the promoted students.
43. Lorrie A. Shepard, Mary Lee Smith, and Scott F. Marion, "Failed Evidence on Grade Retention," *Psychology in the Schools* 33, no. 3 (1996): 251–61; Lorrie A. Shepard, Mary Lee Smith, and Scott Marion, "On the Success of Failure: A Rejoinder to Alexander," *Psychology in the Schools* 35, no. 4 (1998): 404–7.
44. Also, see Karl L. Alexander, "Letter to the Editor," *Psychology in the Schools* 35, no. 4 (1998): 402–4; and Shepard, Smith, and Marion, "On the Success of Failure: A Rejoinder to Alexander."
45. Karweit, *Grade Retention.*
46. It is curious that *USA Today* gave this study national editorial coverage, when it had not been published formally and its findings were not covered by any national news service except Gannett, which owns *USA Today*. A. Gary Dworkin et al., "Elementary School Retention and Social Promotion in Texas: An Assessment of Students Who Failed the Reading Section of the TAAS" (Houston: Sociology of Education Research Group, University of Houston, August 1999).
47. *Comprehensive Biennial Report on Texas Schools*, p. 42.
48. Lorrie A. Shepard, personal communication, 1999.
49. Grissom and Shepard, "Repeating and Dropping Out of School."
50. Judy A. Temple, Arthur J. Reynolds, and Wendy T. Miedel, "Can Early Intervention Prevent High School Dropout? Evidence from the Chicago Child-Parent Centers," discussion paper 1180-98 (Madison: Institute for Research on Poverty, University of Wisconsin-Madison, November 1998).
51. *1997–1998 Guidelines for Promotion in the Chicago Public Schools* (Chicago: Chicago School Reform Board of Trustees, Bureau of Student Assessment, 1997).

52. Anderson, "Paths through Secondary Education."

53. Russell W. Rumberger and Katherine A. Larson, "Student Mobility and the Increased Risk of High School Dropout," *American Journal of Education* 107, no. 1 (1998): 1–35.

54. Ibid., p. 24.

55. Ibid., p. 27.

56. Reardon, "Eighth-Grade Minimum Competency Testing and Early High School Dropout Patterns," pp. 4–5.

57. Ibid.

58. Ibid.

59. Shepard and Smith, *Flunking Grades.*

60. For a discussion of possible claims of discrimination based on race or national origin, see National Research Council, *High Stakes,* Chapter 3.

61. Steinberg, "Chancellor Vows to Fail Students Lacking in Skills"; Jacques Steinberg, "Crew's Plan to Hold Back Failing Students Has Familiar Ring," *New York Times,* April 26, 1998.

62. Mary Catherine Ellwein and Gene V. Glass assumed that the intervention, that is, retention, was not as beneficial as promotion to the next grade level. Mary Catherine Ellwein and Gene V. Glass, "Ending Social Promotion in Waterford: Appearances and Reality," in Shepard and Smith, *Flunking Grades,* pp. 151–73.

63. Daniel M. Koretz et al., "The Effects of High-Stakes Testing on Achievement: Preliminary Findings about Generalization across Tests," paper presented at the annual meeting of the American Educational Research Association and the National Council on Measurement in Education, Chicago, April 1991.

64. *Preparing Your Elementary Students to Take Standardized Tests* (Chicago: Chicago School Reform Board of Trustees, Bureau of Student Assessment, 1996); *Preparing Your High School Students to Take Standardized Tests* (Chicago: Chicago School Reform Board of Trustees, Bureau of Student Assessment, 1996).

65. "CPS Ninth Grade Students Excel in Summer School," press release, Chicago Public Schools, 1997; "CPS Test Results of Individual Schools Show Improvements," press release, Chicago Public Schools, 1998.

66. In the Chicago public schools, each retest is based on an alternative form of the Iowa Test of Basic Skills.

67. Melissa Roderick et al., *Ending Social Promotion: Results from the First Two Years* (Chicago: Consortium on Chicago School Research, 1999).

68. Shepard, Kagan, and Wurtz, *Principles and Recommendations for Early Childhood Assessments;* American Federation of Teachers, *Passing on Failure: District Promotion Policies and Practices* (Washington, D.C.: American Federation of Teachers, 1997).

69. General intervention strategies employed throughout grades K–12, as described to the Committee on Appropriate Test Use by James Watt of the Southern Regional Education Board, include having clear core-content standards for each grade and course, clear communication of these standards to teachers and parents, expert faculty, professional development for teachers, and extra instruction beyond the regular school day.

70. In the Long Beach School District in California, children are assessed beginning in kindergarten. When problems are found, interventions include parent-teacher conferences and mandatory summer school after grade 2. If after completing grade 3 and subsequent summer school a student has not reached the first grade reading level, he or she is retained in the third grade until reaching the first grade reading level. No one test holds students back (interview with Lynn Winters of the Long Beach School District). Cincinnati uses grouping and intervention as well as intensive instruction and smaller classes to help children who appear to be having difficulty staying at grade level (American Federation of Teachers, *Passing on Failure*).

71. In Chicago, there is a standard summer program for students who fail the Iowa test at designated grades. Many schools also offer extended-day programs aimed at helping students pass the test. The decision to offer these programs, as well as their content, is made at the school level. Funds for such programs must be found in each school's annual lump-sum allotment (American Federation of Teachers, *Passing on Failure*).

## Notes to Chapter 9

1. National Research Council, Committee on Appropriate Test Use, *High Stakes: Testing for Tracking, Promotion, and Graduation*, Jay P. Heubert and Robert M. Hauser, eds. (Washington, D.C.: National Academy Press, 1999).

2. Ibid., p. 4.

3. Regarding tests used to end social promotion, for example, "much of the public discussion and some recently implemented or proposed testing programs appear to ignore existing standards for appropriate test use" (ibid., p. 116).

4. Ibid., p. 3.

5. Ibid.

6. American Educational Research Association, American Psychological Association, and National Council on Measurement in Education, *Standards for Educational and Psychological Testing* (Washington, D.C.: American Psychological Association, 1999), Standard 13.5, p. 146 (hereafter *Joint Standards*).

7. National Research Council, *High Stakes*, p. 278.

8. *Debra P. v. Turlington*, 474 F. Supp. 244 (M.D. Fla. 1979); aff'd in part and rev'd in part, 644 F.2d 397 (5th Cir. 1981); rem'd, 564 F. Supp. 177 (M.D. Fla. 1983); aff'd, 730 F.2d 1405 (11th Cir. 1984).

9. "Cumulative" failure rates are the proportions of students who still fail the graduation exam after multiple opportunities to take the test; see Natriello and Pallas, this volume.

10. Under the 1997 amendments to the Individuals with Disabilities Education Act, most students with disabilities must be included in large-scale state assessments, with appropriate accommodation, for purposes of system accountability. Federal

law does not require that students with disabilities be subject to retention in grade or denial of high school diplomas, but some states apply the same high stakes to students with disabilities as they do to nondisabled students (National Research Council, *High Stakes*); J. E. Ysseldyke et al., *Educational Results for Students with Disabilities: What Do the Data Tell Us?* (Minneapolis: National Center on Educational Outcomes, 1998).

11. These estimates are based on the proportion of students scoring below "basic" on the NAEP. For example, in 1996, 40 percent of students taking the eighth grade math test scored below "basic," and in the District of Columbia public schools roughly 80 percent scored below "basic" (Robert Linn, "Assessments and Accountability," paper presented at the annual meeting of the American Educational Research Association, San Diego, Calif., 1998, figure 14, citing Clyde M. Reese et al., "NAEP 1996 Mathematics Report Card for the Nation and the States," National Center for Education Statistics, Washington, D.C., 1997).

12. In Massachusetts, roughly 40 percent of white students failed the "MCAS" in 1999, compared with 80 percent of black students and 82 percent of Hispanic students. Passing the MCAS is not now required for graduation, but soon will be.

13. As noted earlier, students with disabilities consistently fail state tests at rates thirty-five to forty percentage points higher than those for nondisabled students (Ysseldyke et al., *Educational Results for Students with Disabilities*). If the failure rate for nondisabled students is 40 percent, the estimated failure rate for students with disabilities would be in the range of 75 to 80 percent.

14. Paul Weckstein, "School Reform and Enforceable Rights to an Adequate Education," in Jay P. Heubert, ed., *Law and School Reform: Six Strategies for Promoting Educational Equity* (New Haven: Yale University Press, 1999).

15. National Research Council, *High Stakes*, pp. 247–92.

16. The author served as study director for the NRC's Committee on Appropriate Test Use, which wrote *High Stakes*.

17. The draft, dated December 14, 1999, is entitled *The Use of Tests When Making High-Stakes Decisions for Students: A Resource Guide for Educators and Policymakers*.

18. National Research Council, Committee on Child Development Research and Public Policy, *Placing Children in Special Education: A Strategy for Equity*, Kirby A. Heller, Wayne H. Holtzman, and Samuel Messick, eds. (Washington, D.C.: National Academy Press, 1982).

19. National Research Council, *High Stakes*, pp. 2–3.

20. See ibid., Chapters 4–7.

21. Whether a promotion test is a placement test or a mastery test depends on how educators use the test in a particular situation. If the test is intended to help assess a student's readiness for work in the next higher grade, it is a placement test. If it is used to help determine whether a student has learned what he or she has already been taught, it is a mastery test.

22. Tracking may be defined as "forms of placement whereby individual students are assigned, usually based on perceived achievement or skill level, to separate

schools or programs; classes within grade levels; groups within classes (at the elementary level); and courses within subject areas (at the secondary level)" (National Research Council, *High Stakes,* p. 91).

23. Ibid.; *Joint Standards,* p. 146, Standard 13.5.

24. Linda Darling-Hammond, "The Implications of Testing Policy for Quality and Equality," *Phi Delta Kappan* 73, no. 3 (1991): 220–25; Lorrie Shepard, Sharon Lynn Kagan, and Emily Wurtz, eds., *Principles and Recommendations for Early Childhood Assessments* (Washington, D.C.: National Education Goals Panel, 1998); Lorrie Shepard, "Negative Policies for Dealing with Diversity: When Does Assessment and Diagnosis Turn into Sorting and Segregation?" in Elfrieda H. Hiebert, ed., *Literacy for a Diverse Society: Perspectives, Practices, and Policies* (New York: Teachers College Press, 1991); Robert Stake, "Some Comments on Assessment in U.S. Education," *Education Policy Analysis Archives* 6, no. 14 (1998): http://epaa.asu.edu/epaa/v6n14.html.

25. National Research Council, *High Stakes,* pp. 275–76; Milbrey McLaughlin and Lorrie Shepard, eds., *Improving Education through Standards-Based Reform* (Washington, D.C.: National Academy of Education, 1995). For a careful analysis of the resources that New York would have to expend to enable its high schools to meet new state graduation requirements, see Gary Natriello, *The New Regents High School Graduation Requirements: Estimating the Resources Necessary to Meet the New Standards* (New York: Community Service Society, 1998).

26. National Research Council, *High Stakes,* p. 7.

27. Ibid.

28. Ibid.

29. Ibid., p. 81. Robert Linn also emphasizes this point: "The gender difference in percentage passing based on the NAEP proficient level criterion varies considerably by subject. . . . The point is that construct choice . . . matters." Linn, "Assessments and Accountability"; Warren W. Willingham and Nancy Cole, *Gender Bias and Fair Assessment* (Hillsdale, N.J.: Lawrence Erlbaum Associates, 1997).

30. Susan E. Phillips, "Legal Defensibility of Standards: Issues and Policy Perspectives," *Proceedings of the Joint Conference on Standard Setting for Large-Scale Assessments,* September 1996, pp. 379–98.

31. "Test questions are a sample of possible questions that could be asked in a given area. Moreover, a test score is not an exact measure of a student's knowledge or skills. A student's score can be expected to vary across different versions of a test—within a margin of error determined by the reliability of the test—as a function of the particular sample of questions asked and/or transitory factors, such as the student's health on the day of the test. Thus, no single test score can be considered a definitive measure of a student's knowledge" (National Research Council, *High Stakes,* p. 2).

32. Placement tests, for example, should test students separately in each subject in which the student is to be placed. A reading test would not measure validly which mathematics course available in a school would be most beneficial for a

particular student any more than a math test would be valid in making a place-ment decision for reading or social studies.

33. National Research Council, *High Stakes; Joint Standards,* p. 146, Standard 13.6.

34. The *Joint Standards* address this issue in several ways. For example, they state: "When credible research reports differences in the effects of construct-irrelevant variance across subgroups of test takers on performance on some part of the test, the test should be used if at all only for those subgroups for which evidence exists that valid inferences can be drawn from subtest scores" (p. 81, Standard 7.2), and that "research should seek to detect and eliminate aspects of test design, content, and format that might bias scores for particular groups" (p. 81, Standard 7.3).

35. National Research Council, *High Stakes,* p. 279.

36. *Joint Standards,* p. 146, Standard 13.7.

37. *Trends in State Student Assessment Programs* (Washington, D.C.: Council of Chief State School Officers, 1998); *Making Standards Matter 1998* (Washington, D.C.: American Federation of Teachers, 1998).

38. Walt Haney, "Testing and Minorities," in L. Weiss and M. Fine, eds., *Beyond Silence: Class, Race, and Gender in United States Schools* (Albany: State University of New York Press, 1993); Sean Reardon, "Eighth Grade Minimum Competency Testing and Early High School Dropout Patterns," paper pre-sented at the annual meeting of the American Educational Research Association, New York, April 1996.

39. Lee J. Cronbach, "Test Validation," in R. L. Thorndike, ed., *Educational Measurement,* 2d ed. (Washington, D.C.: American Council on Education, 1971); Lorrie Shepard, "Evaluating Test Validity," *Review of Research in Education,* vol. 19 (1993): 405–50.

40. National Research Council, *High Stakes,* p. 276.

41. *Improving America's Schools Act of 1994,* 20 U.S.C. sec. 6314(b)(1), 6315(c)(1), and 6320(a)(1); Weckstein, "School Reform and Enforceable Rights to an Adequate Education."

42. *Joint Standards,* p. 146, Standard 13.5. Indeed, federal statutes impose affir-mative obligations to "assess limited-English proficient students in the language and form most likely to yield accurate and reliable information on what stu-dents know and can do" (Nancy Kober and Michael Feuer, *Title I Testing and Assessment: Challenging Standards for Disadvantaged Children* [Washington, D.C.: National Academy Press, 1996], pp. 1–2), and "if students with limited English proficiency are tested in English—in areas other than language arts—and then classified on the basis of their scores . . . this constitutes discrimination under Title VI" (*Letter Report from Richard Shavelson, Chair, Board on Testing and Assessment, to Norma Cantu, Assistant Secretary of Education for Civil Rights* [Washington, D.C.: Board on Testing and Assessment, National Research Council], June 10, 1996). Federal law also requires that most students with dis-abilities be included in large-scale assessments, with accommodations for the construct-irrelevant effects of their disabilities (*Individuals with Disabilities Education Act,* 20 U.S.C., sec. 40 et. seq.).

43. National Research Council, *High Stakes,* p. 82.

44. *Letter Report from Richard Shavelson,* p. 4, quoting Samuel Messick, "Validity," in Robert L. Linn, ed., *Educational Measurement,* 3d ed. (New York: Macmillan, 1989), pp. 13–103.

45. *Joint Standards,* p. 82, Standard 7.5: comment.

46. National Research Council, *High Stakes,* p. 281.

47. *Joint Standards,* p. 83, Standard 7.10.

48. Under the *Joint Standards,* "when test scores are . . . used as part of the process for making decisions for educational placement [or] promotion . . . empirical evidence documenting the relationship among particular test scores, the instructional programs, and desired student outcomes should be provided" (p. 147, Standard 13.9). According to *High Stakes,* "valid placement requires evidence that students are likely to be better off in the setting in which they are placed than they would be in a different available setting. Such evidence, in psychometric terms, shows an aptitude-treatment interaction in terms of outcome measures of learning and well-being" (p. 96).

49. National Research Council, *Placing Children in Special Education.*

50. Ibid.; Shepard, Kagan, and Wurtz, *Principles and Recommendations for Early Childhood Assessments.*

51. C. Thomas Holmes, "Grade Level Retention Effects: A Meta-analysis of Research Studies," in Lorrie A. Shepard and Mary Lee Smith, eds., *Flunking Grades: Research and Policies on Retention* (London: Falmer Press, 1989); Stuart Luppescu et al., *School Reform, Retention Policy, and Student Achievement Gains* (Chicago: Consortium on Chicago School Research, 1995); James B. Grissom and Lorrie A. Shepard, "Repeating and Dropping Out of School," in Shepard and Smith, *Flunking Grades;* Douglas K. Anderson, "Paths through Secondary Education: Race/Ethnic and Gender Differences," Ph.D. thesis, University of Wisconsin-Madison, 1994; National Research Council, *High Stakes,* p. 283. *High Stakes* describes ways in which educators "can avoid the simplistic alternatives of promoting or retaining students based on test scores"; these include combining early and effective remedial education with multiple opportunities for students to retake different forms of the promotion test (pp. 132–33).

52. National Research Council, *High Stakes,* pp. 280–81.

53. Ibid., p. 3.

54. Ibid.

55. *Joint Standards.*

56. Joint Committee on Testing Practices, *Code of Fair Testing Practices in Education* (Washington, D.C.: American Psychological Association, 1988).

57. *Joint Standards,* p. 145.

58. American Educational Research Association, "Ethical Standards of the American Educational Research Association," *Educational Researcher* 21, no. 7 (1992): 23–26; National Council on Measurement in Education, *Code of Professional Responsibilities in Educational Measurement* (Washington, D.C.: Board on Testing and Assessment, 1995).

59. American Psychological Association, "Ethical Principles of Psychologists," *American Psychologist* 36 (1981): 633–38.
60. Office of Technology Assessment, *Testing in American Schools: Asking the Right Questions* (Washington, D.C.: U.S. Government Printing Office, 1992), p. 62.
61. The Educational Testing Service (ETS), for example, declined to provide the National Teacher Examination (NTE) to Arkansas when then-governor Bill Clinton proposed to use the test to evaluate experienced teachers; ETS claimed that the test was not valid for that purpose. In the 1970s, when South Carolina decided to use NTE scores in certifying teachers and determining teachers' salaries, ETS filed an amicus brief in the Supreme Court, asserting that such uses were inappropriate; South Carolina nonetheless prevailed. *U.S.* v. *South Carolina*, 445 F. Supp. 1094 (D.S.C. 1977, aff'd per curiam sub nom). *National Education Ass'n* v. *South Carolina*, 434 U.S. 1026 (1978).
62. National Research Council, *High Stakes*, pp. 126–27.
63. Office of Technology Assessment, *Testing in American Schools*.
64. Walt Haney and George Madaus, "The Evolution of Ethical and Technical Standards for Testing," in Ronald K. Hambleton and Jac N. Zaal, eds., *Advances in Educational and Psychological Testing: Theory and Applications* (Boston: Kluwer Academic Publishers, 1991); S. D. Kohn, "The Numbers Game: How the Testing Industry Operates," in Paul L. Houts, ed., *The Myth of Measurability* (New York: Hart, 1977), pp. 158–82; George Madaus et al., *A Proposal to Reconstitute the National Commission on Testing and Public Policy as an Independent, Monitoring Agency for Educational Testing* (Boston: Center for the Study of Testing Evaluation and Educational Policy, 1997); *From Gatekeeper to Gateway: Transforming Testing in America* (Boston: National Commission on Testing and Public Policy, 1990); Office of Technology Assessment, *Testing in American Schools*.
65. Testing programs have been challenged, under the U.S. Constitution's equal protection clause, on two grounds: (1) that a test was adopted with discriminatory intent; and (2) that a test, while not itself discriminatory, preserves or carries forward the effects of prior illegal racial segregation. However, as *High Stakes* points out, most of these challenges have been unsuccessful (pp. 52–57). With very few exceptions, courts have been unwilling to find that large-scale testing programs were adopted or implemented with racially discriminatory intent. Similarly, most courts acting today would be disinclined to rule that testing programs carry forward the effects of illegal segregation, chiefly because most findings of illegal segregation were made more than a decade ago. Under current law, the most promising constitutional basis for challenging high-stakes testing programs arises not under the equal protection clause but under the due process clause. In *Debra P.* v. *Turlington* (1981), a federal appeals court ruled that it would violate the due process clause for Florida to deny high school diplomas to students unless it could show that the test measured what the student test takers had actually been taught. As noted in the section on principles of appropriate test use, this principle has been incorporated into the *Joint*

*Standards.* As promotion and graduation tests increasingly reflect world-class standards, and the discrepancy between what tests measure and what students are taught grows, claims such as those made in *Debra P.* are likely to become more frequent.

66. 42 U.S.C. sec. 2000d.
67. 34 C.F.R. sec. 100.3(b)(2).
68. *Board of Ed. of New York v. Harris,* 1979: 151.
69. *Elston v. Talladega County Board of Education,* 1993: 1412.
70. *New York Urban League, Inc. v. New York,* 1995; *American Assoc. of Mexican-American Educators v. California,* 1996.
71. *Larry P. v. Riles,* 1984; *Sharif v. New York State Ed. Dept.,* 1989.
72. Compare, for example, *Georgia State Conference of Branches of NAACP v. Georgia,* 775 F.2d 1403 (11th Cir. 1985) with *Simmons on Behalf of Simmons v. Hooks,* 843 F. Supp. 1296 (E.D. Ark. 1994). In the 1985 Georgia case, the 11th Circuit affirmed a finding that homogeneous grouping was educationally necessary to accommodate student needs. In Simmons, however, a district court concluded in 1994 that such grouping practices were not justified educationally. For cases involving assignment of students to classes for students with educable mental retardation (EMR), compare *Larry P. v. Riles,* 495 F. Supp. 926 (N.D. Cal. 1979); aff'd, 793 F.2d 969 (9th Cir. 1984) with *PASE v. Hannon,* 506 F. Supp. 831 (N.D. Ill. 1980). In the California case, the 9th Circuit characterized EMR classes as educational dead ends, while the Illinois court viewed such placements as beneficial (National Research Council, *High Stakes,* pp. 54–55).
73. In *U.S. v. Fordice,* 505 U.S. 717 (1992), for example, the U.S. Supreme Court rejected Mississippi's exclusive reliance on the American College Test (ACT) composite scores in making college admissions decisions, because the *ACT User's Manual* called instead for admissions standards based on ACT subtest scores, self-reported high school grades, and other factors. Similarly, a federal district court, relying on the *ACT User's Manual,* found that the ACT was not valid for use in admission to an undergraduate teacher training program (*Groves v. Alabama State Bd. of Educ.,* 776 F. Supp. 1518 [M.D. Ala. 1991]). Another district court relied on the manual for the Scholastic Aptitude Test (SAT) in concluding that the SAT was not designed to measure student achievement in high school (*Sharif v. New York State Education Dept.,* 709 F. Supp. 345 [S.D.N.Y. 1989]).
74. See, for example, *People Who Care v. Rockford Board of Education,* 111 F.3d 528 (7th Cir. 1997), in which the court disregarded extensive evidence on the harmful educational effects of low-track placements on the ground that such educational questions are beyond the competence of judges.
75. *High Stakes* identifies four possible supplementary strategies for promoting appropriate test use (Chapter 11). These include deliberative forums, a test-monitoring body (Madaus et al., *A Proposal to Reconstitute the National Commission on Testing and Public Policy as an Independent, Monitoring Agency for Educational Testing*), better information about the content and purposes of particular tests, and increased government regulation.

76. 20 U.S.C. sec. 1681.
77. 29 U.S.C. sec. 1794.
78. Equal Employment Opportunities Commission, *Uniform Guidelines on Employee Selection Procedures,* 29 C.F.R. sec. 1607 et seq.
79. *Occupational Safety and Health Act of 1970,* 29 U.S.C. sec. 655 (1998). "National consensus standard" is defined in 29 U.S.C. sec. 652(9) (1998) as a "standard . . . [that] has been adopted and promulgated by a nationally recognized standards-producing organization. . . ."
80. These include the American Society for Standards and Materials and the National Fire Protection Association. Personal conversation with Dr. Mark Mendell, National Institute for Occupational Safety and Health, February 23, 1999.
81. Since all states and school districts receive federal funds, they are subject to Title VI.
82. National Research Council, *High Stakes,* Chapter 2; Natriello and Pallas, this volume.
83. OCR has promulgated investigative guidelines for its own staff's use in testing cases and, as noted in the chapter, it also has circulated drafts of a "resource guide" on high-stakes test use. Like guidelines and policy statements, these may prove valuable as educational tools or as expressions of OCR's opinions on how Title VI should apply. But neither of these is a source of legally enforceable standards of appropriate test use, upon which litigants and judges can rely.

# Index

*Note:* Page numbers followed by letters *f, t,* and *n* refer to figures, tables, and notes, respectively.

237

# About the Contributors

**John H. Bishop** is a member of the Department of Human Resource Studies at the New York State School of Industrial and Labor Relations, Cornell University. He is also executive director of the Educational Excellence Alliance, a consortium of three hundred high schools that are studying ways to improve school climate and student engagement. Prior to coming to Cornell in 1986, he was director of the Center for Research on Youth Employability and associate director, research, at the National Center for Research in Vocational Education. He has served on numerous advisory committees, and he has published numerous articles on education reform and hiring and training policies.

**Marguerite Clarke** is assistant professor of research in the Lynch School of Education at Boston College and associate director of the National Board on Educational Testing and Public Policy. She is a former Fulbright scholar and was a consultant to the National Research Council for their volume, *High Stakes: Testing for Tracking, Promotion, and Graduation* (National Academy Press, 1999).

**Keith Gayler** was a doctoral student at the Harvard Graduate School of Education.

**Robert M. Hauser** is Vilas Research Professor of Sociology at the University of Wisconsin-Madison, where he directs the Center for Demography of Health and Aging. He is a member of the National Academy of Sciences and a fellow of the National Academy of Education. His current research interests include trends in educational progression and social mobility in the United States among racial and ethnic groups and the uses of educational assessment as a policy tool. He is the editor, with Jay P. Heubert, of the National Research Council volume *High Stakes: Testing for Tracking, Promotion, and Graduation.*

**Jay P. Heubert** is associate professor of education at Teachers College, Columbia University, and adjunct professor of law at Columbia Law School. He is the coeditor (with Robert M. Hauser) of the National Research Council volume *High Stakes: Testing for Tracking, Promotion, and Graduation* and *Law and School Reform: Six Strategies for Promoting Educational Equity* (Yale University Press, 1999). In May 2000 he was named a Carnegie Scholar, one of twelve nationally and two in education.

**Mindy L. Kornhaber** is the director of research for K–12 education at the Civil Rights Project at Harvard University and is a reseach associate at the Harvard Graduate School of Education. Her work focuses on how institutions and social policies enhance or impede the development of individual potential. She is coauthor, with Howard Gardner and Warren Wake, of *Intelligence: Multiple Perspectives* (Harcourt Brace College Publishers, 1996).

**Henry M. Levin** is the William Heard Kilpatrick Professor of Economics and Education at Teachers College, Columbia University, and the director of the National Center for the Study of Privatization in Education, a nonpartisan entity. He is also the David Jacks Professor Emeritus of Higher Education and Economics at Stanford University.

**George Madaus** is the Boisi Professor of Education and Public Policy in the Lynch School of Education at Boston College and a senior fellow with the National Board on Educational Testing and Public Policy. He was the executive director of the National Commission on Testing and Public Policy, which produced the 1990 report, *From Gatekeeper to Gateway: Transforming Testing in America.*

**Ferran Mane** is an assistant professor at the Rovira i Virgily University (Spain). He has been visiting fellow at Essex University (England) and at Cornell University. He has published several articles and chapters on vocational education, the effects of on-the-job training on workers' productivity, changes in the American education system, and the effects of technological change on education and occupational structures.

**Linda McNeil** is a professor of education and has been codirector of the Rice University Center for Education, a center for teacher development and research, since 1988. She has taught at the Harvard Graduate School of Education and has been a visiting scholar at the Stanford University School of Education. She served as the vice-president of the Curriculum Studies Division of the American Educational Research Association and is the editor of the Social and Institutional Analysis Section of *American Educational Research*. She is the author of numerous publications on curriculum, teaching, and urban schooling, including *Contradictions of Control: School Structure and School Knowledge* (Routledge, 1986) and *Contradictions of School Reform: The Educational Costs of Standardized Testing* (Routledge, 2000).

**Gary Natriello** is professor of sociology and education in the Department of Human Development at Teachers College, Columbia University. He is the editor of the *Teachers College Record* and the director of the Evaluation Center at Teachers College. He is the author of numerous articles and books, including (with William Firestone and Margaret Goertz) *From Cashbox to Classroom: The Struggle for Fiscal Reform and Educational Change in New Jersey* (Teachers College Press, 1997).

**Monty Neill** is the executive director of the National Center for Fair & Open Testing (FairTest, www.fairtest.org). He has directed FairTest's work on testing in the public schools since 1987 and has taught and administered in preschool, hich school, and college. His publications include *Implementing Performance Assessments: A Guide to Classroom, School and System Reform* and *Testing Our Children: A Report Card on State Assessment Systems*.

**Gary Orfield** is professor of education and social policy at Harvard University. He is codirector (with Christopher Edley, Jr.) of the Civil Rights Project at Harvard University. His most recent books are (with Susan Eaton) *Dismantling Desegregation: The Quiet Reversal of* Brown *v.* Board of Education (New Press, 1996); (with Edward Miller) *Chilling Admissions: The Affirmative Action Crisis and the Search for Alternatives* (Harvard Educational Publishing Group, 1998), and (with Michal Kurlaender) *Diversity Challenged: Evidence on the Impact of Affirmative Action* (Havard Educational Publishing Group, 2001).

**Aaron M. Pallas** is professor of sociology and education in the Department of Human Development at Teachers College, Columbia University. He is the editor of *Sociology of Education* and a past chair of the Sociology of Education Section of the American Sociology Association.

He studies the interrelations of educational stratification, the social organization of schools, and the life course of individuals.

**Angela Valenzuela** is associate professor of education and of Mexican American studies at the Univesity of Texas at Austin. Prior to this position, she taught at Rice University. Her book *Subtractive Schooling: U.S. Mexican Youth and the Politics of Caring* (State Univesrity of New York Press, 1999) was awarded the American Educational Research Association Outstanding Book Award, the highest prize in the United States in education research. She also has been the recipient of a Ford Foundation Post-Doctoral Fellowship.